SAMUEL JOHNSON'S PARLIAMENTARY REPORTING

SAMUEL JOHNSON'S PARLIAMENTARY REPORTING

Debates in the Senate of Lilliput

By Benjamin Beard Hoover

UNIVERSITY OF CALIFORNIA PRESS
BERKELEY AND LOS ANGELES
1953

UNIVERSITY OF CALIFORNIA PUBLICATIONS
ENGLISH STUDIES: 7
EDITORS (BERKELEY): W. H. DURHAM, JAMES CLINE,
J. J. LYNCH

Submitted by editors April 3, 1953
Issued December 29, 1953
Price, cloth $2.50, paper $1.75

UNIVERSITY OF CALIFORNIA PRESS
BERKELEY AND LOS ANGELES
CALIFORNIA

◆

CAMBRIDGE UNIVERSITY PRESS
LONDON, ENGLAND

FOR ELIZABETH

CONTENTS

INTRODUCTION ix

I. HISTORICAL BACKGROUNDS: SAMUEL JOHNSON AND PARLIAMENTARY REPORTING IN THE EIGHTEENTH CENTURY   1

Parliamentary reporting in periodicals, 1711–1737, 6; The dominance of the *Gentleman's Magazine* and the *London Magazine,* 15; The decline of reporting in the magazines, 29

II. THE DEBATES DURING TWO CENTURIES: THE HISTORY OF THE DOCUMENT 33

The *Debates* during Johnson's life, 36; The *Debates* after Johnson's death, 44

III. THE DEBATES AS FACT: A COMPARISON WITH THE COLLATERAL EVIDENCE 55

The method, 57; Reports of the Lords debate of February 13, 1741, 58; Reports of the Commons debate of February 13, 1741, 78; Comparison of the remaining debates, 110

IV. THE DEBATES AS ART: THEIR PLACE IN THE LITERARY CAREER OF SAMUEL JOHNSON 131

The *Debates* as "debates," 132; Johnsonian style and the *Debates,* 142

NOTES 153
BIBLIOGRAPHY 167
APPENDIX 1 171
APPENDIX 2 207
INDEX 225

INTRODUCTION

THE *Debates in the Senate of Lilliput* have always been treated as poor relations of the better known writings of Samuel Johnson. They have never achieved the dignity of completely independent publication or the equality of wholehearted acceptance among the collected writings; under Johnson's name the *Debates* have been printed only as supplementary volumes added to three editions of the *Works*. It seems probable that a misleading title has, at least in part, accounted for the neglect—a title under which the work did not appear during Johnson's life. *Debates in Parliament* has, perhaps, too political a sound to engage the interest of the Johnson enthusiast whose concern is chiefly *literary* history. But even the traditional title may arouse a flicker of interest in the uninitiated: "Was Johnson, then, a member of Parliament?" When it is explained that the *Debates* are magazine reports of parliamentary proceedings written up by Johnson to alleviate the poverty of his youth, the interest vanishes: mere journalism, at best an adaptation of the words of others rather than an independently creative work. The original title, *Debates in the Senate of Lilliput,* brings up literary associations, dispels the prospective reader's assumption that this is simple reporting, suggests the curious circumstances of composition and original publication—in short, conveys more fully the work's interest and its nature.

Nevertheless, the restoration of a more promising title does not justify the reopening of a forgotten book. There is the obvious and irrefutable objection that this is apprentice work. But is it not all the more absorbing for being early Johnson? This is the first large single body of prose that we have from his hand, and therefore worthy of reading and of investigation if Johnson is thus worthy. This study was undertaken, then, with the assumption that the *Debates* are worth bothering about, and was pursued with the conviction that they provide an essential key to our understanding of Johnson's development.

If that conviction must for the moment remain personal, it may quickly be demonstrated that available scholarship on the subject is inadequate. Only one published study of the *Debates* seems to be based on scholarly investigation and a firsthand acquaintance with the whole of the work itself.[1] This is Appendix A of Hill's edition of Boswell,[2] an essay which packs much information into the small compass of twelve pages. Hill contributes a useful introduction to the history of early eighteenth-century parliamentary reporting and the circumstances surrounding the writing and first printing of the work; there is also some bibliographical information, including a list showing the order of publication of the *Debates* in the *Gentleman's Magazine*. If every page reaches valuable conclusions, every page also opens new fields of investigation, fields which must be thoroughly explored before our knowledge of Johnson's *Debates* is at all adequate.

I intend the present study as a step toward that knowledge. My plan is to discuss the results of my investigation in four chapters. Chapter i is concerned with the history of the creation and first printing of the *Debates*. It embodies a discussion of eighteenth-century parliamentary reporting, Johnson's place in the tradition, the circumstances of the first printing of the work, and the contemporary reaction to it. The second chapter traces the history of the *Debates* from the earliest printing to the present. Studying the succession of reprintings, I follow the course of the text over the years and show the extent to which the *Debates* have been read and the measure of esteem in which they have been held—not always, indeed, as works of Johnson. The third chapter brings us closer to the text of the work itself. Each debate, when possible, is compared in general design and

---
[1] For notes to the Introduction see page 153.

Introduction

minute detail with the corresponding report of the *London Magazine* and other surviving contemporary records. Such a comparison gives a clearer notion of the nature of the *Debates,* of the degree of their originality, of the materials with which Johnson worked, of characteristic ways of handling those materials, of the relation to the *London Magazine* reports. The final chapter is concerned with the *Debates* as literature. Here I have sought to study them as debates and to define the qualities of the prose. It is hoped that each of the chapters has fulfilled its separate purpose without losing sight of the common end: to persuade the reader that the position of poor relation ill befits the *Debates in the Senate of Lilliput,* that the work has high importance, historical and literary, as an original creative work.

It is a pleasure to express my thanks to those who have aided me. I have for a number of years been instructed and encouraged by Professor Bertrand H. Bronson, director of the dissertation from which this book is taken. To him my debt is great. For valuable information and numerous kindnesses I must thank Professor James L. Clifford. I wish also to acknowledge the suggestions, generously given, of those others who have read the book in manuscript: Professors Donald Cornu, George H. Guttridge, Edward A. Bloom, and Harold Kelling.

I am grateful for the consideration shown me by the editors of this series and the staff of the University Press. The assistance of the University of California Library should not go unmentioned, especially that received from the Loan Department, Documents Division, and Interlibrary Service Department; and I am pleased to acknowledge aid from the Research Fund of the Graduate School, University of Washington. Finally I must thank my wife for the performance of tasks, great and small, that have made a book possible.

CHAPTER I

HISTORICAL BACKGROUNDS: SAMUEL JOHNSON AND PARLIAMENTARY REPORTING IN THE EIGHTEENTH CENTURY

Addison, writing the eighty-sixth *Tatler* from his "own Apartment, October 25," 1709—some month and a half after the birth of the Great Moralist—describes the London visit of a group of country gentry led by Sir Harry Quickset of Staffordshire. These "persons of so much state and rusticity" entered Dick's Coffeehouse and "marched up to the high table." There "Sir Harry called for a mug of ale and Dyer's Letter. The boy brought the ale in an instant; but said they did not take in the Letter. 'No! (says Sir Harry,) then take back your mug; we are like indeed to have good liquor at this house!'"[1]

The anecdote throws light on the status of parliamentary reporting in the year of Johnson's birth. Addison was attempting to amuse his readers by drawing a typical scene. London's polite world, or at least the male part of it, congregated in the coffee shops, where political news and political disputes were as much the stock in trade as coffee and ale. Important sources of parliamentary news for the coffeehouses and the chief source for the Sir Harry Quicksets, the squires of the provinces, were the newsletters—manuscript sheets made up by London scriveners. Writers got them up at their peril; coffeehouses took them in at their peril, and it was perhaps for this reason that "Dick's" was unable to provide "Dyer's Letter,"[2] for John Dyer was "the first of the 'news-writers' to attempt to penetrate the hooded mystery of the House of Commons, in the interest of his readers."[3]

[1] For notes to chapter i see pages 153–158.

Because we are now accustomed to considering legislative debates as directed to the world outside the chambers, we may forget that Parliament at this stage of its development guarded jealously its privilege of secrecy, that parliamentary news was contraband. Vestiges of the tradition remain today. Visitors to Parliament are called "strangers": the public galleries are the "Strangers' Galleries" and the means of clearing the house for a secret session (as in time of war) is to announce, "Mr. Speaker,— I spy strangers."[4] Indeed, it is said that, according to resolutions technically remaining in force, every English newspaper that reports the proceedings of Parliament violates the law.[5] The *Journals of the House of Commons* give abundant evidence of the severity with which the rules were applied at the end of the seventeenth century. On December 21, 1694, "a Complaint being made to this House, that *Dyer,* a News-Letter-Writer, has presumed in his News-Letter to take notice of the Proceedings of this House,"[6] it was resolved that he should next day attend. The bare record of the *Journals* conveys some of the awful dignity visited upon the offending Dyer:

The House being informed, That * *Dyer,* the News-Letter-Writer, attended, according to the Order of Yesterday;
He was called in; and heard touching the Complaint made against him; and acknowle[d]ging his Offense, humbly begged the Pardon of the House for the same.
And then withdrew.
Ordered, That the said * *Dyer* be brought to the Bar, and upon his Knees, reprimanded by Mr. Speaker for his great Presumption.
And accordingly he was brought in, and reprimanded.
Ordered, That the said * Dyer be discharged, paying his Fees.
Resolved, That no News-Letter-Writers do, in their Letters, or other Papers, that they disperse, presume to intermeddle with the Debates or any other Proceedings, of this House.[7]

It was a resolution often to be renewed in years to come. But Dyer was not diverted from his intermeddling career; his name recurrently crops up in the Commons *Journals* throughout the

Historical Backgrounds 3

following decade. Nor was the newsletter writer alone subject to the censure of the house. In 1695, Jeremiah Stokes, keeper of Garaway's Coffeehouse, was brought before the house with the letter writer Griffith Card, because Card's paper was distributed at that establishment.[8] Later in that year two prisoners "were fined for taking in Dyer's news-letters at the Old Bailey."[9] The House of Lords, though it did not at this time often take notice of violations of its privilege of secrecy, expressed itself with no less firmness. In 1699 it was resolved: "That it is a breach of the Privilege of this House for any Person whatsoever to print, or publish in Print, any Thing relating to the Proceedings of this House without the Leave of this House; and that the said Order be added to the Standing Orders, and set on the Doors of this House."[10]

At the time of Dyer's first reprimand, the desire for privacy in the houses of Parliament had already had a long history. We have no information on the attitude of medieval parliaments, but the statement of John Hooker, a member of the House of Commons writing, about 1560, "the earliest impartial and careful description of the actual procedure,"[11] records a tradition seemingly long established: "No manner of person, being not one of the parliament house, ought to enter or come within the house, as long as the sitting is there, upon pain of imprisonment, or such other punishment as by the house shall be ordered and adjudged."[12] On the question of disseminating parliamentary news, Hooker had this to say: "Also every person of the parliament ought to keep secret, and not to disclose the secrets and things done and spoken in the parliament house, to any manner person, unless he be one of the same house, upon pain to be sequestered out of the house, or otherwise punished, as by the order of the house shall be appointed."[13]

We must undoubtedly regard the tradition of secrecy within the houses as a natural accompaniment of the long struggle between Parliament and the Crown, which, beginning in Elizabeth's day, ran its course through much of the seventeenth century. To keep its words within its chambers and away from the ears of the king was, for Parliament, simple prudence. There seems to have been little concern with enforcing the rule in Elizabethan times. Many members kept diaries, and much information leaked out; still, there was no systematic dispersal of parliamentary news, nor was there a reading public with a thirst for such news. The *Journals,* kept at that time solely for the members' use, early in the seventeenth century were giving extended information about the debates. Perhaps because Charles "used to send for the *Journals* and peruse their contents,"[14] the House of Commons, three years after that monarch came to the throne, resolved that entries concerning the debates were unwarranted and implied that they should be discontinued.[15] When the Short Parliament met (April, 1640) after Charles's long period of personal rule, it was necessary for Commons to direct the clerk assistant not to "take any Notes ... without the precedent Direction and Command of this House, but only of the Orders and Reports made in this House."[16] Later in the same year the Long Parliament ordered that the clerk "suffer no Copies to go forth of any Argument or Speech whatsoever."[17] With the overthrow of the Star Chamber in February, 1641, the stringent regulation of the press became disorganized, and "during two or three years there was practically no control over authors and printers."[18] A flood of sheets and pamphlets containing parliamentary news spread over the country. The Long Parliament met the situation by putting new restrictions on printing and by disseminating its own view of the news in officially licensed newsbooks known as *Diurnals.*[19] Newsletters became extremely important conveyors of news as control of the press was tightened under the Commonwealth and the Protectorate. After the restoration, Charles II, by his Licensing Act of 1662, further stifled the reporting of domestic news, and this included news of the happenings within the legislative houses. Some

Historical Backgrounds

members (Andrew Marvell and Anchitell Grey are two of the best known) kept notes of the debates of Commons, but they were not made public at this time. In 1680 the House of Commons voted to lift the fringes of its veil of secrecy by ordering the printing of the *Votes* of the house. In 1681 the order was repeated and extended to read *and Proceedings,* "and from that year votes and proceedings were regularly printed and placed on sale to the public under a resolution taken at the beginning of each session, except during 1702-3."[20] But the *Votes and Proceedings* containing only the bare record of motions passed and petitions received, could not unsupplemented satisfy the demand of the coffeehouse public.

When, by the Glorious Revolution, Parliament emerged victorious from its struggle with the Crown, the tradition of secrecy survived its justification and experienced a curious reversal of direction. Parliament, which under the now-established limited monarchy felt little need of protection from the king, became deeply concerned with shrouding its activities from the people. The maintenance of privacy had the sanction of usage, and perhaps beyond that there was a feeling among the members that Parliament in substituting itself for the Crown as the source of power must accentuate its authority by surrounding itself with mystery. The action against Dyer in 1694 was, after the constitutional settlement, the first move in a long contest with the people. But the enlarged reading public gathered in the coffeehouses was not to be denied. Newsletters, pamphlets, and (of course) the *Votes and Proceedings* (within limits) continued to supply the news. Less to be depended upon for parliamentary information were the newspapers; not until 1722 was the resolution against newsletter writers extended to include printers or publishers "of any printed News Papers" who might "insert in any such Papers any Debates or any other Proceedings of this House or any Committee Thereof."[21]

Parliamentary Reporting in Periodicals, 1711-1737

By the end of the first decade of the eighteenth century, Parliament's privilege of secrecy had made irregularity and partiality important elements in the tradition of debate reporting. There was no regular flow of accounts from any one source; reporting was spotty and erratic. Because the risk was great, it could be taken only when there was some motive other than "the simple desire for truth"; as a result, debates were put forward to gain political ends.[22] The writer was expected to take sides.

In January, 1711 (about a year and a half after Johnson's birth), began a new phase in the tradition of debate reporting—a phase in which Johnson, twenty-seven years later, was to take his place. With the publication of the first number of the *Political State of Great Britain,* regularity of issuance and impartial accuracy were combined as recognized and realized virtues. The *Political State* took the form of a pretended monthly letter of news from an English writer to his friend in Holland, and the proceedings of Parliament, including the debates, had a place in it from the beginning. The editor, in his preface, made plain his aim of impartiality: he would present *"a fair and true Representation of Things, without Passionate Aggravations, or uncandid Extenuations."*

The founder of the *Political State* was Abel Boyer, a literary handy man of some versatility.[23] He wrote histories, manuals, translations, and a French-English dictionary that was the most enduring of his works and continued to be issued under his name down past the middle of the nineteenth century. There is a link between Boyer and Johnson other than their common participation in the tradition of parliamentary reporting: a mutual friend. Richard Savage supplied Boyer with one thousand words for his dictionary (so Boyer stated in its preface) and aided him with subsequent manuals, compilations, and translations.

Until 1729, Boyer supplied the public with parliamentary

Historical Backgrounds

news. Only once did Parliament challenge his right to do so, and then but a few months, curiously, after the founding of the periodical. The House of Lords on March 2, 1711, was informed that "contrary to a standing order of this house, there is a Book printed intitled the *Political State* of Great Britain." On March 6 Boyer attended, confessed his guilt, and was taken into custody. Six days later, "expressing his Sorrow for his Offense" and paying his fees, he was released.[24] Boyer did not have occasion thereafter to express his sorrow to either house. It is difficult to explain Parliament's failure to restrain him. Probably his genuine attempt at impartiality had its effect. Many members must have come to accept with toleration a neutral and fairly accurate report of their proceedings. At least we have the word of Boyer that many members aided him by supplying notes.

Boyer's debates were not got up without a measure of caution. He never brought them forth as literal narratives. These were "the Heads of some of the most remarkable Speeches." He was cautious in the printing of names. The usual device for disguising them was the use of the first and the last letter separated by a blank: Mr. "P—y" and "Lord H—x." But the *Political State* was even more wary of invading the Lords' privacy than that of the Commons. A complex method is used in identifying the speeches of the Lords on the Septennial Act in 1716. The twenty-four speakers are first listed without disguise and the names numbered. The speeches then follow with most of the speakers not identified, but in the order of the list. The report of the debate in Commons on the same subject identifies the speeches directly and with undisguised names.[25]

Interference with Boyer's activities came subsequently not from Parliament but from the printers of *Votes and Proceedings* of the House of Commons. In the preface to the *Political State* of 1729, the editor reprints this letter from his publisher:

Sir,—The *Proprietors* of the *Votes* have been with me, desiring me to acquaint you, That if you meddle with the *Parliamentary Proceed-*

ings, in your *Political State,* you will *certainly* be taken into *custody* for the same. I thought it my Duty to acquaint you therewith, That you may proceed accordingly, and am, Sir, Your humble Servant,

Thomas Warner.

In answer, Boyer denounces the "proprietors" for their "high Presumption and Indiscretion" in seeming to anticipate "the Resolutions, *Censure,* and *Judgment*" of the house. Still, he thinks "fit to *cancel* a whole Half-Sheet ... which contain'd an Account of the *Parliamentary Proceedings* of the month of *January.*" The *Political State* had previously been able to publish the parliamentary account soon after the events occurred, month by month. Now Boyer waited until the session of 1729 had ended before giving, in one issue, a much abbreviated account, "The History of the Last Session."

In delivering their warning the printers of the *Votes* can have been interested only in protecting their copyright, which certainly did not extend to the debates themselves. Boyer probably had other cause to consider imminent the wrath of Parliament. In the *Journals* of the Commons we find evidence that the sentiment of the house had begun to shift toward a more energetic restriction of news. On March 4, 1728, the complaint was made that the *Gloucester Journal* had presumed to take notice of the proceedings of the house. Robert Raikes, the publisher of the paper, testified before Commons that he had received his information from a clerk of the post office in London, one Edward Cave. Cave accordingly appeared on March 30 and admitted having "sent to Robert Raikes several News Letters which did contain Intelligences (relating to the Proceedings of this House)," and said that he had received the news from four others. Cave, Raikes, and three of the other four were committed to the custody of the sergeant at arms and not released until they had been publicly reprimanded by the speaker toward the middle of April.[26] In February, 1729, Raikes was again brought before the house because he had printed matter concerning its proceedings.

Historical Backgrounds

This time it was not Cave but another postal employee who had supplied him with the news. On this occasion Commons added to its usual resolution: "That, upon Discovery of the Authors, Printers, or Publishers of any such written or printed Newspaper, this House will proceed against the Offenders with the utmost Severity."[27] Boyer was well advised to modify his parliamentary reporting during the last months of his life.

After Boyer's death, in 1729, the *Political State* was carried forward by other hands, but news of Parliament was severely curtailed for several years. After the session of 1730 had ended, only one debate was printed. In 1731, when Parliament had been prorogued, the *Political State* gave the debate on the address at the beginning of the session with the speakers' names printed in full; and in the September issue a debate on public offices which had occurred in February was printed with the names obscured by blanks. In 1732 and for several years thereafter the periodical gave full reports much in the style of Boyer's time, but the accounts of a session were never begun until that session had ended, upon the assumption that the resolution against publishing its proceedings was in force only while Parliament was sitting.[28] Actually, this limitation applied only to the House of Commons. The House of Lords was "a Court of Record, and as such, its rights and privileges never die."[29]

That the *Political State* was a success we may infer not only from its long life but also from the fact that it inspired an imitation. The first quarterly issue of the *Historical Register* was published in 1716, for the benefit of policyholders in the "Sun Fire-Office." The preface informs its readers that "The Company of the Sun Fire-Office have resolved to give their Subscribers for the future a Quarterly Book instead of their Weekly News-Paper," a quarterly that will endeavor to supply a "full, true, clear, disinterested, and impartial Account of all the memorable Occurrences" during the three months preceding publication.[30] The *Historical Register* gave a selection of parliamentary news, copied out of the

Political State, a selection that became fuller over the years. (Since the reports of the *Political State* were unauthorized, Boyer held no copyright and so could not protest the plagiarism.) In a recent study, Mary Ransome, after comparing the periodical reports of debates from 1727 to 1737, concludes that "those in the *Political State* and *Historical Register* are generally word for word the same,"[31] and the *Political State* publication was always the earlier.

The Edward Cave who supplied the *Gloucester Journal* with parliamentary news in 1728 now reënters the narrative in a larger role. In 1731 he established the *Gentleman's Magazine, or Trader's Monthly Intelligencer,* "the first magazine." The term "magazine" as then understood and Cave's purposes are explained in the advertisement to the first volume: "Several Gentlemen" have been induced "to promote a Monthly Collection, to treasure up, as in a Magazine, the most remarkable Pieces on the Subjects above mentioned, or at least impartial Abridgments thereof, as a Method much better calculated to preserve those Things that are curious than that of transcribing."[32] Parliamentary news at first was brief and was unostentatiously buried within the "Monthly Intelligencer," a regular department of the magazine. References to proceedings might be found also within the summaries of recently printed essays. In January, 1732, the king's address at the opening of Parliament was printed, and in July the first genuine debate report was begun in the back pages, under the heading "Proceedings and Debates of the Last Session of Parliament."[33] The account was of the debate on the address earlier printed. In August the report was continued under the shortened head "Debates in the Last Session of Parliament," and the importance which Cave attached to the new feature is revealed by the fact that it now led off the magazine. Its increasing importance is indicated by the title pages issued for bound volumes. That of 1732 lists first "An impartial View of the *Weekly* ESSAYS," and "Debates in PARLIAMENT" follows close behind. On

Historical Backgrounds

the 1733 title page, "Proceedings and Debates in Parliament" heads the list.

The *Gentleman's Magazine,* in its debate reporting, from the beginning followed its established general policy of summarizing previously published material. The first accounts were therefore summaries of those printed in the *Political State*. As in that periodical, the names of speakers were riddled with blanks, and speeches often not quoted but described: "Mr. Cl—b—ck seconded the Motion, and declared that . . ." A note found at the end of the debates for August, 1732, disavows any claim to literalness and brings to mind the similar disclaimer in the *Political State:* "N.B. The farther PROCEEDINGS and DEBATES will be continued in this Manner in our future Numbers. We don't pretend to give the very Words of every Speech, but hope we have done Justice to the Arguments on each Side."[34]

The success of the *Gentleman's Magazine* soon brought forth an imitator. In April, 1732, a group of booksellers began to issue the *London Magazine,* or *Gentleman's Monthly Intelligencer*. In every respect the new magazine modeled itself on its predecessor. The rival followed the *Gentleman's Magazine* by one month when it initiated "Proceedings and Debates" in August, 1732. In both magazines the debates were leading features for that month. It thereafter became the custom of the two magazines to begin to print accounts of parliamentary debates at the session's end (or actually, by necessity, after the *Political State* had begun its reports) and to continue publication until the end of the year. The *London Magazine,* finding its debates still incomplete in the December issue, added to the 1732 volume a supplement that brought the report of parliamentary proceedings to a close. Of this practice the *Gentleman's Magazine* became the imitator and put out its first supplement at the end of the 1733 volume. Thereafter the supplement was issued annually by both magazines.

The *Political State* continued for several years as virtually the sole source of parliamentary intelligence printed in the two magazines. C. L. Carlson states, "A careful comparison of the accounts of the debates in the *Political State* with the accounts in the *Gentleman's Magazine* shows that except for some rearrangement of the speeches, they were copied almost verbatim from the *Political State* as long as the periodical continued to publish the debates."[35] The two versions do seem to have been nearly always similar, but the *Gentleman's Magazine* did not invariably copy from the *Political State*. Miss Ransome came to a conclusion similar to Carlson's, that the debates up to 1737 "are, with a few minor exceptions, the same in all the magazines. Those in the *Political State* and *Historical Register* are generally word for word the same, while the reports in the *Gentleman's Magazine* and *London Magazine* differ only in being shortened by the omission of a few unimportant words or phrases."[36] In most of these years the *Political State* began its reports in the May issue, and the two magazines began in June. The dependence of the *Gentleman's Magazine* on the *Political State* is amusingly demonstrated in the issues of 1735. The latter periodical announced in its May number that the accounts would start in June. Next month the *Political State* put off its debates until July. As a result the *Gentleman's Magazine* was forced, in June, to declare that the reports had been delayed. (In that month Cave improved the interval by printing one speech that is independent of the *Political State*.) And in the July issue was announced the *Gentleman's Magazine Extraordinary* to be published "about the 20th day of *August*." Parliamentary news was there resumed and henceforth was carried on as before, a month behind the source.

But Cave's magazine was not always dependent on the *Political State*. A short account of the playhouse bill debate of 1735 does not find a counterpart in the other periodical, and independent separate speeches were sometimes printed.[37] In 1737, reports in the *Political State* became irregular and both that magazine and the *Gentleman's Magazine* generally followed the earlier *London Magazine* versions. It is plain that Cave was endeavoring, by 1735, to inject fresh material into his magazine by getting help from members of Parliament. On July 31 he wrote to Dr. Birch, "I trouble you with the enclosed, because you said you could easily correct what is here given for Lord Chesterfield's speech."[38] (Cave probably enclosed the *Political State* version of the speech.) In 1737, again in July, Cave made a similar request of Birch: "As you *remember* the Debates so far as to perceive the Speeches already printed are not exact, I beg the favor that you will peruse the inclosed: and in the best manner your memory will serve correct the mistaken passages, or add anything that is omitted."[39]

Among the last reports published in the *Political State* in 1737 are speeches copied from the *Gentleman's Magazine*. Before the first of these, a speech of Patrick Lindsay reprinted from the August *Gentleman's Magazine,* the September *Political State* places a querulous note: "Having for so many Years furnished all the Debates to others, we may surely be allowed to make some Reprizals; a Liberty we shall take but seldom and very shortly not at all."[40] Speeches of Hardwicke and Argyle taken from the October *Gentleman's Magazine* follow in November.

The abandonment of parliamentary reporting by the *Political State* suggests that trouble was brewing again. Cave's cautious statement in the Supplement for 1737 is also revealing.

The candid Reader who knows the Difficulty, and sometimes, Danger, of publishing speeches in P—t, will easily conceive that it is impossible to do it in the very Words of the Speakers. With regard to the major Part, we pretend only to represent the Sense as near as may be expected in a Summary Way.[41]

In April, 1738, the storm broke. One newspaper took the liberty of printing the king's answer to an address from Commons before it had been reported from the chair.[42] Onslow made complaint to the house. On April 13 the House of Commons passed unanimously a resolution which made ominously significant departures from the familiar form:

That it is an high Indignity to, and a notorious Breach of the Privilege of, this House, for any News-Writer, in Letters, or other Papers, (as Minutes or under any other Denomination), or for any printer or publisher of any printed News Paper, of any Denomination, to presume to insert in the said Letters or Papers, or to give therein any Account of the Debates, or other Proceedings of this House, or any Committee thereof, as well during the Recess as the Sitting of Parliament; and that this House will proceed with the utmost Severity against such Offenders.[43]

The phrase "as well during the Recess as the Sitting of Parliament" had been added by amendment and was obviously aimed at the magazines. The resolution brought to an end another period of relatively free reporting of debates.

As the original reporting of the debates from 1711 through 1737 was almost wholly the work of the *Political State,* it will be well to inquire how that periodical invaded the secrecy of the houses to procure the raw material for its reports. Boyer in the advertisement to the second edition of the initial seven volumes gives us clues to his methods of gathering news. He speaks of the debates and speeches "which the Author either takes care to collect, with indefatigable Labour and Industry or with which he is befriended by some eminent Members, who are fully apprized of his honest Intention to Serve the Public."[44] We may assume that the "Labour" of collecting was that of entering the house by some means or hiring an agent to enter, as did the French ambassadors who sent parliamentary news to their Foreign Office. We have evidence that access was easier before 1738 than it was thereafter.[45] In the preface to the 1729 volume, Boyer again states that he has been aided by "eminent and public-spirited Members" and adds the names of some of those now dead, "with reverence to their memories": Earl Stanhope, Lord Lechmere, and Mr. Harper.[46]

The reports thus produced before 1737 were apparently more

Historical Backgrounds

accurate than those in the years immediately following. Miss Ransome has found parallel evidence by which fifty-seven of the debates given by the *Political State* and the other periodicals between 1727 and 1737 can be checked. In the fifty-seven debates she finds fourteen "major errors of fact." She concludes, "On the whole the general arguments, names of the speakers, and divisions given in the magazine are confirmed, and sometimes very closely confirmed."[47] The reports, although leaving something to be desired, did not fall far short of the modest representations of the magazines.

THE DOMINANCE OF THE GENTLEMAN'S MAGAZINE AND THE LONDON MAGAZINE

Parliament's action against the magazines was taken but a short time after the beginning of Johnson's connection with the *Gentleman's Magazine*. Johnson had, the previous summer (1737), written to Cave, proposing a new translation of Sarpi's *History of the Council of Trent*.[48] The proposal seems to have gained the publisher's approval, but the project was not begun for another year (and was subsequently dropped).[49] According to Hawkins, "Cave's acquiescence ... drew Johnson into close intimacy with him."[50] "It appears that he was now enlisted by Mr. Cave as a regular coadjutor in his magazine, by which he probably obtained a tolerable livelihood."[51] Johnson made his initial appearance in the *Gentleman's Magazine* with some complimentary Latin verses addressed to Cave ("Ad Urbanum") in the March issue which came out the first of April.[52] Meanwhile, no doubt, preparations were under way for compiling reports of the parliamentary session then in progress so that publication could commence with the beginning of the recess. Two weeks after the world saw "Ad Urbanum," the House of Commons resolved that reports were illegal "as well during the Recess as the Sitting of Parliament."

The anguish of the magazines' publishers may easily be appreciated. For six years they had thought so highly of their "Debates in Parliament" that the feature had taken precedence in the issues in which it had appeared and was the sole justification for the supplements. To discontinue those reports now might mean disaster for two flourishing enterprises. Moreover, questions in Parliament were becoming more hotly contested than ever before within recent memory, and interest in them was growing. Walpole, who had usually had things his own way since 1721, was being charged with the worst varieties of political viciousness by men desperate for a taste of power. Public feeling ran high and was even to force Walpole, in October of the next year (1739), to declare war on Spain. To find some new means of evading the restrictions of Parliament would be to reap increased financial rewards.

A way was found. With the new expedient began a new era in the reporting of debates, corresponding closely to the period of Johnson's link with the tradition. A general account of the magazines' debates during these years will prepare the way for a consideration of Johnson's part in the history.

The *London Magazine* was ready with its answer to the challenge of Commons by the publication date of its May, 1738, number. In the middle of that issue is an article, "Proceedings of the Political Club, &c."[53] It purports to be written by the secretary of "a Club of young Noblemen and Gentlemen who dine together thrice a Week" and "at every Meeting appoint some Question in Religion, Politicks, Law, Trade or Philosophy, to be ... debated in the next." The members have agreed to "speak and argue as much as possible in the Stile and Manner of *Parliament*" and debate in the club "every grand Question in Politicks." Since "it is now rendered unsafe ... to entertain the Publick" with parliamentary debates, the secretary proposes to substitute for them the proceedings of his club. The members will remain anonymous, but will be distinguished "by the great Names of the ancient *Grecians* and *Romans*." The speakers are not to be confused with the original holders of those names, but in discussing ques-

Historical Backgrounds

tions before Parliament "the Speakers upon each Side, assume the Characters of some of their Superiors, and endeavor to speak in the Character they have assumed." The secretary speaks of the club's plan as "so innocent, and at the same time so entertaining." We may be sure that the editor, if challenged, planned to protest the innocence of his entertainment. Indeed, it would have been difficult to prove him guilty, and any attempt to do so could have met only ridicule.

The article is rather wordy, and lacking in imagination and charm. The writer of the debates for the *London Magazine* and, we assume, the author of the introductory piece was Thomas Gordon, distinguished as the translator of Tacitus. The debate itself was a report of that held in the Commons the preceding February on the reduction of the army, and the first speaker was the "Honourable *Scipio Africanus,*" whom the reader was to identify as Lord Noel Somerset. *M. Tullius Cicero* (Walpole) and *M. Cato* (Pulteney) also figured in the debate. How the reader was to be led to these connections we cannot be sure: perhaps by word of mouth, for no key appears to have been printed for some time.

Whether Cave waited for the example of Astley (his rival editor) before devising a disguise for his debates or whether his plan was already contrived when the May *London Magazine* was issued, we cannot know. At any rate, he was a month behind. The first item in the table of contents for the June issue of the *Gentleman's Magazine* is the "APPENDIX to Capt. *Lemuel Gulliver's* Account of the famous Empire of LILLIPUT." The title given on the first page is "DEBATES *in the Senate of* MAGNA LILLIPUTIA."[54]

We doubt not but our readers will be much pleased with an Appendix to Capt. GULLIVER's Account, which we received last Month, and which the late Resolution of the House of Commons, whereby we are forbidden to insert any Account of the Proceedings of the *British Parliament,* gives us an Opportunity of communicating in their Room.

A narrative of the exploits of Captain Gulliver's grandson is then begun. To defend his ancestor against the accusation of falsehood, this gentleman contrived to sail to Lilliput, where he found that the elder Gulliver's exploits now provided subjects for epic poems and annual orations. The new voyager had easy access to the great men of the realm, who gave him, first, a lesson in geography. He was told that *Blefuscu* was not an island, as had been reported by Swift's Gulliver, but a very large empire on the continent of *Degulia,* which the grandson perceived, by the aid of maps, was a miniature Europe. Indeed, inhabited by "this Pigmy Race" was "a World in Miniature," differing from ours only in size and in the fact that it was flat rather than spherical. The writer then embarks on a historical survey of this world that serves to identify *Iberia* as Spain, *Mildendo* as London, *Columbia* as America. His account of the government of Lilliput concludes with the statement: "As we propose to publish every Month such Part of Mr. GULLIVER's Papers as shall seem most proper" to acquaint "our Readers ... with the History and present State of *Lilliput,* we have chosen for this half Year's Entertainment, the DEBATES of the *Lilliputian* Senate" and shall begin with that on the Spanish depradations, a debate that took place "at *Belfaborac* in the 11th Moon of the Reign of Emperor GORGENTI the Second."

The device of indirection hit on by the *Gentleman's Magazine* was more imaginative than that of the *London Magazine* and seemingly more complex, but was actually easier on the reader seeking facts, since the "translations" were quickly learned. The names assigned to speakers were anagrams of their true names or were otherwise altered, but not enough to be unrecognizable. A slight alteration sometimes produced an amusing effect: *Walelop* for Walpole, *Ptit* for Pitt. Only a few of the names were confusing: *Quadrert* (Carteret) and *Castroflet* (Chesterfield) caused the first editor of the *Debates* some trouble, as we shall see later. The *Gentleman's Magazine* had brought forth, on the whole, a happy expedient and had presented it in a vigorous and entertaining essay. "The Autobiography of Sylvanus Urban," on no apparent authority, states that the device and its introduction were both the work of William Guthrie,[55] who by this time had been employed by Cave to "bring home and digest" the debates.[56] George Birkbeck Hill thinks that the device was probably Johnson's and the initial essay certainly his.[57] The Lilliputian disguise would seem to have issued more appropriately from Johnson's fertile mind than from the pedestrian Guthrie's, but it may have been the joint achievement of a number of editorial minds. That the introduction is highly Johnsonian in style can hardly be disputed after one has read the first paragraph-sentence.[58] The reader is referred to Appendix 1 of this study, where the text of the "Appendix to Capt. Lemuel Gulliver's Account" is reproduced.

For several months the magazines were highly conscious of the new clothing of their debates and seemed to put more emphasis on the device than on the real business at hand, to communicate parliamentary intelligence to their readers. The *London Magazine* printed long, heavy introductions in an attempt to explain the terminology of the "Club." No doubt the reader made an easy adjustment and soon forgot that his "Debates in Parliament" were now called "Proceedings of the Political Club." Use of the device was confined to the introductions to debates and the links between speeches. The *Gentleman's Magazine* made extensive use of footnotes that were intended to give hints for the translation of Lilliputian terms. In time the disguises came to be worn more comfortably, but the *Gentleman's Magazine* must occasionally have been found irksome by reason of the heavy sprinkling of grotesque Lilliputian terms within its speeches. However the eighteenth-century reader may have received them, the terms seem appropriate to the air of unreality in the Lilliputian *Debates,* especially as those speeches, in the 'forties, took on the full strength of Johnson's classical eloquence.

20   *Johnson's Parliamentary Reporting*

The *Gentleman's Magazine* went to some pains in order that the reader might not find his reading of the news obscured. At the end of the Supplement for 1738 is printed an advertisement for "Proposals for printing by Subscription ANAGRAMMATA REDIVIVA, or the ART of *Composing* and *Resolving* ANAGRAMS." (This example of what I take to be early Johnsonian high jinks is reproduced in Appendix 1.) Here the reader was given an easy guide to Lilliputian geographical terms, and the similar advertisement in the Supplement for 1739 revealed the English names of the Lilliputian speakers and translated other terms. Some of these (for example, *Hurgos*, or Lords, and *Clinabs*, or Commons) were already sufficiently well known.[59]

At the end of 1738 Cave followed his old custom of concluding the previous session's debates. The magazine was then free of Lilliputian content until June, 1739. The *London Magazine* continued its "Political Club" into the new year with some of the debates on "Politicks and Philosophy" that had been described in the original preface, one on "the original Form of our Government" and another "showing the Benefit that accrues to Society from a general Belief in the fundamental Principles of Natural Religion."[60] In 1740 and thereafter, both magazines kept up the publication of their parliamentary reports after the beginning of a new volume.

Caution was still observed, however, in printing views of a Parliament in session; the custom was, as before, to withhold the debates of a given session until it had come to an end. The *London Magazine*, over the years, tried to maintain a reasonably accurate sequence in printing its debates. The lists of Appendix 2 exhibit the increasingly jumbled chronological order of the debates in the *Gentleman's Magazine*. Hill[61] attributes the confusion solely to caution in printing the debates of a given session while it was still in progress. This does not explain why there are installments of two different debates in most of the magazines, of three in several. Cave may have felt that he would, by keeping several of them going at once over several months, assure continued interest in his magazine—and steady purchase of it. Perhaps, too, he felt that to publish them thus added a further element of indirection to the venture and so made him less likely to be accused of a breach of parliamentary privilege.

Rivalry became more intense after the magazines adopted the new form for their debates. Each magazine chided the other for inaccuracy, for partiality, for lack of originality. In its newspaper advertisements the *London Magazine* frequently accused the rival of stealing debates:

N. B. The two speeches of the Lord Viscount G—ge, which Dr. Urban would impose upon his readers as never before printed, are *stolen* from the *London Magazine* for May last, and several lines omitted, according to that Collector's usual Way of mangling every thing he can lay his Hand on.[62]

And in April, 1742, the *London Magazine* distributed a handbill advertising the Commons debate in the "Political Club" on the motion to remove Walpole, which appeared in its March issue.

N. B. [it reads] The Public may be assured, that those wretched *Scraps* of *Speeches* lately publish'd in the *Gentleman's Magazine* are spurious, and an Imposition on the Public, and have always been so, except in the Year 1737, the latter End of 1740, and the Beginning of the Year 1741, when they were all *stolen* from the LONDON MAGAZINE.[63]

The last accusation is true. We have already seen that the *Gentleman's Magazine* followed the *London Magazine* in its debates for part of 1737. In November, December, and the Supplement, 1740, and in February, March, and April, 1741, Cave's publication derived several debates from the rival, though these were much revised verbally. Later in 1742 the *Gentleman's Magazine* has a complaint to make about its competitor's accuracy. In reporting the debate on Lord Limerick's motion for an inquiry into Walpole's conduct for the past ten years, the writer complains that the earlier *London Magazine* account had evidently been written by "Persons... very little acquainted" with the facts, "even ignorant of the Number of Speakers.... For, as in a former remarkable Debate they had but *six* Speakers instead of *twenty,* so in this, instead of *ten,* they have introduced but *six,* and those in a very confused Manner." They have put one man's speech into the mouth of another and reversed the order of two important speeches." Again the criticism was justified, as will be shown in chapter iii. The *Gentleman's Magazine* usually printed more speeches, the *London Magazine* longer ones.

Neither of the rival magazines during these years abandoned the practice of printing individual speeches of presumed authenticity. These were supplied either by the speakers or by members who had taken notes. That the former was probably the usual means of supply we may deduce from the fact that most of these speeches were delivered by a small group of members. Lord Gage and John St. Aubyn, for example, seem to have been in the habit of sending the magazines copies of their speeches. These were reprinted without "Club" or Lilliputian disguise, usually with the speaker's name veiled by the use of blanks. Both publications often solicited copies or notes of such speeches by means of statements on the title page or its reverse.

Competition seems not to have diminished the success of either venture. The popularity of the Lilliputian *Debates,* according to Hawkins, "increased the sale of Cave's pamphlet from ten to fifteen thousand copies a month." He "manifested his good fortune by buying an old coach and a pair of older horses; and, that he might avoid the suspicion of pride in setting up an equipage, he displayed to the world the source of his affluence, by a representation of St. John's Gate, instead of his arms, on the door-panel."[65] (St. John's Gate was the editorial address of the *Gentleman's Magazine* and a cut depicting it was on the cover of every issue.)

According to the preface in the eleventh volume (1741), the magazine was "reprinted in several presses in *Great Britain, Ireland,* and the Plantations" and its debates were copied "by Some." In March, 1742, it was noted that "the Debates in our

Magazine [were] so well received in Holland, that they are begun to be translated."⁶⁶ Before the Commons debate on the motion to remove Walpole is prefixed (February, 1743) a statement that the report of the debate in the other house had been "translated in the *Etat Politic de l'Europe* printed at the *Hague,* also into *Spanish* and *High-Dutch.*"⁶⁷ The "Proceedings of the Political Club" after 1739 were reprinted by the *Scots Magazine,* a publication lovingly remembered by Boswell when he was writing the *Life.*⁶⁸ There was also a Dublin edition of the *London Magazine.*

We must now fit Johnson more precisely into the narrative of the rise and progress of the *Debates in the Senate of Lilliput.* Which of them are of his sole composition? The answer is less easily arrived at than has often been assumed. Boswell's authority has been relied on most heavily and is, indeed, the most dependable.⁶⁹

He this year [1741], and the two following, wrote the Parliamentary Debates. He told me himself, that he was the sole composer of them for those three years only. He was not, however, precisely exact in his statement, which he mentioned from hasty recollection; for it is sufficiently evident, that his composition of them began November 19, 1740, and ended February 23, 1742–3.⁷⁰

We regret the imprecision of Johnson's statement. Six days before Johnson's death, he requested to see John Nichols, from whom he had borrowed some of the early volumes of the *Gentleman's Magazine,* "with the professed intention to point out the pieces which he had written in that collection. The books lay on the table, with many leaves doubled down, particularly those which contained his share in the parliamentary debates."⁷¹ But Nichols did not think to make a record of the doubling down. This is unfortunate, because Boswell's statement is ambiguous.

It is generally assumed that Boswell intends to say that Johnson reported the debates which took place on and between "November 19, 1740," and "February 23, 1742–3." The dates obviously cannot, as his statement suggests, represent the time of composition, for Boswell could hardly have arrived at them so precisely in the absence of a statement from Johnson. Nor can the dates represent the time of publication, which, for the *Gentleman's Magazine,* was the first of every month during these years. Boswell's interpretation, that it is "sufficiently evident" that the reports of the debates taking place on and between those dates are Johnson's, is surely based on internal rather than external evidence. What are we to say of the dates? The latter must certainly refer to the debate on the spirituous liquors bill (February 22 to 25, 1743), but does the first date refer to the corn bill debate (November 25), as has been the traditional interpretation, or to the debate on the address of thanks for His Majesty's speech (November 18), which is closer to Boswell's date?

We must go back to the *Gentleman's Magazine* for the year 1741 to examine the internal evidence on which Boswell relied. After having printed revised versions of *London Magazine* reports in November, December, and the Supplement, 1740, the *Gentleman's Magazine,* in its January issue, presents an original debate from the Sixth Session of the Eighth Parliament, the session preceding the one in progress. In the following numbers, February to April, appear more revisions of previously published accounts from the *London Magazine,* still of debates of the Sixth Session. We can say with confidence that the copied debates are not of Johnson's composition, though they may have been revised by him. Parliament was prorogued at the end of April, and publication of the reports of the Seventh Session began in the May issue with the previously mentioned debate of November 18, 1740. After several months of dependence on the *London Magazine,* Cave gave his readers an original report. Appearances seem to indicate that the starting of a new series, of a fresh group of reports, the change coinciding with the commencement of the debates for a new session. Since Boswell and other authorities assign all subsequent reports of this session to Johnson, are we

Historical Backgrounds 25

not led, by a consideration of the circumstances of publication, to the conclusion that he wrote this one too? A reading of the debate of November 18 provides convincing proof that the traditional interpretation has been the right one. I feel that this debate has nothing Johnsonian about it and shall try to justify that feeling by an analysis of style in the appropriate place.

Until more evidence is found, it is impossible to reconstruct the circumstances attending Johnson's assumption of full authorship of the *Debates*. The report of the debate that took place on February 13, 1741, may well have been the first written by him. I surmise that, some time after that date, Cave approached Johnson with the proposal that he take over authorship of the parliamentary account. Hawkins lends support to this conjecture:

> The vigorous opposition to the minister, and the motion in both houses of the thirteenth of February, 1740-1 to remove him, were a new aera in politics; and, as the debates on that occasion were warmer than had ever been known, the drawing them up required, in Cave's opinion, the pen of a more nervous writer than he who had hitherto conducted them.[72]

The printing of the debate of November 18, 1740, begun in May, 1741, was concluded in the June issue. Perhaps that report had been written for Cave by an inferior hand before the debate on the motion convinced the publisher that "a more nervous writer" was needed. Cave then published it before the Lords debate on the motion—a debate which he must have known to be more in demand by his readers—because the earlier report was ready for print and he did not wish to waste it, and perhaps because caution was considered desirable in printing a report of the most hotly contested debate of the session immediately after its end. Johnson's report of the debate on the motion (House of Lords) was printed in the July and August issues of the magazine. The subsequently printed reports covering the debates of November 25, 1740, to February 13, 1741, may have been written by Johnson from notes taken by others at the time of the debates or perhaps rewritten from previously completed reports by Johnson's predecessor. This writing may have been done just before the publication of the reports. Unless we assume that they were so written, it is hard to explain the haste with which they were composed.[73] It is possible that some debates may have been set up in type[74] and laid aside until it was felt that a moment safe for publication had arrived. Such an explanation may account for the delayed appearance of the Commons debate on the motion, which was not published until some two years after the event.

There is other evidence besides Boswell's that the debate on the spirituous liquors bill was the last to be reported by Johnson. Hawkins states, "Johnson continued to write them till the passing the bill for restraining the sale of spirituous liquors, which was about the end of the year 1743."[75] If we accept February 22–25, 1743, as the date of the last debate reported by Johnson, the last debate of the series to be *printed* was the Commons debate on the Hanoverian troops, December 10, 1742. This is concluded in the March, 1744, issue of the magazine and is followed in the same issue by a debate of very different character, divorced of all Lilliputian trappings—the names of the speakers represented by initials, dashes, and final letters. This debate is concluded in the April number, and in May the Lilliputian *Debates* are taken up again with news of the next session. There seems to be a significant break here in the sequence. According to Hawkins,[76] the author of the newly resumed Lilliputian *Debates* was Hawkesworth, Johnson's "closest imitator."[77]

Hill would have us believe[78] that Johnson discontinued his labors on the *Debates* because he was shocked to learn that they were taken as fact. In support of his contention he cites the coincidence of the date of the late debate, February 22–25, 1743, with the announcement of the translation of a debate into a foreign language in the February, 1743, issue of the *Gentleman's Magazine*. Nevertheless, the chronology is all wrong. Johnson

Historical Backgrounds

probably did not write the February 22 debate until many months thereafter; and, as a matter of fact, an announcement of another translated debate had appeared a year earlier. Moreover, Hill's theory assumes considerable *naïveté* in a man now past thirty who had been connected with the enterprise for five years. The magazine and Johnson continually protested that they did not pretend to give the exact words of speakers but simply to do justice to the arguments of both sides. Many speeches begin with a reminder of the disavowal: "Sir *Rub. Walelop* spoke next in substance as follows:" "Then the Urg; *Bewlos* spoke in this Manner." No doubt Johnson came gradually to feel uneasy about his part in the venture, but there was no sudden shock.

What of the *Debates in the Senate of Lilliput* printed in the *Gentleman's Magazine* before July, 1741? According to Boswell, "The debates in Parliament, which were brought home and digested by Guthrie, whose memory... was... very quick and tenacious, were sent by Cave to Johnson for his revision."[79] Support of the statement is found in a letter quoted by Boswell. Johnson writes to Cave, "If I made fewer alterations than usual in the Debates, it was only because there appeared and still appears to be less need of alteration."[80] The letter is assigned the date September, 1738, by Powell. That Johnson revised the earlier *Debates* seems certain, but he was making "fewer" corrections at the time of the letter, and the *Debates* may not have become "more and more enriched by the accession of Johnson's genius"[81] (as Boswell puts it) between the years 1738 and 1740. A. L. Reade has given extensive evidence to show that Johnson was not in London from the late spring of 1739 to the early part of 1740,[82] and, if we accept his conclusion, it is probable that Johnson did not revise the *Debates* issued during those months.[83] The *Debates* published during Johnson's absence reveal attributes of style hardly more or less Johnsonian than are found in the *Debates* which precede and immediately follow. Those issued before 1741 do not, on the whole, impress us strongly as Johnson's.[84]

We have concluded that Johnson was "sole composer" of the debates that reflect proceedings from November 25, 1740, to February 25, 1743, but what do we mean by the phrase (which is Boswell's)? If Johnson merely put spoken words of others into more polished written form, we can regard him not as composer or author but rather as editor. Time has made impossible a complete appraisal of the degree to which the *Debates* are original compositions. Such authentic records as exist will, later in the present study, be compared with the *Debates;* and the comparison will give us partial knowledge.

It would be well, at this point, to review the evidence concerning the sort of material with which Johnson worked and the method of its collection. We are sure that Johnson himself did not hear the speeches of the members. According to Hawkins, "he never was within the walls of either house of parliament."[85] Murphy claims that Johnson said, "I never had been in the gallery of the House of Commons but once."[86] At any rate, gathering the news was not part of his job. He worked "from scanty notes furnished by persons employed to attend in both houses of Parliament. Sometimes, however, as he himself told me, he had nothing more communicated to him than the names of the several speakers, and the part which they had taken in the debate."[87] To Nichols, Johnson reported that "they were frequently written from very slender materials and often from none at all,—the mere product of his own imagination."[88] Murphy records Johnson's fullest explanation of the preliminaries to his composition, but Murphy was writing from memory more than nineteen years after the statement was made.

Cave had interest with the door-keepers. He, and the persons employed by him, gained admittance: they brought away the subject of discussion, the names of the speakers, the side they took and the order in which they rose, together with notes of the arguments advanced in the course of the debate. The whole was afterwards communicated to me, and I composed the speeches in the form which they now have in the Parliamentary debates.[89]

Historical Backgrounds

How Cave or his agents made their way into the houses is suggested by the statement that he "had interest with the doorkeepers." According to Hawkins, "Cave had an interest with some of the members of both houses, arising from an employment he held in the post office, that of inspector of the franks."[90] Hawkins also gives a plausible-sounding description of Cave's method of assembling notes.

> I have been informed by some who were much about him, that, taking with him a friend or two, he found means to procure for them and himself admission into the gallery of the house of commons or to some concealed station in the other, and that then they privately took down notes of the several speeches, and the general substance of the arguments. Thus furnished, Cave and his associates would adjourn to a neighboring tavern, and compare and adjust their notes, by means whereof and the help of their memory they became enabled to fix at least the substance of what they had so lately heard and remarked.[91]

Cave's statement before the House of Lords in 1747[92] that he alone attended the sessions of Parliament, "made use of a black lead pencil and only took notes of some remarkable passages; and from his Memory put them together himself," cannot be trusted. He testified at the same time that he sometimes had assistance from members, and, as we have seen, there is evidence that he sought the aid of Dr. Birch. Also, he said that members of the house sometimes sent whole speeches to him. These were probably the individual speeches printed in the *Gentleman's Magazine* without Lilliputian disguise. There is evidence, then, that Cave had the means for gathering a limited amount of parliamentary news.[93] And we have Johnson's words, probably authentically preserved, that the *Debates* "were frequently written from very slender materials and often from none at all."[94]

The Decline of Reporting in the Magazines

The *Debates* did not long survive the severing of Johnson's connection. They continued to be printed through the rest of 1744 and the whole of 1745. In 1746 they appeared in only four issues, and in December the *Debates in the Senate of Lilliput* were brought to a final but an unceremonious end. The *London Magazine's* "Political Club" continued. In March, 1747, both magazines printed, without disguise of any sort, reports of Lord Lovat's trial in the House of Lords. That was an imprudent piece of boldness. For breach of privilege, both Cave and Astley were ordered into the custody of the Gentleman Usher of the Black Rod and were questioned in some detail before the Lords concerning their methods of invading the privacy of Parliament.[95] Both were evasive. Astley said that his information came to him "by Penny Post or by Messenger pursuant to Advertisements frequently inserted in the *London Magazine,* inviting Persons to furnish him with matter of that nature." On being pressed, he offered the name of one Mr. Clarke, "whom he supposed an Attorney," but Clarke could not be questioned; he had been dead since May last. Cave insisted of his debates that "from his memory he put them together himself." No one had ever been employed by him to write them. As for the offending account of Lord Lovat's trial, Cave had printed it from a paper left at his house, by whom he did not know. Both editors were finally released.

The period of Cave's regular parliamentary reporting had ended, but Astley, after an interval of four months, resumed the "Political Club." The newly begun series was prefaced by a letter from the "secretary," explaining that it would be necessary to revert to a former practice and record only the arguments of each side without naming the speakers in any way. (The *London Magazine* had of late dared to print the members' names along with the Roman designations.) Soon the familiar classical names returned and the "Club" was continued until August, 1757; thereafter the department was replaced by a running narrative, "The History of the Last Session of Parliament," in which debates, properly speaking, did not figure.

Historical Backgrounds 31

Some of the public interest in debates had probably begun to wane when Johnson gave up his reporting activities. With Walpole out of office, much of the justification was gone for the abusive accusation and the hot retort. We may assume that when Cave, sensitive as he was to his readers' desires, discontinued the reports in the middle 'forties, there was no longer enough demand for them to offset the risk of offending a continually vigilant Parliament. The task thus abandoned by the magazines was not immediately taken up by other hands. The *Parliamentary History* speaks of "the deficiency of connected Parliamentary Information during the great chasm between the years 1743 and 1774."[96]

Parliamentary reporting, when again seriously resumed, had become the property of the weekly and daily newspapers. Their accounts were at first meager, inaccurate, and partisan. Parliament was still inclined to insist on its privilege. Early in 1771 the House of Commons began action against a group of newspaper printers for "misrepresenting the speeches and reflecting on several members."[97] John Wilkes and his followers took up the cause of the printers and sought to obstruct the orders of the house. Wilkes, Alderman Richard Oliver, and Brass Crosby, Lord Mayor of London, were ordered to appear. Wilkes refused, and Commons wisely let proceedings against him lapse. Oliver and Crosby were sent to the Tower, but not until a mob had broken up Lord North's carriage and "hustled and pelted with stones and mud"[98] the ministerial members. Oliver and Crosby were heroes and the house could only release them at the end of the session. Parliament's legal victory became a practical defeat. Neither house dared again to prevent the publication of news; the modern era of parliamentary journalism had begun.

That phase of the history of debate reporting which extends from the foundation of the *Political State* in 1711 to the discontinuance of the reports by the magazines at mid-century is well defined. During those years the work was carried on regularly, at least while Parliament was in recess, and with impartiality by monthly[99] periodicals. And constantly in the background, shaping the form of the debate reports, lay the fact that the activity was illegal. At the time of Johnson's connection with parliamentary reporting, that phase of the tradition was at its highest level. The proceedings were then most lively; the reports of them, most extensive; the restrictions against the work, most rigid; the means of evading those restrictions, most picturesque. That Johnson should have assumed the position of "writer of the debates" in that period bespeaks the attainment of high standing among writers by profession. When we consider his youth, his late removal from the rusticities of Lichfield, his lack of experience in the world of politics and affairs of state, it is possible to echo the homely enthusiasm of Sir John Hawkins:

That a man, under these disadvantages should be able to frame a system of debate, to compose speeches of such excellence both in matter and form, as scarcely to be equalled by those of the most able and experienced statesman is, I say, matter of astonishment, and proof of talents that qualified him for a speaker in the most august assembly on earth.

Chapter II

THE DEBATES DURING TWO CENTURIES: THE HISTORY OF THE DOCUMENT

Those gathered at Foote's for dinner made an illustrious company. Both Samuel Foote himself and Arthur Murphy were men of the stage: actors and playwrights. Alexander Wedderburne, lawyer and politician, was later to become Lord Chancellor. Dr. Philip Francis was renowned as the translator of Horace. And there were others. The presence, in addition to these, of Dr. Samuel Johnson—"Dictionary Johnson"—gave assurance that there would be good talk. At length the conversation settled on politics.

An important debate toward the end of Sir Robert Walpole's administration being mentioned, Dr. Francis observed, "That Mr. Pitt's speech, on that occasion, was the best he had ever read." He added, "That he had employed eight years of his life in the study of Demosthenes, and finished a translation of that celebrated orator, with all the decorations of style and language within the reach of his capacity; but he had met with nothing equal to the speech above-mentioned." Many of the company remembered the debate; and some passages were cited, with the approbation and applause of all present. During the ardour of conversation, Johnson remained silent. As soon as the warmth of praise subsided, he opened with these words: "That speech I wrote in a garret in Exeter Street."

He proceeded to explain that he had been in the House of Commons but once, that Edward Cave and his employees gained admittance and brought away "the subject of discussion, the names of the speakers, the side they took, and the order in which they rose, together with notes of arguments." From these materials, Johnson composed the *Debates*.

To this discovery Dr. Francis made answer: "Then, Sir, you have exceeded Demosthenes himself; for to say that you have exceeded Francis' Demosthenes, would be saying nothing." The rest of the company bestowed lavish encomiums on Johnson: one in particular, praised his impartiality; observing, that he dealt out reason and eloquence with an equal hand to both parties. "That is not quite true," said Johnson, "I saved appearances tolerably well, but I took care that the WHIG DOGS should not have the best of it."[1]

We are safe, I think, in placing Foote's dinner party in the 1760's.[2] If we put our trust in the anecdote as told by Murphy, the secret had been well kept until then.

That there should have been a secret requires explanation. It may have been considered, at first, that there was danger of parliamentary action. Hill suggests that Cave intended to screen Johnson when, before the House of Lords in 1747, "being asked 'if he ever had any Persons whom he kept in pay, to make speeches for him?' he said 'He never had.' "[3] Johnson may well have felt, when he had gained a measure of recognition, that the hastily written *Debates* might not increase his literary—and might reflect on his moral—reputation. There is evidence that he was aware of the point of view from which the writing of debates, since the public was prone to accept them as fact in spite of insistence to the contrary, might be looked on as deceptive. He expresses that point of view with his usual cogency when, in 1756, he says, in his preface to the *Literary Magazine,* "We shall not attempt to give any regular series of debates, or to amuse our Readers with senatorial rhetoric. The speeches inserted in other papers have been long known to be fictitious, and produced sometimes by men who never heard the debate, nor had any authentic information. We have no Design to impose thus grossly on our Readers."[4] At the end of his life Johnson had come to feel that "the only part of his writings that then gave him any compunction, was his account of the debates in the Magazine."[5]

---

[1] For notes to chapter ii see pages 158–160.

The Debates During Two Centuries   35

Much evidence casts doubt on Hawkins' claim that, once the secret was disclosed, Johnson was "free and indeed industrious in the communication of it."[5] Even to his friends, Johnson was not industrious in communicating information on the subject. As we have seen, he was vague in disclosing his part of the *Debates* to Boswell. Mrs. Thrale, making for her own use, in December, 1777, a "Catalogue of such Writings as I *know* to be his," lists "Debates in Parl^t Pitts 1st Speech,"[7] and thus reveals that she was sure only of his authorship of one speech and imprecise in identifying that one. Johnson must have been even less free in communicating his secret to the world at large. No doubt vague rumors circulated, but Horace Walpole, a man not unfamiliar with the talk of the town, could say that he "never knew Johnson wrote [the *Debates*] till Johnson died."[8]

Because Johnson's authorship of the *Debates in the Senate of Lilliput* did not become common knowledge until after his death, the history of the document has had two phases. During the first, the *Debates* were almost never read as the work of Johnson or of any single man but as the reflection of fact. The subsequent phase found readers—though at first reluctant to give up the assumption that it was essentially a factual report—strongly aware that the work was in some degree Johnsonian. The purpose of the present chapter is to trace the fortunes of the *Debates* through these phases by investigating the forms in which the work has reached print since its appearance in the *Gentleman's Magazine*. The foundation for the investigation lies in the Courtney and Smith *Bibliography of Samuel Johnson*,[9] which, however, records but three of the publications here to be described. The exclusion of the four general collections of debates in which Johnson's compositions were printed seems to have been an oversight by the compilers of the bibliography, for certainly those collections fall within the scope of that volume, the expressed purpose of which is "to give a record of the publication of his writings and compositions."

The Debates During Johnson's Life

The first reissue of the early Johnson reports was begun even before the last had been written. At the time of his "sole composition" of the *Debates,* the intensity of public interest brought forth several "parliamentary histories" covering the period between the restoration and the time of publication. Since the most voluminous accounts of parliamentary information after 1711 were to be found in the periodicals, the debates for those years were appropriated from them and printed in the collections without acknowledgment. Thus Johnson's *Debates in the Senate of Lilliput* had no more than seen print in a monthly magazine when they were snatched up and thrust between the hard covers of a "history." There were, in the early 'forties, two rival collections of this sort. One, originally an Irish production, later reprinted in London, covered the proceedings of both houses (commonly called Torbuck by historians, after its London publisher); the other was a pair of closely related works (Chandler and Timberland) covering separately the history of the two houses.

The Chandler-Timberland collection (since the two complement each other, we may look on them as constituting a single collection) was more carefully prepared and more comprehensive than the Torbuck collection. The volumes of Chandler's *History and Proceedings of the House of Commons* which contain Johnson's work we may, for convenience, refer to as Chandler, Volumes XII, XIII, and XIV; the actual title pages show considerable variation.

The History and Proceedings of the House of Commons from the Restoration to the Present Time...Vol. XII. London: Printed for Richard Chandler and sold at the *Ship* without *Temple-Bar,* and at *York* and *Scarborough.* 1742.

The History and Proceedings of the House of Commons during the Third Parliament of his present Majesty King George II. Held in the Years 1741, and 1742...London: Printed for Richard Chandler...1743.

The Debates During Two Centuries 37

The History and Proceedings of the House of Commons during the Third Parliament of his present Majesty King George II. Held in the Years 1742, and 1743 ... London: Printed: And sold by William Sandby at the *Ship* without Temple-Bar, and at York and Scarbrough [*sic*]. 1744.

In these three volumes are printed complete all but four of the Commons debates traditionally admitted to the Johnson canon (those dated November 25, 1740, to December 10, 1742). The four debates are represented by extended selections of speeches or passages. (The reader is referred to Appendix 2, p. 218, for a more detailed account of the Johnsonian content of Chandler.) The absence of full reprints of the important debates dated February 13, 1741, March 9, 1742, and March 23, 1742, may be attributed to the slowness of the *Gentleman's Magazine* in getting its reports into print. The *London Magazine's* accounts of those debates were used by Chandler in the main historical narrative, because they were published at least six months earlier than the rival's and so were ready for use when a given volume of the collection was put together. Later, when the *Gentleman's Magazine* version was found to contain additional speeches, supplements to the main account were added in the Addenda and Appendix of Chandler. Thus in the Addenda to Volume XIII are placed all the Johnsonian speeches of the debate of February 13, 1741, except those of Sandys, Pelham, Harley, Pulteney, and Walpole—all previously represented in the account taken from the *London Magazine*. The only other debate of Johnson not fully reprinted is found in the main body of the Chandler collection, XIV; there the debate of December 10, 1742, is amalgamated with the *London Magazine* account. The tardiness of the *Gentleman's Magazine* necessitated the wrenching of order elsewhere in Chandler's volumes. The debates of November 25, 1740, and February 24 and April 8, 1741, are not found in the main text of Volume XII, but are relegated to a section at the rear cryptically headed, "Particulars omitted in the last Session which did not occur in the Order of Time." The notably tardy report of December 10, 1740 (printed in the *Gentleman's Magazine* Supplement for 1742, and the January issue, 1743), finds its way into the Addenda of the subsequent Volume XIII.

Bearing in mind that the *Debates* were printed without authorization of writer or original publisher; issued not out of permanent literary interest but out of temporary political interest; and reprinted with the knowledge that the magazine reports were no better than approximations of the original debates—we are not surprised to find a text only reasonably faithful to the original. The comparison of a number of pages from each of the three volumes with the corresponding pages of the *Gentleman's Magazine* reveals no startling verbal alterations (though occasional misprints). Even punctuation and capitalization show no significant variations. The main change in the text is the removal of all Lilliputian paraphernalia. Names of speakers are printed in full. The narrative connections supplied by the *Gentleman's Magazine* are usually altered or replaced by new ones. An additional change, though perhaps excusable in view of the nature of the publication, nonetheless falsifies the Johnson text significantly. That is the omission of the careful qualifications generally used when putting words into the debaters' mouths: "Capt. Carnwoll then rose, and spoke to this effect," "The Hurgo Haxilaf spoke next in substance as follows" become simply "Captain Cornwall," "Lord Halifax."

Since I have had an opportunity to examine only two copies of the Chandler collection, I cannot say how many times it was reissued. It seems safe to assume that there were at least two printings, since the complete set appears in two different forms. One form, apparently the first, divides the whole into two separate series: the first five volumes carry the work down to the death of Anne; the subsequent volumes, again beginning with a Volume I, contain the narrative that commences with the first Parliament of George I.[10] In a set made up in this fashion, the

The Debates During Two Centuries 39

volume designated above as XII is labeled Volume VII (i.e., of the history subsequent to the death of Anne). There is no evidence of a new setting of type in the consecutively numbered set except on title pages and introductory sheets, but the set examined by me was printed on paper of poorer quality and smaller size than the earlier issue.

Chandler's collection must have been popular. Gent, the memoir-writing printer, says of Chandler's "debates" that, "by the run they seemed to take, one would have imagined that he would have ascended to the apex of his desires; but alas! his thoughts soared too high."[11] Chandler fell into debt and shot himself in 1744. Perhaps his business venture had felt the effect of the ebb of public interest in parliamentary news, which partly accounted for Cave's abandoning the reports. The name of Chandler's successor, Sandby, appears on the title of the last volume of the work.

The title pages of the collection published by Timberland give evidence that that bookseller was closely connected, geographically, with Chandler.

The History and Proceedings of the House of Lords, from the Restoration in 1660, to the Present Time...Volume the Seventh, from 1739, to 1741. London: Printed for Ebenezer Timberland in Ship-Yard, Temple-Bar and sold by the Booksellers in Town and Country. 1742.

The History and Proceedings of the House of Lords, during the Third Parliament of King George II. Held in the years 1741 and 1742. London: Printed for Ebenezer Timberland...M,DCC,XLIII.

The volumes were apparently issued in close association with the earlier collection of debates in Commons. There is an advertisement of the Lords debates (that designation on the contemporary binding suggests the popular name of Timberland) facing the title page of Chandler, Volume XIII, which reads, "Just published, Beautifully printed in Eight Volumes Octavo, connected with Chandler's Edition of the Proceedings and Debates of the House of Commons, to which they are a proper Supplement, and together containing a regular Series of Parliamentary Transactions both of Lords and Commons for Eighty two Years past." Typographical similarity between the two collections leads us to the belief that they issued from the shop of a single printer, a belief further substantiated by the presence, in a volume of Chandler (one of the University of California copies), of the Timberland preface mistakenly introduced in place of the correct one.

Appendix 2 (p. 207) shows that for the period of Johnson's authorship the Lilliputian debates of the Lords were printed entire from the *Gentleman's Magazine* with one exception. That one, the debate of February 13, 1741, is represented only by the controversy on the second question of the day; the *London Magazine* report of the debate on the main question was used in place of Johnson's. The text of Volume VII exhibits the main characteristics of the text of Chandler and need not be further described. In the "eighth volume," however, are found some surprising alterations. "So far as it was to be foreseen by human Prudence" becomes: "So far as discoverable by human foresight."[12] "The Senate thus divided and disturbed will perhaps conclude with less Prudence than any single Member, as any Man may more easily discover Truth without Assistance, than when others of equal Abilities are employed in perplexing his Enquiries, and interrupting the Operation of his Mind." This is altered to: "A Parliament thus divided will perhaps conclude with less Prudence than any single Member, as any Man may more easily discover Truth without Assistance, than when others of equal Abilities are employed in perplexing his Enquiries."[13] The changes tend toward condensation. Was the editing done to save type and paper? It seems more likely that the text was felt to need "improvement." The result is more direct but less graceful and less Johnsonian.[14]

The Debates During Two Centuries

The companion Chandler-Timberland histories were, from the beginning, contending with a rival. In the first five volumes of *History and Proceedings of the House of Commons,* asterisks are used in the tables of contents to set off all particulars "omitted in Torbuck's Debates." If Chandler thus admitted himself bettered in priority of publication (Torbuck, London edition, 1741–1742, must, volume by volume, have remained a jump ahead of the Chandler collection, issued during the same years), he nevertheless demonstrated the superiority of his product. The comparison was, as a matter of fact, unfair; it assumed a purpose that the rival did not intend. The debates of both Chandler and Timberland were so set about with additional information (motions, bills, reports, protests, and the like) that the title *History and Proceedings* was justified. It is principally this additional material that Chandler claimed was omitted from Torbuck, but the title of the latter's work announces its more limited scope: *A Collection of the Parliamentary Debates in England.* Both Lords and Commons debates were included, but little more.

Chandler and Timberland, in their volumes issued in 1743, attempted to convey the impression that Torbuck was a trespasser in the field in which he had, as a matter of fact, broken ground before them. On the verso of the title page of Chandler, Volume XIII, is found, "To prevent the Publick being imposed on by any Spurious Accounts of Parliamentary Proceedings from *Ireland* or elsewhere, I subscribe my Name to this only Authentick Edition...Rich Chandler." Timberland signs his eighth volume in similar fashion and, in a preface entitled "The Bookseller to the Reader," refers to "an imperfect Irish Collection of Debates, lately reprinted by one Torbuck." A list follows of "Particulars inserted in my two first volumes only...intirely omitted in the Irish Collection."

Torbuck, alone among the publishers of debate collections, ran into difficulty with Parliament. On February 26, 1741, complaint was made to the House of Lords "of the printing and publishing certain Books intituled '*A Compleat Collection of Debates in Parliament (both Lords and Commons, &c. in Nine Volumes Octavo*'; mentioned to be sold by *John Torbuck*, in *Clare Court, Drury Lane.*"[15] A committee, which was ordered to investigate, reported on March 2 that they "met ... and were ... attended by *John Torbuck;* who owned to the Committee 'That he was the Printer and Publisher of the said Books; and that he printed the same from a printed Copy ... purchased of *John Smith*, Bookseller in Dublin;' but the said John Torbuck refuses to name any of the Persons whom he employed in printing the said Books." The house then ordered that the Gentleman Usher of the Black Rod "forthwith attach the Body of the said John Torbuck for his said Offense; and ... convey, or cause him to be conveyed, to the Prison of Newgate, and delivered to the Keeper thereof, to be by him safely kept during the Pleasure of the House."[16]

The original Irish collection is apparently scarce. There is no printed record of a copy either in the British Museum or in the Library of Congress. It is said to have been "apparently first issued 1739–42 without printer's name or place of publication,"[17] and to have covered the years 1668 to 1741. I assume that the original title was reproduced with the text in Torbuck's reprint:

A Collection of the Parliamentary Debates in England from the Year M,DC, LXVIII to the Present Time ... London: John Torbuck.

Both the first Irish edition and Torbuck's occupied twenty-one volumes. The nine volumes mentioned in the House of Lords must have been those printed up to the time of the complaint received there. In 1743 a sequel[18] to the set issued during the previous two years was published without Torbuck's name on its title page:

An Impartial History of the Proceedings and Debates in Both Houses of Parliament ... B. Cowse: London, 1743.

The Debates During Two Centuries 43

The volume carries the account from December 1, 1741, to July 15, 1742. According to the *Bibliography of British History*,[19] a second Irish edition, brought out during the years 1741-1749 in twenty-four volumes, covered proceedings up to May, 1744, and incorporated the speeches in the London publication of Cowse.

Within the Torbuck collection were printed, in full, at least fourteen of Johnson's *Debates,* and in part, three.[20] The accounts of debates omitted are all taken from the *London Magazine*. Speeches of the three debates printed in part are thrown together with those from *London Magazine* reports. On the whole, the text is verbally more faithful to the *Gentleman's Magazine* than is either Chandler or Timberland. There are, however, extensive changes in typographical form. Throughout, paragraphs of the original are consolidated into longer ones. No nouns except proper nouns are capitalized. (The *Gentleman's Magazine* and the other two collections capitalize all nouns.) All Lilliputian terms are, of course, rendered into English, but the Torbuck collection, unlike the other two, preserves the original introductions to the speeches ("... spoke to the following purpose").

Plainly, the debate collections of Chandler, Timberland, and Torbuck were popular: they were widely distributed and must have been widely read. Johnson's *Debates* were, to be sure, merely part of the mass, but they were placed toward the end of the mass, and we may conjecture that readers found the debates of the early 'forties to have special qualities without knowing why. (Witness the talk at Foote's dinner party.) The official look of the collections and their boasts of authenticity had an effect. The whole of the volumes soon came to be taken as historical fact; readers tended to forget the unreliability of some of the sources. Obviously, the editors collecting Chesterfield's works for publication did not question the authenticity of Timberland or Torbuck. The *Miscellaneous Works,* issued in 1777, printed, as "specimens of lord Chesterfield's eloquence," two speeches on the spirituous liquors bill that had been written by Johnson! Dr.

Johnson was of course delighted: "he laughed, and said 'Here now are two speeches ascribed to him, both of which were written by me: and the best of it is, they have found out that one is like Demosthenes, and the other like Cicero!'"[21]

THE DEBATES AFTER JOHNSON'S DEATH

Few people can have been aware, when he died in December, 1784, that Johnson had "written debates" in his youth. To be sure, the obituary sketch in the *Gentleman's Magazine* (written by Thomas Tyers) contains the statement, "That he had a considerable share in compiling the 'Parliamentary Debates' in your [i.e., the magazine's] early volumes is well known, and will ever be an honour to his memory."[22] But the fact was perhaps not so well known as the *Gentleman's Magazine,* not averse to catching its share of reflected glory, intended that it should be. The statement is, as far as I have been able to determine, the first published announcement of Johnson's authorship. In the absence of a convenient text of the work, exact knowledge of its nature remained vague; firsthand acquaintance, rare.

When, in 1787, a group of London booksellers, headed by one J. Buckland, issued the first edition of *The Works of Samuel Johnson,* the *Debates in the Senate of Lilliput* did not find a place in the eleven volumes. To John Stockdale, publisher, the omission of the other booksellers was regrettable, perhaps, but challenging. He was at the time not unacquainted with printing connected with Parliament, for he had begun in his trade as a porter to Almon, publisher of the compilation of debates (inadequate, to be sure) that carried on the work of Chandler, Timberland, and Torbuck after 1743.[23] Stockdale independently had reissued some of Almon's publications and had himself put out *Stockdale's Guide to Parliament* and a selection of speeches which he called *The Beauties of the British Senate.* His own interest in Johnson as reporter may well have been heightened by the extended account in Hawkins' *Life of Johnson,* which was

The Debates During Two Centuries

printed as preface to the eleven volumes of the *Works*. Why should not the public want to extend its acquaintance with Johnson's *Debates* beyond the extracts given by Hawkins? Stockdale felt himself called upon to satisfy the demand.

His edition of the *Debates,* the first under Johnson's name, was issued the same year. It was supplied with two title pages. The first announced the book as:

The Works of Samuel Johnson, LL.D. In Thirteen Volumes. Volume XII [XIII]. London: Printed for John Stockdale, opposite Burlington-House, Piccadilly. M. DCC. LXXXVII.

The falseness of the title page gives a hint of the "eccentricity of conduct and ... coarseness of manner" for which Stockdale had a reputation.[24] As R. W. Chapman and Allen T. Hazen remark, "Stockdale had no business to represent his volumes as part of The Works in Thirteen Volumes. Printed by John Stockdale, for whom in fact thirteen volumes had not been printed."[25] The general title page was followed by a second:

Debates in Parliament. By Samuel Johnson, LL.D. In Two Volumes. Vol. I [II]. London ...

Stockdale no doubt intended that the general title might be retained or deleted depending upon whether the buyer desired Volumes XII and XIII of the *Works* or simply the *Parliamentary Debates*. Chapman and Hazen, who have examined several copies, say that the general title is often missing. Appearance sets Stockdale's volumes apart from the genuine *Works* of 1787, for his page is more crowded and the paper of grayer tone. The first printing of the *Debates,* then, managed to be neither a bona fide part of an edition of the *Works* nor a completely independent publication.

Boswell says that the editor of these volumes was George Chalmers. If that is true, it may be questioned whether his editing went beyond writing the preface, which is unreliable in its facts, unenlightening in its criticisms. Reading aids consist of a

"List of Fictitious Terms" (i.e., a list of Lilliputian names), a table of contents, and an index of the speakers. Since this was the first edition of the work printed under Johnson's name, a careful editing of the text might have been expected. The necessary task of untangling and assembling complete debates and transcribing them from the *Gentleman's Magazine* was attempted. A date was assigned to each and the debates were placed in chronological order. Finally, the Lilliputian machinery was removed. But in carrying out all this work, the editor, or editors, stopped short of perfection. Since this text has intrinsic importance and was to have a subsequent history, it should be examined in detail.

The task of extracting complete debates from the issues of the *Gentleman's Magazine* was not without pitfalls for the reckless editor. (The parliamentary compilations of the 'forties might have been of assistance, but evidently were not used.) The editor's task was complicated by the absence of dates in most of the accounts as originally printed. To carelessness in performing the job of assembling may be attributed the omission of two complete debates and the concluding paragraphs of another. They are the debates of January 27, 1741, and March 23, 1742, and the final passages in the speech of Lord Cornwall in the debate of March 9, 1742. The omission of the first is hard to explain except on grounds of willful carelessness. It is a short debate on the seamen's bill, and in the *Gentleman's Magazine* stands directly before a subsequent debate on the same issue. Perhaps the editor, undecided whether to print the debate in conjunction with that on the same bill or to print it in its proper chronological position, avoided a decision by omitting it altogether. Or possibly it was overlooked or considered an appendage to the list of provisions of the bill with which the issue of the magazine begins (and which is omittted from Stockdale also). Both the omitted debate of March 23, 1742, and the deleted portion of the debate of March 9 appeared originally in the same issue, July, 1743. This omission may have been the result of an oversight. We should be tempted

The Debates During Two Centuries

to say that the editor was working from an imperfect file of the magazine from which the July, 1743, number was missing, but the issue also contains the second installment of the debate of February 1, 1743, which is reproduced entire in Stockdale. It is possible that the issue was not lost but was defective. The missing speeches of both debates are contained complete in signatures Xx and Yy, which may have dropped out. Curiously, a report of the division is printed below Cornwall's speech where it breaks off in Stockdale, but in a form very different from that found in the *Gentleman's Magazine*. The oversight may have been caught after the page was set up and the line of type containing the division inserted to put as good a face on the matter as possible.

A further omission in Stockdale is more important than these, and can less confidently be ascribed to careless editing. This is the omission of the Commons debate on the motion to remove Sir Robert Walpole (February 13, 1741), one of the best of the Johnson performances. That debate appeared two full years after the event and was the last report printed of the session in which it occurred. This fact may account for its being overlooked until the setting up of the type by Stockdale made insertion in its proper place impossible. But its conspicuousness in three separate numbers discounts oversight. Perhaps the editor felt that the debate would not be missed since that in the House of Lords on the same subject was included. It may be noted that the inclusion of the debate would have gone far toward removing the disparity in bulk between the two volumes.

Whoever assigned dates to the debates in Stockdale must have been satisfied with pure guesswork more than once. The reader is referred to Appendix 2 (pp. 207–218), where he will see that a few errors in dating were so serious that they disrupted the chronological sequence. Sometimes, at the head of a debate, the *Gentleman's Magazine* had inserted such a notation as "the eighth day of sitting," but these hints appear not to have been followed. Nor were the *Journals* referred to. One may wonder how the editor managed to date the majority of the debates correctly.

Stockdale's editor felt that the "barbarous jargon" (as he termed the Lilliputian trappings) detracted from the effectiveness of the *Debates,* and set out to translate it into ordinary English. Again we must complain of incorrectness and inconsistency. The major error here is the assigning of all but one speech of Lord Chesterfield to Lord Carteret. Chesterfield was "Castroflet"; Carteret, "Quadrert," as the list of fictitious names in the first volume of Stockdale asserts. But the "translator," when he came to "Castroflet," wrote Carteret.[26] Other errors of translation appear chiefly in names of places and nationalities. So "Belgian" (which meant Dutch) was transcribed "French."[27] "Mildendo" (London) became "Middlesex."[28] Sometimes the editor gave up: "those that forced the Pass of Schellenbourg and made their way into the Trenches at Blaregnies" is changed to: "those that forced those passes, and those trenches, that other troops would have failed in attempting."[29] The "translator" of the Lilliputian terms is guilty, too, of inconsistencies. He could not always remember, for example, to change "Senate" to "Parliament," "senatorial" to "parliamentary." (It should be noted that the writer—or editor—of the original also occasionally slipped in supplying this sort of Lilliputian dress to his speeches.)

The text itself is an imperfect reproduction of that in the *Gentleman's Magazine.* A careful comparison of the first two debates of Stockdale with the original printing reveals many discrepancies. Little attempt is made to reproduce accurately the introductions to speeches and the bridges between debates. Perhaps it was felt that these were not by Johnson and hence not important to an edition of his works, but we have no evidence that he did not write them, and we expect closer correspondence to the original here than in the debate collections. "The Advocate Campbell spoke next in Terms to this Purpose" is simply not the same as "The Advocate Campbell spoke next to this purpose." The speeches themselves fare somewhat better. Some misprints in the imperfectly printed *Gentleman's Magazine* are corrected. But new misprints rather frequently find their way into the text. We may take as typical two at the beginning of the corn bill debate. There, "any increase of power" becomes "an increase in power." On the last line of the same page of Stockdale the "Patrons of their Country" become "patterns of their country."[30] Most of the capital letters of the original have been removed and punctuation has occasionally been altered. The last changes are of little consequence, since printers (or so it is generally held), rather than authors, determined the style of punctuation in the first place.

An edition at last available, the *Debates* that were Johnson's were read as his and their Johnsonian qualities were recognized. The conscientious historian could no longer quote the words of Pulteney or Pitt without mentioning that Johnson was said to have had something to do with the speeches, but it was difficult to give up the assumption that the Chandler and Timberland collections, in the main, bore a close resemblance to fact. William Coxe, in a careful weighing of his sources for the *Memoirs of . . . Robert Walpole,* presents five reasons for crediting the general accuracy of "Chandler's Parliamentary Proceedings . . . recently called into question." He attacks specifically the notion that any of the debates were products of Johnson's imagination. "Either Johnson deceived himself into an exaggeration of his own powers, or his biographers mistook his assertion." But the only evidence that Coxe can muster to prove his point is that "the Bishop of Salisbury recollects to have seen several . . . notes, which Guthrie communicated to Johnson on the very day on which he obtained them"—a nebulous story.[31] The less painstaking historical writer continued to go without question to the debate collections for "facts." John Almon, in his *Anecdotes of Pitt* in 1791 reprints the "speeches of Pitt" written by Johnson without once raising the question of their authenticity.[32]

The world waited twenty-four years for a second edition of Johnson's *Debates*.

The Works of Samuel Johnson, LL.D. A New Edition. With an Essay on his Life and Genius, by Arthur Murphy, Esq. Volume the Thirteenth [Fourteenth], Forming the First [Second] Volume of the Debates in Parliament London ... 1811.

The two volumes were issued as supplements to the 1810 edition of the *Works*. This edition of the *Debates* may be described briefly as a reprint of Stockdale. The text manifests all the peculiarities noted in the discussion of the earlier printing: the omission of three debates and part of another, the "translation" of Lilliputian terms including the "mistranslations" that have been described, the same errors in dates, and a large portion of the misprints. Though the edition is undistinguished typographically, the printer has seen fit to correct a few of the misprints that produce patently illogical readings. The Murphy edition reprints the preface of Stockdale and the other introductory features (table of contents, lists of speakers, and Lilliputian terms).

The complete series of Johnson's *Debates in the Senate of Lilliput* had still never been reprinted from the *Gentleman's Magazine*. The next year, such a reprinting was accomplished, not in a book devoted to Johnson's works, but in just such a compilation, though more accurate and complete, as had been issued in the 1740's. *Cobbett's Parliamentary History of England* had begun publication in 1806 and by 1812 had got as far as the period of Johnson's authorship of the *Debates*. From the beginning, the printer was T. C. Hansard. With the thirteenth volume, Cobbett's name drops from the title page and finally, in the volume containing the proceedings for 1803, the work becomes *Hansard's Parliamentary Debates,* a series that continued unbroken through 1891, becoming in the end an official record.

The eleventh and twelfth volumes contain the *Debates* of Johnson.

Cobbett's Parliamentary History of England from the Norman Conquest to the Year 1803 ... Vol. XI. A.D. 1739-1741. [Vol. XII. A.D. 1741-1743.] London: Printed by T. C. Hansard, Peterborough—Court, Fleet Street ... 1812.

The Debates During Two Centuries

The editor of these, John Wright,[33] not only acknowledged Johnson's part but made an effort to point out the errors of previous editors. Nevertheless, as compiler of a "history," he was not inclined to reprint the *Debates* without upholding their historical accuracy. This he does in the preface to Volume XI, demonstrating his point by citing the similarity of the reports of the Lords debates to the accounts contained in Archbishop Secker's *Journal*, an uncertain means of proof as we shall see in the next part of this study. The same preface points out the omissions from Stockdale's edition, its errors in dating debates, and the misattribution of the speeches of Chesterfield. The preface to Volume XII gives "a correct List of the Debates compiled ... by Dr. Johnson," the substance of which I reproduce in Appendix 2, page 207.

The volumes containing Johnson's accounts are more carefully edited than those of the *Parliamentary History* earlier printed. The source of each debate, except when carelessly omitted, is indicated by a footnote. For several debates, both the *London Magazine* and the *Gentleman's Magazine* accounts are given, in order that they may be more readily compared. The volumes also print (as footnotes) reports of certain debates of the Lords from the manuscript notes of Secker.

In view of the above-named virtues of the editor's work, his treatment of Johnson's text is unfortunate. The removal of all Lilliputian terms was to be expected, but are not some of the "translations" rather free? Should not "Clinabs" be rendered "Commons" rather than "members"? And is it necessary or proper to change "this assembly" to "this house"? The original narrative bridges are either altered or replaced, and speeches are introduced simply by a name. The speeches themselves are printed in only slightly more dependable form than in the best volumes of the previous century's compilations. Punctuation, capitalization, spelling are adapted to modern usage. The text is not prepared with care. A comparison with the original reveals such verbal changes as "inconveniences" for "inconveniencies," "proportionable" for "proportionate." Most annoying of all, there is a quantity of surreptitious editing. In the Commons debate on the motion to remove Walpole, the speech of Harley is silently omitted, no doubt because the editor found it identical with the speech in the *London Magazine;* a footnote would have been appreciated. Speeches of Shippen and Wager, not from Johnson's account, are introduced without notation into the body of the same report. The editor did not hesitate to correct Johnson where Secker showed him to be in error. Thus, in the debate on the spirituous liquors bill, the speeches of Lonsdale and Oxford are silently transferred to Hervey and Sandwich.

In spite of its own shortcomings, the *Parliamentary History* pointed out important errors in the existing text of Johnson's *Parliamentary Debates.* It was only fair to expect that when that text was next reissued, those discoveries would be taken into account. A new edition did not appear for thirteen years. In 1825 was issued in Oxford the edition of Johnson's *Works* generally taken as the standard.

The Works of Samuel Johnson, LL.D. In nine volumes. Oxford, published by Talboys and Wheeler; and W. Pickering, London. MDCCCXXV.

The supplementary Volumes X and XI contain the *Debates.* The edition as a whole was supervised by Francis Pearson Walesby. He, or another, contributed a new preface to the supplementary volumes, but, in it, no new information. The text of the edition has familiar features. The debates of January 27, 1741, February 13, 1741, and March 23, 1742, are omitted, and the last lines of the March 9, 1742, speech, as well. Some misprints may be found (for example, "an" and "patterns" at the beginning of the corn bill debate). In short, the compiler of the last edition of the *Debates* that we have, instead of returning to the original publication in the *Gentleman's Magazine,* was content to reprint the text hurriedly prepared by Stockdale almost forty years earlier. However,

The Debates During Two Centuries   53

the edition is printed far better than Stockdale's; the fine paper and clear type contrast strikingly with the poor paper and presswork and the dull type of the earlier edition. Evidence that the printing was done with more care is to be seen also in the correction of obvious mistakes in Stockdale. The same errors in "translation" occur.

No collection of Johnson's *Debates* has seen print since 1825. Nevertheless, though the fact that he wrote the speeches has sometimes been forgotten, the speeches themselves have not been forgotten. Publication in the *Parliamentary History of England* had lent new authority to the *Debates* and, in historical works printed in the last century, it is not uncommon to find, unacknowledged, the words of Johnson.[34]

Early in our own century such scholars as Williams and Mantoux, aided by the earlier work of Hill, began the work of clarifying the sources of debate reports of the eighteenth century.[35] As a result of their labors, responsible historians no longer use the *Parliamentary History* indiscriminately. The caution of the historians has not always been emulated. Collections of "orations" seem to have been extremely popular in the last quarter of the nineteenth century and the first quarter of this. In these it is not uncommon to find speeches written by Johnson printed without reservation as the work of Pitt, Walpole, Chesterfield, or Pulteney.[36] One of the most authoritative-looking of these collections, made by Herbert Paul in 1911, reprints two speeches, said to be by Pitt, which may be traced to "Ptit" of the *Senate of Lilliput*.[37] One is Pitt's famous reply to Horace Walpole in the debate on the seamen's bill ("The atrocious crime of being a young man..."), a speech that has had wide currency in our century as well as in the eighteenth. That famous passage has been printed most recently in Mona Wilson's selections from Johnson,[38] a reprint notable for the fact that it reproduces, for the first time, part of a debate in its original Lilliputian form.

It is plain that the *Debates in the Senate of Lilliput* are not forgotten works in the ordinary sense. They have not remained on library shelves, locked away in the files of an ancient magazine, but have been often brought forth and sent into the world anew. They had wide currency in the years following first publication, though not, indeed, as works of Johnson. After his death there was sufficient demand for Johnson's *Parliamentary Debates* to justify three editions. And, in the years that followed, men have at times been roused by bits of British eloquence, unaware that the words were never spoken in Parliament but were written in a garret by a youth who was to become the great literary figure of his day.

Chapter III

THE DEBATES AS FACT: A COMPARISON WITH THE COLLATERAL EVIDENCE

In the generations since Johnson has become less actively read than written and gossiped about, the *Debates in the Senate of Lilliput* have supplied critics and biographers with little more than a lively Johnsonian anecdote and a catch Johnsonian phrase. The anecdote, of course, is Murphy's story of the "great revelation" at Foote's dinner party; the phrase is that which clinches the anecdote: "I saved appearances tolerably well, but I took care that the WHIG DOGS should not have the best of it."[1] Though we may question the reliability of its details, the anecdote is too good to abandon. Still, if we are to read the *Debates*, we must read with understanding, and to do this we must know something of their status as original compositions, Johnson's problems in writing them, and his attitude toward them. The tone of Murphy's story, and especially of the catch phrase that concludes it, is likely to color our reaction to the *Debates* by oversimplifying these problems. Are we to read them as a vast, a Johnsonian, practical joke on the WHIG DOGS?

The *Debates* are not, indeed, a magnificent *tour de force,* but the fruits of a humble employment of Johnson's youth and the chief literary product of three years. Murphy's anecdote is too facile. Although it seems to provide all the answers, every answer raises new questions. The statement that Cave's agents "brought away the subjects of discussion, the names of the speakers, the side they took, and the order in which they rose, together with notes of the various arguments advanced in the course of the debates" sounds too conclusive for ready acceptance. Was just the

[1] For notes to chapter iii see pages 160–163.

same sort of material brought to Johnson over the three-year period? Were the agents always able to bring away this much? Could not other sources have yielded information for the finished debates? Was each debate uniformly well reported to Johnson throughout its length? Was the information always accurate? Were the "notes of the various arguments" not assigned specifically, as the anecdote suggests, to particular speakers? Was Johnson given any clue to the order of the arguments? In short, if Johnson composed the speeches, in what degree and in what sense can we call them original compositions? The statement about the WHIG DOGS has some of the elements of a puzzle. How did Johnson take care that they should not have the best of it: by falsifying their arguments? by allotting less space to the Whigs? by ascribing more vigorous words to the opposition? Is a statement made under such circumstances (always assuming it was made) to be relied upon as uncolored fact? Could the Great Moralist have justified the falsification of a purportedly impartial parliamentary report? Might a bias have crept in unintentionally as well as by design?

There is no conclusive way of answering these questions. Internal evidence tells us next to nothing; we must go outside the *Debates* themselves. Had we the notes supplied to Johnson as well as the finished debates we should have almost the whole story. In the absence of these, we must collect what we can of accounts of the debates other than Johnson's. We must turn to the "Political Club" of the rival *London Magazine* and to the records of a few members who took notes of their own and others' speeches. Johnson's is the sole record of some of these debates, but fortunately parallel records can be found for a part or the whole of sixteen. In comparing these parallel reports with the *Debates in the Senate of Lilliput,* my objective has been to clarify the nature of the *Debates:* to state the degree to which each debate is an independent creation or a journalistic report, to estimate the fullness of the notes from which Johnson worked,

The Debates as Fact

to measure his dependence on the *London Magazine*, to determine in each debate the degree of impartiality, or bias, and its kind.

A comparison of the *Debates* with collateral materials for these purposes has never been carried through systematically.[2] Hill in his appendix to the first volume of the *Life* and Michael MacDonagh in *The Reporters' Gallery*[3] have brought together a few isolated passages that show either striking similarity or remarkable (or amusing) disparity. Neither attempts to discuss several accounts of a whole debate or even of a whole speech. Mary Ransome has made a more systematic survey in an article the title of which suggests her scope and purpose: "The Reliability of Contemporary Reporting of the Debates of the House of Commons, 1727–1741."[4] The Commons debates of these years have been studied here in an effort to estimate the usefulness of each of the magazine series as records of historical fact. She has looked for and has counted "errors in argument" and other "major errors" in each debate report. The difference between Miss Ransome's purpose and methods and my own may be more clearly seen by a comparison of her statements and mine with respect to the debate on the motion to remove Walpole.[5]

The Method

My method has been to look first at each debate as a whole in relation to its parallel material. Are the speakers the same? Do the main lines of arguments agree? Is there a comparable movement of debate? Then each speech has been examined closely. The object has been not only to compare the arguments as arguments but also to compare their arrangement, the relative weight given to each by space and forcefulness of expression, the manner in which the argument has been supported by concrete evidence, and, most intangible, the tone in which the argument is advanced.

A step-by-step examination of two debates, in conjunction with the collateral evidence, will, I hope, give a sense of the nature of the materials and the method. I shall then discuss each debate for which supporting material is available, concerning myself more with important evidence and conclusions than with the steps used to arrive at them. The two debates that I have chosen for the demonstration of procedure display interesting similarities and differences. They are the debates in the House of Lords and in the House of Commons on the motion to remove Walpole. Concerned as they are with the most notable debate of this period, they are among the better known of Johnson's performances in this form, though the Commons debate is unaccountably omitted from all editions bearing Johnson's name on the title page. The date of the two debates is the same, February 13, 1741, but a long interval must have separated Johnson's composition of the two reports. If I am correct in my surmise that Johnson wrote the reports in the order of their appearance in the magazine, the Lords debate was the first produced by Johnson in his period of exclusive authorship. The Commons debate was printed over a year and a half later, and, again if I am correct in my surmise, represents a fairly advanced stage in Johnson's parliamentary reporting.

Reports of the Lords Debate of February 13, 1741

Besides Johnson's, there are two purportedly full reports of the Lords debate on the motion to remove Walpole: that of Archbishop Secker and that printed in the *London Magazine*. In their relation to Johnson's work, these obviously constitute two different sorts of evidence. Secker apparently writes for the sole purpose of keeping a personal record. He "appears, from his own representation in the MSS., to have first taken down Notes of the Debates in short-hand, and afterwards written them out at large."[9] To judge from the nature of his entries, he was not proficient at shorthand, if shorthand it was. The manuscript consists of a series of statements and phrases without connectives. Its in-

The Debates as Fact 59

coherence in some spots must be attributed in the main to Secker's failing to put down all the points that were handled. In spite of its shortcomings, the Secker account is straightforward and unadorned, and its manner carries conviction; it brings us as near as we can come to the events that took place in the house on February 13, 1741.[7] The *London Magazine* report is a different sort of record. In purpose and in method of composition it stands in parallel relation to the debate reported in the *Gentleman's Magazine*. These two records of the debate, then, can be studied in the light of Secker's, and their fullness, accuracy, and bias compared. The *London Magazine* account has a further possible relationship to Johnson's. It appeared in the May, June, and July (1741) issues of the magazine; Johnson's followed in July and August. Thus the *London Magazine* becomes a possible source for two-thirds of the debate appearing in the *Gentleman's Magazine*.[8]

We can see, by reference to Secker, that the actual debate consists of two parts: the main debate on the motion itself, "That an humble address be presented to his Majesty, most humbly to advise and beseech his Majesty, that he will be most graciously pleased to remove the Right Honorable Sir Robert Walpole ... from his Majesty's Presence and Councils for ever"; and a supplementary debate on the resolution, "That any attempt to inflict any kind of Punishment on any Person without allowing him an opportunity to make his Defence, or without any Proof of any Crime or Misdemeanor committed by him, is contrary to natural Justice, the fundamental laws of this Realm ...." According to Secker, nineteen lords spoke in the first part of the debate; the *Gentleman's Magazine* reports eleven speeches, the *London Magazine* but five. Johnson's speakers correspond exactly to Secker's, but with Hervey's speech (the eleventh in Secker) the account of this part of the debate ends. The *London Magazine* prints Carteret's opening address, but omits the seconding speech of Abingdon. Newcastle, Argyle, and Hardwicke follow as in Secker. The *London Magazine* then skips to the speech of Bathurst, the eighteenth according to Secker. The *Gentleman's Magazine* continues with the second part of the debate directly after its report of Hervey's speech, and gives an account of nine speeches. This compares with Secker's seventeen, though he records no more than the name of the speaker in several instances. The Lilliputian version alters the order of speakers here. The *London Magazine* omits this part of the debate entirely.

No major arguments mentioned by Secker are omitted by either magazine, nor does either add any. The main subjects of debate are those early announced by Carteret in his address: the constitutionality of the motion, Walpole's conduct of foreign affairs, his conduct of domestic affairs. All speakers reported by the *London Magazine* and the *Gentleman's Magazine* are put on the correct side of the argument, but the nature of some of the speeches differs greatly.

The progress of the debate as recorded by Secker is what we might expect. The principal address is given by the motion maker, Carteret; it is both orderly and detailed. The seconding speech of Abingdon is miscellaneous in content, bolstering the previously stated arguments here and there. Newcastle follows with an orderly and detailed rebuttal of Carteret. Argyle, in answer, touches on a wide variety of secondary arguments. Hardwicke gives most attention to the constitutional question, citing historical precedent not mentioned before. And so the debate continues, as we should expect a debate at this stage to continue, with speeches that either support a single point or clarify a number of different points.

In both the *London Magazine* and the *Gentleman's Magazine* reports, this pattern of debate is altered in the direction of increased artificiality, but toward different sorts of artificiality. The *London Magazine* tends to put the speeches more consciously into debate form. Each speaker refers to his predecessor on the floor and attempts to answer his arguments specifically. The

The Debates as Fact

speech of Bathurst is not only a final rebuttal but a summing up. There is a strong sense of the debate as a whole. Johnson, on the contrary, tends to look on each individual speech as a unit. Each is formally organized into beginning, middle, and end, but the speeches have little relation to one another. So much is true of the first and main part of the debate; his account of the supplementary debate is strong in argumentative interchange, though he does not convey so lively a sense of it as does Secker in his notes. The relations of the speeches to one another and to the whole debate, as presented in each of the reports, will emerge more clearly as we treat the speeches separately.

The opening remarks of Carteret's address, as they appear in the three versions, present an interesting verbal contrast. According to Secker, the speaker begins: "I am glad to see the house so full. The honour of the nation is at stake. And the oldest man hath not seen such circumstances as we are in." The *London Magazine* Carteret is more formal, less matter-of-fact: "My lords, I have a Motion to make to your Lordships, which, as a Friend to our present happy Establishment, as a Friend to his Gracious Majesty now on the Throne, as a friend of my Country, and as a Member of this House, I think I am in Duty bound to make." Johnson's Carteret speaks an essay in his first sentence:

As the Motion which I am about to make is of the highest Importance, and of the most extensive Consequences; as it cannot but meet with all the Opposition which the Prejudices of some, and the Interest of others, can raise against it; as it must have the whole Force of ministerial Influence to encounter without any Assistance but from Justice and Reason; I hope to be excused by your Lordships for spending some time in endeavoring to shew, that it wants no other Support, that it is not founded upon doubtful Suspicions, but upon uncontestable Facts; that it is not dictated by private Interest, but by the sincerest Regard to publick Happiness; not abetted by the personal Malevolence of particular Men, but enforced by the Voice of the People; a Voice which ought always to be attended to and generally obey'd.

According to Secker's account, Carteret follows his opening remarks by a plain statement of the plan of his speech: "I shall, 1. go through the Foreign Transactions of several years. 2. The Domestic. 3. Prove that what I am about to propose is a parliamentary method." The *London Magazine* and the *Gentleman's Magazine* reports make the same tripartite division, but alter the sequence: the constitutionality of the method is treated first, then foreign and domestic affairs. The announced method of procedure is followed closely in Secker's account. Gordon (in the *London Magazine*) and Johnson allow the clear division of the argument to become obscured at the very end of Carteret's speech, Gordon by returning after the discussion of domestic matters to the subject of foreign affairs (the Spanish depredations and the misconduct of the war) and thereafter to the principle that "common fame" is sufficient grounds for such an address; Johnson also by returning briefly at the end to the "common fame" of Walpole's misdeeds.

In comparing the three accounts of these main topics of Carteret's speech, we shall follow the order adopted by the *London Magazine* and by Johnson. Secker (who records the fact that Carteret actually discussed last the legality of his motion) notes that the speaker begins this part of his address by saying that "the method I propose is not hard or unparliamentary." And the usage of Parliament is the law of the land. In dealing with such a situation as this, "there are two ways in parliament quite regular": impeachment and an address. The first is a "criminal process," and there must be proof. The second is "removing from place," and is not a punishment. "If the generality of the people of all ranks think things would be better were one obstacle removed," that is sufficient cause for removal.

The Carteret of the *London Magazine* and the *Gentleman's Magazine* conducts the argument in an elaborated fashion, but the line of thought is the same. We have the impression that Secker here omits much, and, since the elaborations are logical

The Debates as Fact 63

extensions of the line of thought recorded by the archbishop, they may indeed have been Carteret's own. Both magazines begin by emphasizing the duty of Parliament. To give advice to the sovereign is a duty of Parliament, says the *London Magazine.* It is the duty of the house to remove from office those found wanting in ability or virtue, according to Johnson's Carteret. Then, according to both magazines, the motion maker proceeds to discuss method. The *London Magazine* goes farther than Secker here and announces four means of removing a minister: by impeachment, by bill of attainer, by bill of pains and penalties, and by humble address. The first three require proof of "criminal Facts." For the last, proof of "common Fame" is enough. By the Johnson account, Carteret asserts that there are several "violent and vindictive Methods" (Secker mentions only impeachment), but does not name them. He points out the moderation which must certainly recommend the method to those who think the minister honest but mistaken. According to both magazines, the speaker then proceeds with an argument not mentioned by Secker: while the minister remains in office, proof of crimes cannot be brought against him because of fear and corruption, but if the motion were passed he could then be charged with specific crimes.

In the magazines, Carteret passes now to the question of Walpole's conduct of foreign affairs, which by Secker's account was the first topic discussed. Here again the three accounts present essentially the same arguments. The main purpose is to show that Walpole has upset the balance of power in Europe by favoring the French interest. In all the accounts the method of demonstrating this contention is to survey continental European affairs and England's relation to them since the Treaty of Utrecht.

According to each of our records, Carteret begins by the enunciation of the principle of England's foreign policy. In Secker the principle is stated chiefly by implication.

I remember great approbation given to the Treaty of Utrecht and in a little time the makers of it impeached. The capital fault of it was making France too strong and Germany too weak. And if the House of Austria hath ever been powerful since, it is a great justification of the Treaty of Utrecht.

Johnson expresses the principle forcibly.

Blefuscu [France], my Lords, is the constant and hereditary Enemy of Lilliput, so much divided from her in Religion, Government, and Interest, that they cannot both be prosperous together; as the Influence of one rises that of the other must by consequence decline...It has been therefore, my Lords, a settled Principle of every wise Administration...to attend with the highest Degree of Vigilance to all the Designs of the *Blefuscudians,* and oppose with incessant Diligence every Attempt to increase their Force or extend their Influence, and to check their Conquests, obstruct their Alliances, and forestall their Trade.

The "Maxims" put in the mouth of Carteret by the *London Magazine* express a more complex view of the balance of power.

The Maxims established ever since the Revolution, and the Maxims upon which both the late heavy Wars were founded, have been, to prevent the Increase of the power of *France,* to support and increase the Power of the House of *Austria,* as a balance to that of France, and to prevent, if possible, an Union between the Kingdoms of *France* and *Spain.*

Having stated the principle, Carteret proceeds, by an account of England's adventures in foreign entanglements, to show how Walpole has violated it. In the outlines of this narrative, the versions of the two magazines differ little from each other or from Secker's record. The principal topics are the Treaty of Utrecht, Walpole's misinterpretation of the Treaty of Vienna between Austria and Spain, the Treaty of Hanover which "delivers us tied into the hands of France" (Secker), the Treaty of Seville, the agreement with the emperor in 1731 (approved by Carteret), the breaking of most of these treaties by Walpole and the resulting resentment of all the European powers, the slowness to take offense at the Spanish indignities, and the lethargic and inefficient conduct of the war with Spain.

The magazines' reports of Carteret on foreign affairs differ from Secker's mainly in the omission or addition of minor evidence. There is no great significance in finding material supplementing that recorded by Secker. Such material need not be fabrication by the magazines, but may represent authentic parts of Carteret's speech omitted by Secker out of carelessness or the necessity of selection. An example of such an addition is the argument that England did not take advantage of the rift between France and Spain that was caused by the Infanta's being returned from the court of France. Secker does not mention the incident of the Infanta. Another example is the elaboration of detail on the dispute with Spain and Walpole's handling of the war when it came. In Secker's notes, these topics are not given detailed treatment.

The *omission* of a point recorded by Secker is of far more importance, since we may be well assured that such a point was brought up by the speaker in the original debate. Both the *London Magazine* and the *Gentleman's Magazine* fail to make Carteret cite the allowance of the restoration of Dunkirk as important evidence of Walpole's inefficiency and his involvement in the French interest. According to Secker's notes, Carteret dwelt at some length on this topic.

Lest it be concluded that the evidence is pointing neatly toward Johnson's dependence on the *London Magazine* for the foreign-policy section of Carteret's speech, let it be noted that at one point there is definite evidence of a separate source of information. In discussing Walpole's misconception of the dangers of the Austrian-Spanish alliance, one of the Secker notes is, "Yet read the King's speech, 17 January 1726." The *Gentleman's Magazine* has it, "This his late Majesty was advised to assert in his Speech from the Throne which I desire may be read." The speech is then quoted at length. The speech is not mentioned by the *London Magazine*.

"The noble lord was long upon Foreign Affairs, short upon domestic," says Newcastle in his answer to Carteret (Secker's version). This gives a strong indication of the proportionate length of Carteret's treatment of domestic affairs; and indeed, according to the notes of Secker, Carteret has little to say on domestic affairs, but that little is concrete and specific. He discusses at greatest length the mishandling of the sinking fund, citing a number of figures. He mentions the place bill. He deplores the fact that men have been turned out of office for opposing the minister, and cites the case of the Earl of Stairs.

In the *London Magazine* the discussion of domestic affairs is made to develop naturally from the foreign-policy section. See the effect of this policy on domestic affairs, says Carteret. We must keep expensive armies, and malt and land taxes are therefore insufficient. We contract new debts instead of paying off the old. Our trade, especially with the New World, has been interrupted. The financial policy has led to high interest and low private credit. The *London Magazine's* Carteret mentions the excise scheme, and the speaker then returns to foreign affairs, the Spanish depredations and the lack of vigor in the prosecution of the war. Reverting to domestic affairs at the end of his speech, he charges that there is corruption in government. The general opinion of corruption throughout the nation establishes it by common fame. The divergence of this account from Secker's will be noted. Carteret's emphasis on the sinking fund (corroborated by Secker's notation that Newcastle in his rebuttal states, "What hath been said about Domestic affairs is chiefly in the wrong application of the Sinking Fund") is absent from this account; indeed, the fund is not mentioned by name.

The emphases of the *London Magazine* are echoed by Johnson. Trade has declined. By useless armaments, taxes have been increased without diminishing the nation's debts. The sinking

The Debates as Fact

fund is not mentioned by name. The excise scheme would have condemned the nation to slavery. Corruption runs riot in Parliament. Men are turned out of office for disagreement with Walpole, even the "greatest general in Lilliput." "Common fame" is sufficient evidence for the corruption of government and the fact that this man is "sole minister."

Unless Secker unintentionally distorts, Carteret is moderate in his closing remarks.

> If he could lead us out, I should be willing to let him do it. I put no reason into the motion because I would not do anything offensive. I do not mean a prosecution. I bequeath my fame to posterity on this affair.

By Gordon's interpretation, Carteret is shriller, almost threatening.

> As the Weakness of our late Measures is manifest to the whole World, as the Unpopularity of this Minister is known to every Man that converses with any independent Person in the Nation, and as he is generally suspected of being a most notable Corrupter, if you put a Negative upon the Motion I am to make, I am afraid it may affect the Honour, the Character, and the Dignity of this House, by making the World suppose the very Negative to proceed from the Influence of Corruption.

Johnson is less violent, but his implication that revolt is imminent is an even more radical interpretation of Carteret.

> ... such is the present unhappy State of this Nation, and such is the general Discontent of the People, that Tranquility, Adherence to the Government, and Submission to the Laws, cannot reasonably be hoped, unless the Motion ... be complied with.

In the arrangement of main divisions and the elaboration of specific points, the two magazine versions are closer to one another than to Secker. This fact strongly suggests that Johnson at least read and assimilated the *London Magazine* report of the speech before writing his own. But there are several indications of a source of information independent of the other magazine. One indication has been mentioned, and another, perhaps more striking, may be cited here. Secker records Hardwicke's statement: "yet a noble lord [Carteret]° says *superior respondeat,* which is laying down a rule for a prime minister; whereas the noble duke was against any." This is Johnson from the next-to-last paragraph of the Carteret address: "The objection that there is no sole Minister, will create no great Difficulty, if there be many concerned in these Transactions, *respondeat superior...*" The Latin phrase is not in the *London Magazine.*

The two magazines are similar, too, in the violent tone of their criticisms, a tone which is absent from Secker's notes. We assume that such a tone would be much less strongly conveyed by unelaborated notes of the facts of the argument. Still, if the original tone had been violent, we should have expected to gain a sense of it. Instead, we gain the impression of a man who is attempting to win the vote of the moderate by the use of moderation in argument. There seems to be a significant divergence in emphasis and in tone between the two magazines, caused by Johnson's insistence on the "voice of the people," which "ought always to be attended to, and generally to be obeyed." To the *London Magazine,* the voice of the people is the common fame that makes the proof of misdeed unnecessary, but to Johnson it is a fact that must be recognized (or "appeased") if orderly government is to be maintained.

The seconding speech of Abingdon is not reported by the *London Magazine.* According to Secker, Abingdon begins by saying that "common fame" (the first mention of the phrase in Secker, though it is a key phrase in the magazines' account of Carteret) is sufficient grounds for impeachment, but that he would not go so far. He proceeds to mention some points neglected in Secker's account of Carteret: the increase of expenses caused by the increase of an army "to conquer nobody but ourselves," the neglect of the naval force, the undue influence on the

The Debates as Fact

elections. Johnson in his account simplifies and generalizes. Did the notes given him record only Abingdon's first point? At any rate, Abingdon's speech becomes in his hands an essay on "common fame" and nothing more.

For the answering address of Newcastle, all three reports must be taken into account. Secker's notes make it clear that the speaker follows Carteret in organizing his arguments. After brief reference to the lack of parliamentary precedent for the motion, he answers in detail Carteret's objections to the administration's foreign policy and its conduct of domestic affairs, and answers the argument that the method of proceeding is legal. The magazines rearrange the divisions in the order of their accounts of Carteret: the legality of the method first and then foreign and domestic affairs.

Since the Johnson report is the focus here, the points will be discussed in the order in which they are found in the magazines. In regard to the legality of the motion, Secker notes that Newcastle asserts there is no precedent except the House of Commons' addressing the queen to remove Bishop Lloyd. The House of Lords objected to that action because the accused was not heard, nor was there legal proof. The houses differ in their nature. The Lords is a house of judgment, and judgment is impossible without proof. In the other house, common fame is a possible foundation for addressing the king or the House of Lords. Neither magazine records this distinction in the function of the two houses. In the *London Magazine,* Newcastle is made to say that, although there may be a precedent for addressing the king for the purpose of removing a minister, the action has been taken only in troubled times. The basing of such an address on general charges rather than on specific crime is a precedent that puts the king himself in danger. The case of Strafford and Charles I is cited. The motion, moreover, in spite of the statement to the contrary, acts as a punishment because it adversely affects a minister's reputation.

Johnson's argument deviates somewhat from both the others. He puts emphasis on the unreliability of common fame. According to him, Newcastle begins by challenging the contention that Walpole must be removed from office before proof of crimes can be brought against him. The disaffected, those who have been turned out of office, would be willing to bring forth proof if there were any. As a matter of fact, these and other bitter men, in the absence of proof, have expended their efforts in poisoning the minds of the people against the administration. Common fame, then, cannot be relied on, since popular discontent is based on unfounded accusations. If the "patriots" were once allowed in office they would demonstrate to the public that their accusations had been brought solely for private advantage, and the people's discontent would be heightened rather than appeased. On the subject of the motion's constitutionality the magazines both deviate, but in independent directions, from the line of argument clearly recorded by Secker.

According to Secker, Newcastle, after his opening remarks, plunges directly into the topic of foreign affairs. To refute Carteret's arguments, he attempts to show that affairs are not so upset as they have been pictured, that where matters are amiss the measures taken by the administration are not to blame, and that Walpole cannot personally be held accountable for most of England's diplomatic actions. Secker notes that Newcastle is at some pains to show that the danger of the alliance between Austria and Spain was not exaggerated. In this connection he orders the proceedings of the house relating to the Treaty of Hanover to be read. He adds that Walpole had no part in the formulation of this last treaty. The Treaty of Seville did no harm, and the Treaty of 1731 put affairs in good shape. Only the emperor's ministers were to blame for what happened after this treaty and the earlier Treaty of Hanover. A brief reference to Dunkirk is made.

The Debates as Fact

The argument in the magazine accounts does not differ greatly in outline from Secker's. The *London Magazine* is more detailed, the *Gentleman's Magazine* less so. In both magazines a preliminary to the treatment of foreign affairs is the observation that it is easy now "to *foresee* the Past" (as Johnson puts it). When measures are taken, administrations can only guess the course of future events; error, when it occurs, is neither surprising nor reprehensible. The *London Magazine* emphasizes the contention that, since most of the measures of the English were good, the present state of affairs is attributable to the misconduct of other nations, especially Austria, and to chance. When the peace between France and Austria brought Europe into a "happy Situation for this Kingdom," the balance was upset again solely by "the late Emperor's happening to die." The concrete arguments in this part of Johnson's version are rather meager. Much is made of the dangers inherent in the close tie between Austria and Spain, and of the avoidance of those dangers by the alliance with France. By the account of both magazines, Newcastle spends some time defending the policy toward the Spanish depredations and the conduct of the war, subjects not included in the Secker report. But the concrete detail of the reading of the proceedings of the house, as recorded by Secker, is omitted by the magazines.

Domestic affairs are treated briefly by all the accounts. Secker notes only Newcastle's answer to the objections to the misuse of the sinking fund: everything relating to it has been approved by Parliament. Johnson omits domestic affairs almost entirely, limiting Newcastle, on this head, to the refutation of the argument that Walpole is "sole minister." The *London Magazine* says that debts have increased because expenses have increased. In this report Newcastle attempts to justify the excise scheme. In neither of the magazine reports is the sinking fund mentioned or the argument recorded by Secker used.

The debate has now, if we put our faith in Secker's notes,

arrived at the stage at which speakers no longer argue in general terms or in organized addresses, but have become interested in specific arguments. Argyle's answer, according to Secker, is a list of miscellaneous small points rather than a discourse arranged around large generalities. He concentrates on one area of thought at the beginning of the speech, though not in organized fashion. That area is Walpole's handling of financial affairs. No man is better in the affairs of the Treasury, says Argyle; his faults cannot be ascribed to lack of ability. The misuse of public money is then discussed.

The *London Magazine* gives a well-ordered answer to the speech of Newcastle. Argyle, in this report, counters the statement that such an address to the king arises only in troubled times (attributed to Newcastle by the *London Magazine* alone) with the assertion that these are indeed troubled times and this is the sole method of obtaining redress. So neat an answer to a silly argument seems to have been contrived to put the Whigs in a bad light. He answers also Newcastle's citation of the case of Strafford (again an exclusive feature of the *London Magazine's* Newcastle). He states later that he will take the suggestion of Newcastle and examine public measures in the light of events at the time the measures were adopted, but he does not carry out the promise. The remainder of the speech is made up of a demonstration that there is truth in a number of "superstitions" held by the nation concerning Walpole.

Johnson has Argyle begin as if he were delivering an essay on the "voice of the people." (There is a connection here with Newcastle's speech, but it is not expressed.) They are not "a Herd to be led or driven at pleasure"; if they are mistaken, they are mistaken with plentiful evidence on their side. Argyle (in Johnson's account) shows what proofs exist for the people that Walpole is sole minister. A switch is then made to foreign affairs, and two main arguments are pursued: the misrepresentation of the Treaty of Vienna and the misconduct of the war. Johnson's account ends with the opinion that the unfortunate state of affairs that is obvious to every Briton and the likewise obvious, sole responsibility of Walpole make his removal necessary. The magazine accounts differ greatly from the record of the archbishop but just as markedly from one another. In the light of the general dissimilarities between Johnson's and Secker's accounts, a similarity in one detail seems to have some significance: by both accounts, Argyle says that he would have been glad to lead the forces in America if he had been asked.

Hardwicke, the next speaker, is revealed by Secker to have been concerned principally with one topic, the illegality of common fame as grounds for an address. However, he begins by covering a number of topics briefly, treating first foreign, then domestic, affairs. The part of his speech dealing with the irregularity of the motion's method summarizes the arguments already expressed and brings forth much new evidence. He makes a historical survey of addresses in the attempt to show that there is no precedent for the present proposal.

The *London Magazine* report, though touching some of the same points, shows no similarity to Secker in essential detail or over-all plan. Hardwicke's speech is organized as a direct answer to the *London Magazine* speech of Argyle, beginning with a reference to the "troublesome and factious times" which he says have been brought on by the personal animosities of the opposition. He then answers the "suspicions" that have been referred to in the *London Magazine* speech of Argyle.

Johnson, too, makes Hardwicke answer the previous speech, and the answer is much closer to the trend of Hardwicke's actual remarks. This version, too, is concerned with common fame, but the direction of the argument differs. Johnson's Hardwicke asserts with some eloquence the unreliability of common fame. He then shows that no proof has been advanced for the contention that Walpole is sole minister. Without proof of that fact there is no justification for the motion, because Walpole cannot be held solely responsible. After a digression to the Treaty of Vienna, Hardwicke ends with the declaration that the motion is not "supported by legal evidence" and is therefore unworthy of being passed.

The *London Magazine* at this point drops from the debate. The one additional speech given in that publication, Bathurst's, is not included in Johnson's report and therefore not of interest to the present study. This version of the Bathurst speech has little relation to Secker's record, but is a summing up of arguments for the motion. As we continue, we have but two documents to compare.

Johnson has Carlisle reply to the speech of Hardwicke by the argument that the question of common fame as reliable evidence is beside the point, for evidence is not needed. If discontent has spread over the nation to such an extent that it must be appeased by removal of the minister to avoid danger to the crown, it is the duty of Parliament to inform the king of the state of affairs. This is the substance of Johnson's version of the speech. As recorded by Secker, it is a miscellaneous affair. Several minor points are pursued. The only reference to common fame is to the fact that the last previous impeachment in Commons was on the basis of common fame and that the "person now under question" favored it.

Johnson's version of Cholmondeley's speech has no similarity to the speech of Secker's manuscript. By Secker he is shown to dispute the contention that Walpole is sole minister. A new argument is advanced, that Commons will resent an attack on a member of their house. Then several famous names are cited for an uncertain purpose. Johnson has Cholmondeley make just one important point: that to be swayed by the clamors of the populace is not better than to subscribe to the dictates of a minister. The people have no right to sit as judges.

The remaining speeches are, according to the Secker notes, short ones. The next three speeches, those of Halifax, the Bishop

The Debates as Fact

of Salisbury, and Bedford show no similarities in the two versions. Johnson's account of the first of these is interesting in that it continues the debate on the voice of the people. The others repeat old arguments. The last speech, that of Hervey, reveals a close relationship in the two reports. In both, the main arguments are that a man should not be condemned without a hearing, and that the charges are incapable of proof.

Next comes the appended debate on the motion that an attempt to inflict punishment on any man without hearing him or proving any crime is contrary to "natural Justice, the fundamental Laws of this Realm, and the Ancient establish'd Usage of the Senate, and is a high Infringement of the Liberties of the Subject." As we have seen, Johnson reports little more than half of the speeches and alters their order. The purport of the arguments is the same in both versions. Those who support the motion say it expresses a principle that ought to be declared after the farce of the previous debate of the day. The opposition replies that the motion is a truism, but that to pass such a motion on this day would be interpreted as a censure of certain members of the house. The two versions show no remarkable correspondence in the similarity of particular points attributed to particular speakers except in the interchange between Talbot and Cholmondeley. The two accounts of this provide an interesting comparison. Secker has it thus:

Talbot. Should this motion go, it would be observed how many in place supported it and *v.v.* The lords who have spoken for it are in great places. I hope they will not be influenced by them, I will not say of any man that he is influenced by a place.

Cholmondeley. Such words will do no lord any good. I do not desire they should be taken down, but I hope the noble lord will guard himself. It is wanting respect to the whole House.

Talbot. By the eternal G—, I will defend my cause everywhere—[But the lords calling to order he recollected himself and made an excuse].

Johnson's version is much longer and will be quoted only in part. Talbot's words are:

Let us my Lords, consider the circumstances of the three noble Lords by whom this Motion has been made and supported, let us take a View of their Conduct, and consider the visible Motives to which it may be ascribed, their Places, their Dependence—

The Hurgo Sholmlug *spoke next in Substance as follows:*

My Lords,

I rise thus abruptly to preserve that Order and Decency which is essential to public Councils, and particularly suitable to the Dignity of this Assembly, which can only become a Scene of Tumult and Confusion by such methods of Debate, and lose that Respect which it has hitherto preserved, not only by the Justice of its Determinations, but the solemn Grandeur of its Procedure...

The Hurgo Toblat *then resumed:*

My Lords,

Whether anything that has escaped from me deserves such severe Animadversions, your Lordships must decide. For what I might intend to say, since...I was hindered from proceeding, I shall not be accountable.

[Three paragraphs are omitted.]

When I reflect, my Lords, on the Distresses of my Country, when I observe the Security and Arrogance of those whom I consider as the Authors of the public Miseries, I cannot always contain my Resentment, I may perhaps Sometimes start out into unbecoming Transports, and speak in Terms not very ceremonious of such abandon'd such detestable—But as this is perhaps, not the Language of the House...

The debate ends with the passing of the second motion.

If, after this detailed examination, we look back on Johnson's debate as a whole, several conclusions can be ventured. First, we can now say something more about the apparent nature of the notes from which Johnson worked. The record he received con-

The Debates as Fact

tained an accurate account of the order of the speakers, though minor deviations appear toward the end of the debate. The notation, at the end of each of the two parts of the published account, that there were further speakers shows that even the speeches omitted in Johnson's working of the material probably were represented by at least a name in his notes. We have no reason to conclude, from our study, that the notes contained errors. We may surmise that they varied in fullness from speech to speech, becoming more meager as the debate progressed. There seems a strong indication, too, that the note taker recorded the details of argument, perhaps not discriminating accurately between the important and the unimportant, but did not concern himself with the main points of a speaker. The *London Magazine* in its fuller handling of detail of some arguments, especially those on foreign affairs, bespeaks a writer with either fuller notes or a fuller acquaintance with the subject matter. The account of the whole debate is certainly much fuller in the *Gentleman's Magazine* than in the rival magazine, but the difference probably is due to the concentration of the latter account rather than to the inaccuracy of its notes. Was the *London Magazine* a source for Johnson's *Debate?* The examination, I think, has made clear that it could not have been, except for Carteret's speech. Here the arrangement of material and the echo of details suggest that Johnson had at least read the other report. Factual details in the *Gentleman's Magazine,* omitted by the other magazine, demonstrate conclusively that the latter cannot have been the sole source of Johnson's version.

Our general impression is that the two sides of the argument are treated equally. Certainly the *London Magazine's* report is biased in favor of the opposition. Note the significant fact that Johnson ends the main part of the debate with a Whig speaker, and the *London Magazine* ends with an overwhelmingly long, almost wholly fabricated speech of the opposition. A comparison of the space given to each side substantiates the impression. The

London Magazine gives sixty-five columns in favor of the motion and twenty-six against it. On the main question, the *Gentleman's Magazine* has thirty-seven columns favorable and twenty-five opposed. Johnson is even more generous to the Whigs than Secker's record indicates he need have been.[10]

One preoccupation, peculiar to Johnson's report, is worthy of note. By mass of words and emphasis of language, he lays great stress on "common fame" and the "voice of the people." Two conclusions seem obvious: Johnson is more interested than Gordon or the speakers themselves in the larger moral aspects of the debate, and he is highly interested in the relation of the people to their government.

REPORTS OF THE COMMONS DEBATE OF FEBRUARY 13, 1741

We might, even before examining any documents, conjecture that the debate in the House of Commons on that same motion differed little in its essential character from that in the Lords; all possible significant arguments on the question would seem to have been advanced and elaborated among the peers. And indeed, reference to the available evidence gives weight to the presumption that the members of the two houses were, during that long day, engaged in saying the same things. Certainly the magazines were conscious of the sameness. Both the *London Magazine* and the *Gentleman's Magazine* saw fit, in printing their reports of the two debates, to observe such an interval between them that the passage of time might contribute to the second an illusion of freshness. The "Political Club" report of the Lords debate appeared in the May, June, and July, 1741, issues of the *London Magazine;* the Commons debate was not printed until March and April, 1742. Though in the *Gentleman's Magazine* the two debates were separated by a still wider gap (from July and August, 1741, for the Lords to February, March, and April, 1743, for the Commons), it was felt necessary to preface the report with an explanatory statement: since the other report was of interest, the present "will not be disagreeable to our Readers."

As the Arguments used in both Houses were nearly the same, we shall endeavor in this Account to pass slightly over those Articles of Accusation or Defense, which have already been sufficiently explained, and dwell upon those Parts of the Debate, which arose from Circumstances peculiar to the House of Clinabs, or upon Arguments which the Hurgoes do not appear to have so fully disclosed.

A search for firsthand accounts of this debate to be used as the basis of comparison with the magazine reports yields rewards far less gratifying than for the Lords debate. The House of Commons seems to have contained no man possessed of the impulse that led Secker to keep his journal. For the debate as a whole we must depend on sketchy accounts (some of them hearsay): an entry in a diary, a "narrative of the motion" said to have been prepared by Walpole, letters from men of the town to the politically minded and geographically separated. But of the two principal speeches we have full notes: Walpole's notes on his own answer to the motion (freely "edited," to be sure), and notes taken by Fox of the arguments of the motion maker, Sandys. We also have a brief record of another important speech, that of Pitt.

Evidence independent of the magazine reports indicates that this debate, like that in the House of Lords, was actually a "double debate," but here the secondary debate was on a different question and occurred in the middle rather than at the end of the main debate. The House of Lords had argued a second motion censuring the principal motion. The Commons, apart from its controversy on the motion itself, argued at length the question whether Walpole should be asked to withdraw while the accusation against him was being debated. We cannot, of course, be as specific about the course of this debate as we were of the other, but the broad outlines emerge. Sandys opened the argument and made the motion. He was seconded by Lord Limerick, "and then Wortley Montagu got up, and moved that Sir Robert might make his answer to the charge and withdraw. Precedents were demanded and searched ... for the House's ordering a member accused to withdraw whilst his case is debated."[11] The proposal that the accused withdraw was "strongly opposed,"[12] but we do not know who the speakers were. We are told that the argument against this motion centered on the lack of precedent for forcing an accused member to withdraw while other members make "general" accusations against him (those made without reference to particular facts), accusations that he cannot hear and so defend himself against.[13] This phase of the debate came to an end when its "proposer" dropped the second motion without a division.[14] Then the long debate on the main question was resumed.

We have already named the speeches of which we have a record: Sandys', Pitt's and Walpole's. For the rest we can, from sources outside the magazines, collect only a handful of names and a few hints of remarks. "The House would not have divided but by the eager warmth of Mr. Lyttleton."[15] Harley spoke, to the surprise of many, against the question.[16] Shippen declared that "he would not pull down Robin upon republican principles," and withdrew without voting.[17] Lord Cornbury, Bowes, and Southwell were others considered to be notable speakers against the motion.[18] There is evidence that Wager made a telling point of defense,[19] and we are told by the French ambassador that Doddington arose three times, but opened his mouth "sans réussir à trouver son voix" and sat down again.[20] Since Sandys began at one in the afternoon and the question was finally put at three the next morning, there must have been many other speakers.[21] One account, obviously biased, summarizes the arguments in support of Walpole, although it names none of the speakers.

Sir Robert Walpole's friends exposed, in a strong and masterly way, the violence and injustice of proposing to have a member of the House, and a person of his high station, punished by the loss of his character and reputation, by several allegations which were not proved to be crimes, and which had received in former examinations and debates, the approbation and consent of parliament; and in making Sir Robert Walpole the author and adviser of the things alleged without any other evidence than that of notoriety or common fame."[22]

We approach firmer ground toward the end of the debate. Pulteney, we learn, had remained silent, hoping to be allowed to answer Walpole after the latter had made his defense. But now Sir Robert saw his design and forced Pulteney to speak first.[23] Walpole followed and, after the question was put, the motion was defeated 290 to 106.

With the general contours of the debate as outlined above there is no violent disagreement in Johnson's version. Of the speakers named, Bowes, Southwell, Wager, and Shippen are not in Johnson's cast of characters, but, with the exception of Shippen and Wager, we have no strong evidence that these men produced important or individual arguments, and we have already learned that the shortage of magazine space often made it necessary for actual speakers to be omitted. Keeping in mind the outline drawn up from the past, we can summarize the whole debate as Johnson sets it down. Sandys begins with a speech (to be more fully discussed below) that introduces the charges against Walpole in an organized way. Limerick seconds briefly, adding no real argument. Wortley Montagu now breaks in with his motion that Walpole withdraw. He is seconded by Gybbon, who cites the precedents of Coke, Churchill, Falkland, and Manley.[24] Bromley, Howe, and Bladen oppose the motion. Erskine supports it and Gybbon speaks once more in its favor. Finally, Johnson has Pulteney warn against being "diverted from the principal question by Considerations of Small Importance," and conclude, "I think it may very properly be left to his own Choice to stay or retire on this Occasion." The secondary debate at an end, Fox arises to deliver the first speech of rebuttal. Considering the important position of this speech, it is surprising that in none of our other sources of evidence is Fox named a speaker. However, we are tempted to support the possibility that the surviving notes of

Sandys' speech were taken by Fox in preparation for an answer; he may in actuality as well as in Johnson's account have opened the arguments in favor of Walpole. Pitt, who follows, does not advance the whole accusation again, but concerns himself with some particular assertions of Fox. He also, near the end of his speech, introduces a theme, "the people," that is taken up successively by Howe and Heathcote. Pelham then speaks, confining his remarks mainly to the question of constitutionality. Now two of the opposition, Harley and Cornbury, rise to censure the method of the motion. Sir Robert Walpole, "perceiving the House silent and Pulteney not yet spoken," requests that all accusations against him be heard before his reply. Tyrconnel supports him in this, and Pulteney is forced to speak. Walpole answers, and the debate is complete.

The *London Magazine* version is telescoped, as it was in the Lords debate. There are six speeches (compared to the *Gentleman's Magazine's* twenty-two). Of the speakers, five correspond to those of Johnson's debate; one, Barnard, is not found in Johnson's or any other account. The "double" nature of the debate is absent, no mention being made of a proposal for Sir Robert to withdraw. At the end of the debate we are only indirectly made to see Pulteney's maneuver for the position of last speaker; he is made to begin by saying that he had intended to hear Walpole's defense before speaking, but finds himself obliged to alter his intention. Even if first on the job, the *London Magazine* offered a poor value with its foreshortened version spread over three issues.

The detailed comparison of the versions of this debate will begin with an examination of the three speeches for which we have evidence outside the magazines. Subsequently the two versions of three other speeches shared by the two magazines will be compared. The interesting features of the remaining speeches of Johnson's debate may then be summarized.

The Debates as Fact

Thomas Carte in a letter to the Pretender described Sandys' accusation of Sir Robert as "strong, clear and methodical."[25] A sense of the clarity and method that gave Sandys' speech its strength may be gained from Fox's notes.[26] As a matter of fact, the notes bespeak an utterance more ordered than the essays that stand for the speech in the *Gentleman's Magazine* and the *London Magazine*. According to the notes of Fox, Sandys began his speech with a lamentation and an outline. He "lamented the miserable condition of the nation, engaged in a war, without an ally abroad, and under the pressure of an immense debt at home." He "said he would enquire how we came into this situation and then make the proposal . . ." In pursuing the first part of his plan "he would first   our foreign   then   our domestick affairs and lastly the conduct of the present war."[27] The plan thus announced is perhaps best restated in outline form:

> The misconduct
>   Foreign affairs
>   Domestic affairs
>   The war
> The proposal.

The speech as reported by the magazines does not follow this outline. The *London Magazine* arranges its material under three main headings not unrelated to headings in the outline but in reverse order: the constitutionality of the motion, domestic affairs, foreign affairs (the war is lumped under foreign affairs). By this account, Sandys, without general accusations, plunges immediately into the argument on the first point.

Among the many Advantages arising from our happy Form of Government, there is one which is reciprocal to King and People, which is, a legal and regular Method by which the People may lay their Grievances, Complaints and Opinions, before their Sovereign, not only with regard to the Measures he pursues, but also with regard to the Persons he employs.

Johnson sets out in Brobdingnagian fashion:

> The Motion which I am about to offer, being made necessary by the present State of the Nation, its Reasonableness is to be evinced, as the Approbation of the House to be gained, by a view of our foreign and domestic Affairs, by an impartial Comparison of our present Condition with our past, by an accurate Balance of our Losses and Acquisitions for near twenty Years, and an examination to whom we are to impute our Sufferings, or ascribe our Acquisitions.

It is a thorny sentence containing implications of not-to-be-fulfilled promises as well as of aim and plan. Though neither the comparison of the present with the past nor the *balance* of losses and gains is methodically carried out by Johnson, the whole speech is directed toward proving that it is to Walpole that "we are to impute our Sufferings." The bulk of it can be placed under "foreign and domestick Affairs." Unlike Sandys' speech as recorded by Fox, this has no separate treatment of the conduct of the war; any discussion on this head is included in the "View" of foreign affairs. Nor is there extended consideration of the precedent for the motion. (This last omission need not be ascribed to the inaccuracy of Johnson's raw material, but may have been considered one of those "Articles ... already sufficiently explained" in the Lords debate—though to us foreign and domestic matters seem to have been equally worked over.)

Since we should expect Fox, in the notes of his adversary's speech, to omit the obvious rhetorical flourishes, it is difficult to say if, after "lamenting" briefly and announcing his plan, Sandys began directly on his first point. ("As for the first," as Fox has it.) Johnson may have had more complete notes here or may have felt that at the outset of an attack propriety required something further. At any rate, in his version the speaker dwells on the painfulness of the task of looking at the present situation.

> That some vigorous Execution of our Privileges, some Effort of our Constitution is now necessary, must be evident to every Man who looks round on the State of the Continent, or turns his Eyes upon the

The Debates as Fact 85

Face of our own Country; he will indeed find little Relief by changing the Prospect, nor when he withdraws his Eyes from Devastation, Slaughter, Discord, and Confusion, will be able to fix them upon any other Objects than Poverty, Oppression, and Discontent.

The notes of Fox indicate that Sandys gave much attention to details of foreign policy. This section of the speech centered around the afflictions arising from the tying of England's interest to that of France and the mismanagement of affairs with Spain. Our troubles are often attributed to the Treaty of Utrecht, he said, but it was the Treaty of Hanover that upset the balance of power (the phrase is not used in the notes) and resulted in our having "abandoned and lost our old and natural allies." The Congress of Cambray, the sending back of the Infanta, "our refusing the mediation," and the Treaty of Vienna were mentioned as preliminaries to the Treaty of Hanover, the purposeless exploits of the fleets in the Baltic and West Indies, the lack of French intervention in the siege of Gibraltar, and the reparation of Dunkirk as its sequels. Concerning relations with Spain, he mentioned the "preliminaries," the Act of the Pardo, the Treaty of Seville, and Walpole's failure to pursue vigorous measures against the depredations. After agreeing to support the emperor (by the second Treaty of Vienna), said Sandys, we failed to live up to our commitments. That great man Admiral Vernon spoke out against these things, "and it was contrived that he should not be of the next parliament, and he was likewise denied his rank."

Johnson begins this portion of the speech in a manner that reminds us of the corresponding section of his Carteret in the companion debate. He enunciates the principle of England's foreign policy: "it has been the perpetual maxim of Lilliputian Policy to obviate the Designs, and to check the Power of the Blefuscudian Empire." Is there not a reminiscence here of the "settled Principle" of Carteret's speech: "to attend with the highest Degree of Vigilance to all the Designs of the Blefuscudians, and oppose with incessant Diligence every Attempt to increase their

Force or extend their Influence"? Johnson proceeds to an account of the history of Anglo-French relations long before the time of Walpole's accession to power, an account weighty in language but airy in substance. Beginning with the emergence of France as an ambitious world power, the summary of events is broader in scope than that recorded by Fox. But where a parallel period is treated, Johnson is both far more voluminous and much less particular and concrete. There is a marked difference in tone. We could not logically expect Fox to preserve the exact emotional color of Sandys' remarks in notes of this nature. Still, we should think that some sense of the speaker's tone would inevitably come through, but the Sandys of Fox impresses us as reasonable, persuasive, straightforward, and the Sandys of Johnson as acidly and rather violently ironic.

Johnson moves forward deliberately from the beginnings of Anglo-French relations and comes to rest on the Treaty of Utrecht. The treaty is universally condemned and yet, says Sandys (by Johnson), those who then strongly opposed it and impeached its supposed author might, "when the Power was transferred to their hands," have been expected to act "in pursuance of their own Principles." But the present ministry found instead "that to dispute every Claim of the Blefuscudian Monarch was a vexatious and laborious Task." Despairing of resisting France, it decided to befriend her by the Treaty of Hanover. Johnson has Sandys turn the full force of his sarcasm on this agreement. A sentence will convey the gist of several full columns of this attack.

It is not possible, Sir even for those who have the quickest Sense, and the most extensive Views of the Consequences of this contemptible Conduct, to forbear some Degree of Merriment at the Exultation which it produced in those who had projected it; every Man was eager to be thought the Author of so judicious an Expedient and it may be ascribed to the Modesty of the President of the ministerial Counsels, that having secured us from the Pretender and his airy Troops of

Iberians and *Allemannuans* who were to have landed from the Clouds upon the Coast of *Lilliput,* he did not demand a Statue, inscribed *To the Deliverer of his Country.*

The usefulness of the new allies was soon discovered. They not only failed to aid England when her merchants were being plundered and Gibraltar besieged by the Spanish; they did not even remain neutral, but put restrictions on the English fleet sent to the West Indies to intercept the treasure ships.

The focus now shifts to Anglo-Spanish relations. Another treaty "equally judicious with that of Hanevro" was negotiated. (The Treaty of Seville is referred to, but Johnson, apparently wary of being too particular, leaves it without a name.) The concessions made by that treaty, rather than buying "an interval of Quiet," persuaded the Spanish "that nothing but Insolence, Rapine, and Obstinacy, was necessary to enslave the *Lilliputian* Nation." The depredations were the result. The public was aroused and "the Minister saw his Schemes in Danger of Miscarriage, and his Country rising once more into Reputation and Dignity." While he was obliged to make "an Appearance of Preparation for War," he at the same time contrived to conciliate the Spanish by the Convention, which would even have questioned the "Right to free Navigation in the Columbia [i.e., American] Seas." ("I ... am astonish'd they did not propose Commissaries to debate our Pretensions to the city of Mildendo [London].") But though at length "the Minister could delay the Appearance of War no Longer," the conflict was a farce, for he could not "gratify his *Blefuscudian* Allies by any other Method than that of obstructing the Success of those Forces which he was obliged to raise, and of prohibiting those Fleets to molest the *Iberians* which were fitted out against them."

The rest of Johnson's discussion of foreign affairs, except for a brief digression on the ministry's complacency in the face of the reparation of Dunkirk, is concerned with the prosecution of the war. Sandys, if we are to credit Fox's notes, treated this subject separately after his discussion of domestic matters. We can only guess how much broader the treatment was than the notes suggest. "Then he came to the entrance into and conduct of the present war." As a matter of fact, Fox preserves only two points of discussion, centered around two admirals: Vernon and Haddock. The accusation that Walpole failed to supply Vernon, as had been promised, is presented in detail, with an accurate citation of dates. Haddock's want of supply is mentioned, the escape of the Cadiz and Ferrol squadrons, the shortage of convoys in spite of Haddock's care in providing them, the cruisers in the channel.

Johnson has Sandys remark that the war, though forced upon Walpole, had this "Convenience," that it disrupted the economy by means of embargoes and the impress of sailors. Haddock and Vernon are discussed, but with none of the exactness of detail that we find in Fox's notes on the latter. "Our Admiral in the *Middle Seas* [the Mediterranean; i.e., Haddock] a strict Observer of his Orders, floated with an idle Pomp of Hostility from Port to Port" and did not obstruct the sailing of the enemy from Cadiz to Ferrol and from Ferrol to America. Vernon, in spite of lack of support, gained a victory at Porto Bello, and "the Friends of the Minister alone held their Heads in Dejection." Johnson is long upon negligence in the protection of shipping during the war. A point not mentioned in Fox's notes but dwelt on by Johnson is the inexperience of the army sent against the Spanish in America: "Soldiers without Discipline, conducted by Officers without Experience," "a Collection of Boys," their embarkation delayed until the enemy had "made all necessary Preparations for Obstinate Defence." Johnson's account of Sandys on foreign affairs ends with a summary: he has "deserted our Allies, aggrandized our Enemies, betrayed our Commerce, and endangered our Colonies."

In the "Political Club," L. Junius Brutus (Sandys) devotes three columns of the *London Magazine* to foreign affairs.[29] (Johnson's account has seventeen.) He gives a mere sketch, but

The Debates as Fact

it does not impress us as being less full of fact than Johnson's Sandys. There is none of Johnson's irony. The treatment is chronological, beginning with the Treaty of Madrid. Soon thereafter the ministry "entered into that close Friendship and Correspondence with the Court of France, which, to the infinite Disadvantage of this Nation has continued ever since, and which has now at last brought the Balance of Power into the utmost Danger if not to inevitable Ruin." The Treaty of Hanover, "the most pernicious of all his pernicious Measures," gave birth to the "Negotiations, Preliminaries, Pacifications, Conventions and Treaties" (here not further named) that constitute "a perfect Series of Blunders." From the last treaty, the Convention, there was perhaps some profit, for it forced England into war. But the war was as unsuccessful as the negotiations that kept the peace. "In Time of Peace, he made us become the Scoff of the Nations around us, by the Tediousness and Perplexity of his Negotiations: In Time of War he has made us an Object of Scorn to our Enemies, and an Object of Pity to our Friends, by the Vastness of his Preparations and Pusilanimity of his Actions." In this section of the *London Magazine's* speech there seems to be no more correspondence with Fox's notes than we would expect chance (and the widely current criticisms of Walpole) to produce.

Sandy's view of domestic affairs, as the record of it has been preserved by Fox, was a practical view, thick with facts and figures but empty of general theory. "He began with stating the national debt in 1716, then mentioned the debts of the army, which, computed at 400,000 came out, by the ingenuity of the commissioners appointed to state them, to be two millions; then the S.S. scheme..." He compared England's South Sea Scheme with that of France's Mississippi Scheme, finding that the latter paid the country's debts while England's did harm. "He stated the debts and sinking fund in 1727" and noted that the debt was still the same, though the sinking fund had produced fifteen million, "spent in Spithead expeditions and Hyde-park reviews."

That is all that Fox records of Sandys' treatment of internal affairs.

Johnson handles the matter in very different fashion. The national debt, the sinking fund, and the South Sea Scheme are not mentioned. Johnson gives, instead, a grandiloquent lecture on the liberty of the people and the danger of subverting it. The irony that characterizes the first part of the speech, but not the extravagance of the language, disappears. To follow Johnson closely here, reproducing many of his own phrases, will expose much of the peculiar and significant vehemence with which he conducts his attack.

Sandys (Johnson version), turning from foreign to domestic affairs, strikes first at the standing army, maintained, he says, for the sole purpose of restraining a universally discontented people from rebelling. Walpole's adherents, justifying the army, profess fear of the Pretender, but the Pretender cannot come into power except by "the Concurrence of the Majority, and that Concurrence can only arise from the Disapprobation of the present Government." But why would the people wish to be subject to a prince of a different religion, "to a Monarch educated among their Enemies, in Countries governed by arbitrary Power"? "How miserable must be the Condition of the People, whom an Army is necessary to restrain from a Choice like this?" Actually, such a choice is impossible; the people are "too well acquainted with their own Rights, to think that when they cannot deliver themselves from Misery, the Pretender will be able to deliver them." But the discontent of the people exists, and those in power, "to dissipate their own Fears...have established an Army in opposition to the fundamental Laws of the Empire." Here Johnson must be quoted at length:

> It may reasonably be expected, that the People will not always groan under their Burdens, in Submission; that after having enquired why they were imposed, and from what Necessity it arises that they are every Day increased, they will at length resolve to shake them off, and

The Debates as Fact

resume into their own Hands that Authority which they have intrusted to their Governors, that they will resolve to become Judges of their own Interest, and regulate those Measures, of which they must support the Expence, and in which nothing but their Advantage ought to be regarded.

When this important Period shall arrive, when Justice shall call out for the Corrupters of Their Country, the Deserters of Their Allies, and the Enemies of Commerce; when Liberty shall publish the Crimes of those by whom she has been long ridiculed and oppressed; when the cries of the exasperated People shall be too loud to be repressed, and Vengeance shall impend over those Heads Which have so long been lifted up with Confidence, against Truth, and Virtue, then will be the Time in which the Army must become the Refuge of those who have so long supported it.

Then will the Corrupter and his Associates, the Lacqueyes of his Train, and the Slaves of his Levee, then will those who have sold their Country for Opportunities of Debauchery, and wasted the Rewards of Perfidy in the Pleasures of the Stews of the Court, implore the Protection of their military Friends, and request them to repay those Benefits which they have formerly received. What is then to be expected, but that either they will be given up to Punishment by those whom they have pampered at the Expence of the Publick, to secure them from it, which is most ardently to be hoped? or that the People will have recourse to Arms in Assertion of their Demands, and that the Nation will be laid waste with all the Devastations of a civil War? that at length either the *Lilliputians* will be forever deprived of their Liberty, that all our Rights will be extinct and our Constitution at an End? or that Victory will declare on the Side of Justice, that the Arms of the People will be successful, and that the Courtiers, and their Protectors will perish together?

Such are the alternatives facing that country which maintains a standing army: "the Ruin of the Nation, or the Destruction of those who have introduced it for their own Advantage."

But Johnson is quick to temper the hints at revolution by the statement that any rebellious tendencies of the people are not directed against the Crown. "The Murmers of the People" are not a sign of disaffection toward His Majesty.

...they desire a Change not of their Sover[e]ign but of his Minister. ...It may be asked why their Resentment is directed against this Person, why they have singled him out from the Croud with which he is surrounded.... [It is] because they see him as the Source of Wealth and Power....

They select him from those that encompass him by the same Tokens that distinguish an Idol from its Worshippers, they see all that surround him cringing to his superior Power and making humble Offerings of their Consciences, their Voices, their Liberties and their Posterity.

What are the measures that have drawn universal hatred upon him? He has destroyed alliances, diminished commerce, obstructed arms, but most important of all he has tried to destroy the national liberties. It is important to understand the source of liberty in government:

...to enjoy Liberty, is to be governed by Laws not arbitrarily imposed, but enacted by the consent of those whose Obedience is required of them.... The People can only consent by the Voices of their Deputies, [and] therefore can only be free by the Possession of a free Choice of their Representatives.... this Foundation of all our Privileges, this Basis of our Constitution...it has been the hourly Labour of the Minister to weaken by imperceptible Degrees. No expedient has been forgotten that might diffuse Corruption, and promote Dependence; Fear and Hope have been equally employed; those who could not be terrify'd have been caressed, and those whose Understanding enabled them to discover the Tendency of false Caresses, have been harassed with Menaces and Hardships.

A spoils system has been set in motion and "penal Laws have been multiply'd which may be relax'd or enforc'd at the Pleasure of the Minister." The result of these schemes is that Walpole "can now sit in his Closet, and nominate a great Part of those Men who yet assume the Stile of Representatives of the People."

But his most vicious attack on liberty, "his most masterly Attempt for the Establishment of universal Slavery...was the Scheme of extending the Laws of Excise." "As the Tyrant of old

The Debates as Fact

wished to destroy Mankind at a Blow, our Minister not less heroically wicked endeavored by one fatal Vote to oppress Liberty forever." Had the law been passed it would have afforded him an incomparable weapon against individual liberties. He would have been able to diffuse "his Spies and Agents over the Nation," have been "enabled to govern every Man in his own Dwelling." Can it be wondered that "the People hold that Man in Abhorrence..."?

Johnson has Sandys conclude his discussion of domestic affairs (and thus bring his whole speech to an end) in an impractical, even desperate way—by returning to the charge of corruption in the very legislative body he is trying to win over. The Senate (Parliament) now meets "only to tax the People, and to flatter the Court, to offer Addresses, and to vote Supplies." The minister has filled "this House with Dependants on the Court, by scattering lucrative Employments amongst them, which are to be held by no other Tenure, than that of an implicite Submission to his will, and a Resignation of all private Opinions to his unerring Dictates." The speaker sees in the House so many men whose determination he already knows before the motion is made that it seems rather pointless to make it; still, if action is to be taken it must be taken now, "while yet the Right of offering any Motion against the Minister remains."

In the *London Magazine,* that part of the speech falling under the head of "particular Branches of Misconduct" in domestic affairs[29] is divided into three main accusations: the failure to discharge the national debt, the menace of the excise scheme, and the underhanded method of obtaining approval of the Convention. The discussion of the national debt reveals close correspondence with Fox, though the account is greatly expanded. The amount of the debt in 1716 is stated. The swelling of the army debentures is mentioned. By this account Sandys names the amount of the debt in 1725 and adds that it has not changed. (According to Fox, the year cited by Sandys was 1727.) The treatment of the excise is conventional, without the zeal of Johnson. (It will be remembered that Fox does not mention this subject.) The examination of Walpole's misrepresentations to Parliament made in order to gain its support of the Convention with Spain is curious in its length (three columns) and elaboration, considering that it is not, in the treatment of domestic affairs, an issue of importance equal to the two previously raised. It is an argument peculiar to the *London Magazine* version.

Since the version of the debate written by Samuel Johnson is the focus here, we cannot linger on that part of Sandys' speech ignored in the *Gentleman's Magazine* but included in the *London Magazine* report. Gordon's treatment of the nature of the motion itself—its precedent and constitutionality—does not differ essentially from that recorded by Fox, though the two accounts are not parallel throughout. That the *London Magazine* is here more elaborate than Fox need not surprise us. But there is one line of argument in the notes not followed in the *London Magazine*. In answer to the anticipated objection that the motion condemned Walpole for acts that had been approved by Parliament, Sandys replies that Oxford had been accused by Walpole in spite of parliamentary sanction of Oxford's measures. Moreover, parliaments might alter their opinions when they found they had been misled by false information. The *London Magazine* acknowledges the possible objection, but answers (or sidesteps) it by asserting that Walpole is solely responsible because he is sole minister. In short, between Fox's notes on parliamentary precedent and the magazine treatment of it there is no striking likeness of detail or general correspondence in order of argument, tone, or verbal quality.

Considering the three versions of Sandys' speech as a whole, we are more impressed by differences than by similarities. The *London Magazine* account, to be sure, presents many arguments which remind us of those recorded by Fox, especially in the realm of domestic affairs. Still, the logical order is completely dissimilar

The Debates as Fact 95

and there is no correspondence in phrasing. The opinion may be ventured that either of the magazine versions of the speech could have been written without the help of notes taken within the house, if the writer were reasonably familiar with the common arguments against Walpole, widely current in conversation, in pamphlets, and in the magazine reports of other debates. Johnson's preoccupation with liberty, an essential ingredient in his version of the speech, is in no way suggested by Fox's notes, and the hints at revolution would, if there had been a counterpart in reality, surely have left so strong an impression as to have been recorded by a witness.

We cannot be sure of the position of Pitt's speech in the debate. Johnson places it directly after the speech of Fox, which, in turn, he makes the first speech of rebuttal in the debate on the main question. The evidence of the content of Pitt's speech, apart from the *Gentleman's Magazine,* is rather mysterious in origin, compact—even sketchy—in form. It consists of a paragraph in the main text of Coxe's book, the source of which is identified by a footnote as "Heads of Pitt's speech, in Sir Robert Walpole's Parliamentary Memorandums."[30] Coxe's information, we may assume, comes from the Walpole family manuscripts to which he had access, but we do not know the extent of his editing. The paragraph is short and may be quoted in full.

Pitt observed in emphatic language, "That during the administration that was the object of censure, at home debts were increased and taxes multiplied, and the sinking fund alienated; abroad the system of Europe was totally subverted, and at this awful moment, when the greatest scene was opening to Europe that has ever before occurred, he who had lost the confidence of all mankind should not be permitted to continue as the head of the king's government."

If these are, indeed, merely the "heads" of Pitt's speech, it must have been comprehensive, covering much of the ground already well worked by Sandys.

Pitt's speech as given by Johnson is simply a different speech.

It is quite short, and presents little more than a single argument. Though it becomes uncertain in organization toward the end, the speech begins with a single theme: time. "Time is the Test of Opinions." Fox (by Johnson's account) has protested that the opposition has brought forward no new arguments; Pitt answers that the supporters of Walpole have found no new defense. Time has supported the arguments of Walpole's accusers and confuted those of his defenders. It is to be hoped that members who have voted mistakenly in the past will not now, in the face of time's verdict, be predetermined against the present motion.

Time indeed may not always produce new Arguments against bad Conduct, because all its Consequences might be originally foreseen and exposed, but it must always confirm them, and ripen Conjecture into Certainty. Though it should therefore be truly asserted that nothing is urged in this Debate which was not before mentioned and rejected, it will not prove that because the Arguments are the same they ought to produce the same Effect; because what was then only *foretold* has now been *seen* and *felt,* and what was then but *believed* is now *known.*

Pitt now makes application of his generality by examining the manner in which time has vindicated the arguments made against the Treaty of Hanover.

The final paragraphs drop the time theme. The minister, says Pitt, deserves a censure more severe than that intended by the present motion; he "should be deprived not only of his Honours but of his Life." As for this motion, the discontent of the people is sufficient justification, for whether right or wrong in their accusation of the minister, their opinion is manifest and they "should believe their Interest favoured, and their Liberties protected." If we put any faith in the "heads of Pitt's speech," it seems probable that the speech written by Johnson is pure fabrication.

Again we turn to Coxe's *Memoirs of ... Robert Walpole* for evidence, this time for evidence of the speech of the minister

The Debates as Fact

himself. The note at the bottom of the first of its twelve pages is heartening: "The substance of this speech is taken from parliamentary minutes in the handwriting of Sir Robert Walpole—Orford Papers—Chandler."[31] Here certainly is a report in which we can put complete faith! It is only after we read the account with knowledge of the magazine versions of it that we become dismally conscious of the significance of that last word of the footnote. Coxe has filled out his authentic notes with passages from Chandler's collection of debates, and since it is the *London Magazine* version of the Walpole speech that Chandler reprints it is obvious that the original source is the "Proceedings of the Political Club."[32] It is pointless, then, to compare the record of the speech as it stands with the magazine reports. We must do what we can toward filtering the *London Magazine* out of the Coxe mixture, on the assumption that pure Walpole will then remain. We shall reverse our procedure and summarize the magazine accounts before investigating the source of collateral evidence.

The speeches appearing in the two magazines are almost identical in length, but there close likeness ends. According to the *London Magazine,* Walpole observes that since "all Objections now made to the Conduct of the Administration, have been already answered . . . I need only repeat a few of those Answers that have been made already." And those answers constitute his speech in this version. Again we have the division into foreign affairs (including the conduct of the war) and domestic affairs. This core of the minister's speech is rounded out by a beginning paragraph protesting that he is being asked to answer for charges that could be directed equally against "Kings, Lords and Commons," and a paragraph at the end warning that the motion represents an encroachment against the prerogative of the crown. The treatment of foreign affairs contains the stock answers to the stock accusations and need not be analyzed here. Domestic affairs are, for the most part, handled in similarly commonplace fashion. Two arguments stand out by virtue of their particularity from the surrounding generalities. The first is an answer to the charge that the public debt has not been lowered by use of the sinking fund. Eight million of the debt has been discharged by application of the sinking fund, and seven million from the fund has been "applied to the Ease of the Land Tax." The second argument is in answer to the charge made by Pulteney (in this version, of course; we have no authentic evidence of Pulteney's speech) that Walpole had conspired with those who bought up army debentures at a discount just before they were paid off. Walpole replies that this incident had occurred before he was in power, when he was still "the Country Gentleman;" and he proceeds to explain and justify the occurrence.

Johnson does not summarize the conduct of foreign and domestic affairs from Walpole's standpoint. After a brief introduction in which Walpole asserts his innocence and remarks that "the Gentlemen who have already spoken in my Favour have ... freed me from the Necessity of wearying the House with a long Defense," the substance of the speech consists of two parts, about equal in length. The first follows out the familiar line of defense that Walpole cannot be punished for actions that have received the approbation of the legislature, that his responsibility for the conduct of affairs was that of one among many, that "till they have proved the Criminal their Declamations upon the Crimes are empty Sounds ... Arrows shot without a Mark."

The other part of Walpole's speech is concerned with "some Transactions of a more private Kind in which it may be suspected that I was personally engaged." He does not number among these the matter of army debentures, he says. That affair was settled before he came into power. The first of the "Transactions of a private Kind" is the topic of employments given to his family. The purest of his accusers, "Had he been able to obtain the same Interest," would have employed it to the same end. He himself has received fewer rewards from the Crown than any

The Debates as Fact

man in his position: "a little House," "the little Ornament upon my Shoulder"—that is all. He concludes with protestations of his innocence. The speech is a peculiarly perfunctory performance by Johnson. Though of approximately the same length as the *London Magazine* account, it seems much shorter because Johnson is more expansive and does not cover as much ground in similar compass. The speech seems especially brief in contrast with the extended speeches of the earlier part of the debate. Perhaps time and space had both run short.

In the Coxe version, Walpole begins by shrewdly promoting discord among the members of his opposition. The passage of several pages has no counterpart in the magazines and so must be taken from the "parliamentary minutes." The whole direction of the remarks is so appropriate to the speaker and the situation that it carries conviction where the magazine accounts do not. Walpole, before speaking, must have heard the issue of the debate in the Lords and had already observed in his own house the lack of unanimity in the opposition's support of the motion. Certainly the minister, the master politician, must have realized that he could do much more than defend himself against a motion that must certainly be defeated. Why not press the advantage of an assured victory, widen among the elements of the opposition the division fostered by dissatisfaction with the motion? "From whence does the attack proceed?" he asks. "From the passions and prejudices of the parties combined against me; who may be divided into three classes, the Boys, the riper Patriots, and the Tories." He pays a backhanded compliment to the Tories. "The tories I can easily forgive"; they oppose Walpole because he keeps them from power. Certainly they who have always been treated with justice cannot support a motion "contrary to principle and precedent." Walpole levels his heavy accusations against the "men of yesterday, the boys in politics," and "the mock patriots whose practice and possessions prove their selfishness and malignity." Patriots? They spring up like mushrooms! "I have raised many of them in one night. It is but refusing to gratify an unreasonable or an insolent demand, and up starts a patriot." Since the magazines were in urgent need of following fresh directions of thought in the debate, it is surprising that they did not exploit this one. We can only surmise that the notes from which they worked were deficient.

Walpole, in the speech Coxe has given us, now turns to the accusations that have been made against the ministry's conduct of affairs, dividing them into the same three categories Sandys had earlier used and taking them up in the same order. The greater part of the material that Coxe puts together as Walpole's refutation reproduces, with only the slightest alteration, passages from the *London Magazine*. However, the fact that Coxe rejects the sequence of ideas in the magazine ("the conduct of the war" being separated from "foreign affairs" and placed after "domestic affairs") is a strong indication that Walpole did actually record the fact that he defended his "misconduct," and in the order appearing in Coxe, though not in these words. As a matter of fact, within the first and last divisions of this defense, passages not from the *London Magazine,* clearly separated from passages that are, have probably been extracted from Walpole's parliamentary minutes.

The foreign-affairs section begins with material that is not found in the magazines. Walpole is quoted as saying that the opposition speakers have unfairly massed together all treaties and negotiations. Each, however, should be considered in the light of the circumstances in which it was made and the "peculiar situation in which I stand." Is he to be considered "sole minister" of all Europe? Must he answer for the conduct of other countries? Coxe interrupts his quotation to summarize: "he entered into a luminous recapitulation of the principal compacts," beginning with the Peace of Utrecht, which had altered the balance of power in Europe. The reference to Utrecht must be authentic; there is no parallel in the magazine. Coxe then resumes his quotation of Walpole with the first event in the *London Magazine's* recapitulation of foreign negotiations, the refusing of the sole mediation offered by Spain. From this point on the summary of foreign affairs is pure magazine. Next comes a non-magazine paragraph, probably quoted or adapted from the minutes, protesting that all treaties have had the approval of Parliament and that any mishaps in foreign affairs must be attributed to the actions of foreign powers. We must assume that between this paragraph and the earlier reference to Utrecht the parliamentary minutes of Walpole contained such references to other treaties as to justify Coxe in including the extended account from the *London Magazine*. We need not assume that the magazine material closely paralleled that in the minutes. If those notes had been full, Coxe probably would have been content with them and would not have turned to Chandler. By the same token, the notes probably contained very little on domestic affairs, for passages on that subject are lifted almost verbatim from the *London Magazine*.

The treatment of the war's conduct consists of a single paragraph, the first two-thirds from the *London Magazine,* the last third apparently from the minutes. The latter passage appears to be complete in itself, and was no doubt all that appeared on the subject in the minutes. The *London Magazine* section of the paragraph attempts to defend the ministry's prosecution of the war; the rest states simply, "I could, with great ease, have an incontrovertible defense; but as I have trespassed so long on the time of the house, I shall not weaken the effect of that forcible exculpation so generously and disinterestedly advanced by the right honourable gentleman who so meritoriously presides at the admiralty." A statement similar to this last is not included in either magazine report, nor did either magazine, for that matter, seem aware that Wager had made an important speech defending the conduct of the war.

The rest of the speech as given by Coxe is a weakly organized series of statements. Walpole inquires (and this must come from the minutes, since not even the idea is paralleled in the magazines) why he should not speak in his own favor. Why should he not point out his accomplishments? He has revived credit, encouraged trade, kept the peace. Now he turns to a denial of the charge of exorbitant power; this denial, we are surprised to find, is in a passage, slightly altered verbally, from the Johnson version of the speech. We say "surprised" because Chandler does not print Johnson's report of this speech, and Coxe has given us only two sources for his compilation: the Orford papers and Chandler. Two explanations are possible: the first, simplest, and most probable is that Coxe went to the *Gentleman's Magazine*, found and liked this passage, and incorporated it without acknowledgment;[38] the second, that the passage appeared in Walpole's notes of the speech and that Johnson received a verbatim report of this passage and worked it into his report. The fact that the passage sounds Johnsonian inclines us away from the latter alternative. The passage paralleling that in the *Gentleman's Magazine* ends, but the verbal echoes continue in the next few paragraphs. Walpole refers, as in the Johnsonian version, to "the little ornament" on his shoulder and protests that "many may [Johnson has "must"] be pleased to see those honours which their ancestors have worn, restored again to the commons." There are echoes, too, in Walpole's justification of having given his family positions in government. The speech given by Coxe concludes with the final paragraph of the *London Magazine's* debate.

Having established the probable content of Walpole's own record of his speech, we can say that Johnson's version has almost no relation to it if we expect some possible verbal similarities toward the end. We might conjecture that Coxe uses passages from the *London Magazine* version of the speech because the authenticity of those passages is assured by Walpole's notes, but even if we accept that doubtful supposition it must be admitted

The Debates as Fact

that the most distinctive aspects of the speech are absent from that magazine's account.

A contemporary political pamphlet bears a curious relation to all three of the versions we have been examining. This anti-Walpole pamphlet purports to be *A Review of the Late Motion... by a Member of Parliament.*[84] The writer refutes about a dozen statements that are represented as being quoted from Walpole's speech. Each of our three versions contains two or more passages that verbally parallel parts of these quotations. Their similarity to passages in Walpole's parliamentary minutes probably indicates that the quotations in the pamphlet are a fairly accurate record of some of the minister's utterances, and the similarity to passages in the magazines may be explained by surmising that Johnson and Gordon knew the pamphlet and appropriated what they desired. The alternatives to this theory—that Coxe, too, knew the pamphlet or that all four versions go back to independent but authentic notes—seem unlikely. Probably Coxe, finding passages from the pamphlet source in the magazine accounts, was led by the look of authority in those passages to a stronger belief in the authority of the reports as a whole. It is interesting to note that both of the "particular" references in the *London Magazine* account of domestic affairs—to army debentures and the public debt—have, if our theory is sound, been taken from the pamphlet.[85] The "Transaction of a more private Kind" in Johnson's speech, the family employments in the government, the "little house," and the "little ornament," all have close counterparts in the pamphlet. It may have been the authenticity of these references that produced the verbal echoes on two of these points in the Coxe version of the speech.

Our comparison has demonstrated the probability that, aside from the facts that were to be gleaned from this, and perhaps other, pamphlets, neither of the magazine writers of debates had any genuine knowledge of Walpole's remarks. Indeed, now that we have completed the examination of the speeches for which there is authentic evidence, we must conclude that Johnson and Gordon appear to have been working here with even more meager notations of actual fact than were available to them for the Lords debate.

Besides the two already studied, three speeches are shared by the two magazines: those of Pelham, Harley, and Pulteney. A brief comparison of the two versions is particularly interesting because the *London Magazine's* debate was published so far in advance of the Johnson account that it may well have been the source for it.

The very different position of Pelham's speech in the two magazine versions of the debate makes necessary a dissimilar content. In the *London Magazine,* Pelham's debate comes directly after Sandys' speech and is the first speech of rebuttal on the motion (thus paralleling dramatically Johnson's Fox speech, to which it has no real relation). Since, in the *Gentleman's Magazine,* Pelham speaks toward the end of the debate, after the main issues of the motion-making speech have been seesawed back and forth, there is no need for a comprehensive speech. As a matter of fact, the *London Magazine* does not make Pelham as comprehensive as he should be in view of his place in the debate. He does not answer Sandy's accusations in an orderly way. Is the *London Magazine* here showing bias? Pelham begins by challenging the constitutionality of the proposal. He admits that the mob may oppose the minister, but not "the better Sort of People," and even these cannot judge his conduct. Those who do so must have the knowledge "that can be acquired by none but those of high Rank." The constitution does not allow a minister to be turned out because of a general clamor. Do not these arguments depend on admissions and assumptions that carry little conviction? Pelham, by this account, does not answer all Sandys' charges of misconduct, but makes the general statement that no new arguments have been advanced; the old arguments have not only been answered, but those answers have already been ap-

The Debates as Fact

proved by Parliament. Therefore, only a few of Sandys' specific accusations are discussed: excise, the Treaty of Hanover, and the Convention. The conduct of the war is generally and weakly defended. Pelham then demands proof of particular crimes, and ends lamely with a tacked-on refutation (in small type) of the argument that the mere length of Walpole's administration is cause to remove him.

Johnson confines Pelham to the question of the motion's constitutionality. It is a moderate speech. Pelham begins by being astonished that this motion should be promoted "by Gentlemen, whose zeal for Equity and Regard to the Laws of their Country, I never before had any Reason to suspect." The speaker suggests that the members of the house lay aside all considerations of the character of the man under attack and consider only the precedent that might be established. Under the constitution a man is considered innocent until proof of guilt is established. The proposal before the house would convict the minister of unnamed crimes while depriving him of an impartial trial. Though it is possible that Johnson received from the *London Magazine* the hint for the subject elaborated by Pelham, he does not owe the magazine anything in the treatment of it.

Though it is a simple matter to state the relation of the two magazine versions of Harley's speech, it is not a relation simple to explain. The magazines print the same speech.[30] It is a short speech (one column) and a direct one, beginning with the words, "I do not stand up at this Time of Night either to accuse or to flatter any Man." Harley simply wants to assert that, though he has opposed the measures of the administration, though he deplores the state of the nation to which they have led, he must vote against this motion. He cannot censure any man not convicted "from Facts and Evidence." "A Noble Lord to whom I have the Honour to be related" and who has been mentioned in this debate (Oxford) was impeached and imprisoned, prosecuted by the subject of the present question without support of evidence. "I am now, Sir, glad of this Opportunity to return Good for Evil, and do that Hon. Gentleman and his Family that justice which he denied to Mine." Why would Johnson, who is at such pains elsewhere in the debate to avoid any suggestion of following the *London Magazine,* copy Harley's speech directly from the earlier report? We can hardly believe it possible, and without further evidence can only suggest that copies of Harley's speech had such currency outside either magazine account that Johnson, by using any other words than these, would call into question the authenticity of his report. Or might not Harley himself, anxious to vindicate the stand he had taken, have supplied each magazine with a copy of his speech?

Pulteney's speech occupies the same position in each of the two magazines; it comes just before Walpole's. Two points the versions have in common. By both accounts Pulteney begins in protest against being required to speak before Walpole makes his defense, but the *London Magazine's* reference is not entirely clear to us without the knowledge of the situation that we gain from the *Gentleman's Magazine.* The other point of similarity is the accusation concerning army debentures. This must necessarily be introduced by both magazines in preparation for Walpole's defense, which is likewise included in both versions (and inspired by the pamphlet cited above?) Aside from these, there are few likenesses. The *London Magazine* splits the general material into the old categories of foreign and internal affairs. In the treatment of foreign affairs, nothing of importance is offered that has not been mentioned in these pages. It is interesting that the summary of negotiations begins with a reference to Oxford's impeachment, a reference no doubt inspired in Gordon by the reminder in Harley's speech placed directly before this one. In treating domestic affairs, Pulteney is made to say that Walpole governs by bribery and corruption, has prevented the payment of the public debt, and saw to it that his friends bought army debentures at a discount. The speech ends with Pulteney chiding

The Debates as Fact

Harley for his misunderstanding. Since this is not an impeachment, it is not necessary to present proof of particular crimes. A motion requesting the king to remove the minister is justified if the tenor of his conduct shows bad intentions or weakness.

Johnson, in writing up a speech for the latter part of a debate, often confines himself to a single theme. This is true of his handling of Pulteney's speech. The idea itself may have been suggested by the last argument in the *London Magazine* version, or Johnson may have come on it independently. The theme is "proof." The nature of the defense up to this point in the debate has been, says Pulteney, to urge the insufficiency of proof rather than to attempt to vindicate the measures. Such a defense is fallacious. Proof is not required because the motion has no parallels with a criminal trial. The accused is not a felon with whose character the judge is unacquainted. Judges judge those they have not previously heard, but we are to consider facts with which we are all familiar and understand to the full. "If a Criminal were to stand before Judges who had been Witnesses of his Crimes, and who could refer him to no other Judicature," would it "be necessary for them to acquit him for want of Proof?" But since more proof is required, Pulteney will produce such circumstantial evidence as would "convict a House-breaker, a Pick-pocket, or a Murderer." That there is influence and corruption is proved by those who are without merit but live in luxury. That he alone disposes of "Places of Profit" is proved by the number he has settled on members of his family. That he is "Master of the National Treasure" is proved by his "Profusion." Some of the sources of his wealth are indeed easily traced—to army debentures, for example. Pulteney concludes that it is time to take this man's power away and divide it among others. The relation—or lack of relation—of the speech to the other magazine version is obvious.

All the other speeches in Johnson's debate exist in his version only. To study them by means of comparison is impossible, but a few observations on some of them may be worthy of consideration. For example, it is necessary to recognize the importance of Fox's speech to the design of Johnson's debate. It occupies the position of chief speech of rebuttal and thus must balance the address of Sandys. This it does both by virtue of its length (it is even slightly longer than the other) and its incisiveness. Fox's speech, although it lacks the vehemence of expression in Sandys', gives us the sense of its deliverer's complete mastery of the situation. Fox is made to begin by saying that he will answer for every part of Walpole's conduct in the order in which his "imaginary Crimes have been ranged." Two things must be kept in mind, however: first, since nothing new has been argued, there can be nothing new to reply; second, to point out the fact that none of the measures censured was transacted without the concurrence of other ministers and of Parliament is a method of defense so important as to vindicate those measures. Detailed answers are offered to Sandys' specific charges of misconduct in foreign and domestic matters; then Fox returns to the other line of defense. Setting aside all other considerations, is this a proper motion? The "Fallacy of the Argument" consists in supposing "what is principally to be proved," that Walpole is not only the chief but the sole director of affairs. Since he is neither, the motion is unjust and establishes a dangerous precedent. The efficiency of Fox's defense of the government suggests that Johnson was at pains to draft a strong Whig defense to a strong accusation.

All the individual speeches of first importance in Johnson's account have now been examined. It will be necessary only to point out an interesting preoccupation that runs through several addresses in the latter part of the debate. It is a theme introduced by Sandys: the place of "the people" in government. Though Fox answers the accusation behind it, he does not dwell on the theme itself. Pitt reintroduces the theme at the end of his speech. The discontent of the people is sufficient reason for passing the motion; "it is necessary to the Prosperity of the Government that the People should believe their Interest favoured, and their Liberties protected." Howe, toward the latter part of his speech, opposes Pitt's theory. The business of Parliament is to "hold the Ballance between the Court and the People, and to preserve at once the Dignity of the Crown and the Rights of the Nation." We cannot let the king's servants be torn from him by popular fury. Heathcote in reply describes the hatred of the people for Walpole and concludes that "it cannot be expected that his Majesty should long retain the Affections of the People" while a man like this enjoys his confidence. It is proof of loyalty to support the present motion.

What general statements can be made now about the whole debate as Johnson gives it to us? As far as we can determine from the evidence available, its broad outlines parallel actual occurrence. If Johnson omits speeches that were delivered, he has included the interesting aspects of the debate: its double nature and the duel between Pulteney and Walpole for the position of last speaker. Johnson, then, must have worked with a fairly accurate list of speakers. The comparison of three addresses with more authentic evidence, however, leads us to a belief that Johnson had little knowledge of the speakers' actual remarks. He was evidently called upon here to employ his imagination and his political knowledge in far greater measure than in the Lords debate on the same question.

Johnson's success in preserving the main design of the debate is not matched in the *London Magazine*. But if that magazine gives only a handful of speeches made up of repetitious arguments, it also comes nearer, perhaps by chance, to reflecting at a few isolated points particular arguments found in the original evidence. The *London Magazine* account is strongly weighted, whether by intention or not, in favor of the opposition. Johnson, however, displaying his naturally forensic nature, elaborates for the Whigs persuasive arguments that must have run counter to his convictions.

To define our impression of the mind that produced Johnson's debate is difficult. Perhaps, after all, the quality that strikes us most forcibly is the violence displayed in Sandys' speech. But this violence does not pervade the whole performance. We are impressed everywhere with Johnson's habit of thinking in general terms, and that impression is deepened by comparison with other versions. I do not mean simply that he avoids particularity; often there is an amplitude of details. But Johnson, never becoming engrossed with the details, endeavors always to bring particular arguments into a design of larger outline. The manner, for example, in which the Sandys treatment of domestic affairs is made to embrace a theory of human liberty demonstrates a profound concern with the broadest questions of human conduct and the ordering of human affairs.

Comparison of the Remaining Debates

Step by step, the available versions of two debates have been examined. It is hoped that the detailed account has accomplished its purposes: to convey not only the results of the investigation but a full sense of the materials under consideration and the methods employed. But to continue to record the actual processes used in comparing the remaining debates of Johnson with the collateral evidence would be, within the present study, neither possible nor desirable. It will be sufficient now to record the significant likenesses and differences that are revealed by a correspondingly close reading of the other Lilliputian debates and their known counterparts, and to reinforce those findings with such illustrative material as may enlighten and enliven. Because nearly every debate presents separate problems and suggests separate conclusions, it will be necessary, even in this more abbreviated account, to treat them one at a time. The materials available for each have prescribed the methods of study and may now govern the order of presentation.

The Johnsonian debates that remain may be divided into five groups. The first group consists of nine debates for which no

The Debates as Fact

parallel account has turned up. The second group comprises whole debates for which we have two sorts of verifying evidence: magazine and non-magazine, or, as we may put it, the contrived and the authentic. It is immediately apparent that the Lords debate on the motion to remove Walpole is an exemplary member of this group, and there are, besides this one, four. The debate in Commons just considered is the prototype of the third group. In this class we place the debates of which two complete magazine versions exist but for which the historical evidence is deficient. That deficiency may be complete or only partial; of those under study the debate already examined is perhaps least deficient. There are four debates in this group in addition to the one already studied. The fourth group consists of three debates for which we have authentic evidence of the whole but no magazine version other than Johnson's. Into the fifth group go the rest, which can be given but piecemeal comparative study because only evidence of isolated speeches exists outside Johnson's account.

Of the second group, the Lords debate of December 4, 1741, on the address of thanks for His Majesty's speech, is, of those not yet discussed, chronologically first. Johnson's version first appeared in the July, August, and September issues of the *Gentleman's Magazine*. Though the *London Magazine* possessed the advantage of a prior example (its report appeared in the September and October issues of the same year), the editor appears to have been content not to compete in the matter of completeness with his rival. We learn of sixteen speeches in the actual debate from our independent witness, again the conscientious Archbishop Secker; the *Gentleman's Magazine* provides fifteen, the *London Magazine* only five.[37] But the *London Magazine* by the introductions to its speeches seems to disavow the attempt at a complete report: "The next speech I shall give was that of C. Cicerejus ... The last speech I shall give on this Occasion was that of Q. Aemelius Paulus." Johnson was apparently working here with an imperfect list of speakers. The following discrepancies may be noted: Johnson omits four speeches mentioned by Secker and adds three not mentioned by him. Three of the speakers common to both accounts are placed by the *Gentleman's Magazine* out of the sequence recorded by Secker. The five speeches given by the *London Magazine* chance to agree in order of delivery with both Johnson and Secker.

Within the speeches we find a similarity between Johnson and Secker of approximately the same degree as that noted in the Lords debate on the motion. Here, too, is some latitude in accuracy. The speech of Harrington is probably closest to its original, for, different as the details are, the same distinctive content is found both in Secker's *Journal* and in Johnson's account in the *Gentleman's Magazine*. For others of the speeches Johnson may well have worked with no more than a name (and, in view of the inaccuracy of his list of names, some of these may be solely his own choice). The speech of Chesterfield, probably the most important of the debate, may be taken as the mean with respect to accuracy. The main outlines of Johnson's and Secker's versions of this are much the same, though in the finer lines of argument there are no close ties and there are no verbal similarities. Chesterfield, by Secker's account, named numbers of troops, of Spaniards, of ships; Johnson is satisfied with generalities. This time the ironic tone of Johnson finds a counterpart in the authentic version. Secker's "If our administration had been a French one, they would have been the ablest in the World"[38] is matched, for example, by Johnson's "I am too well convinced of the Prudence and Tenderness of the Restrictions by which the Power of our Admirals is limited to expect that our Guns should ever be used but in Salutations of Respect, or Exultations on the Conclusion of a Peace."[39] The *London Magazine* version lacks this tone. It also deviates from the other two in making a detailed chronological survey of foreign affairs and treaties the notable part of the speech. Johnson, too, seems to touch on a consideration typically his when he has Chesterfield say (and there is no hint of this in Secker):

The Debates as Fact

How we shall gratify the Expectation of Foreign Powers, ought not, My Lords, to be our first and Chief Consideration; we ought certainly first to inquire how the People may be set free from those Suspicions which a long Train of Measures evidently tending to impair their Privileges, has raised, and how they may be confirmed in their Fidelity to the Government.[40]

The *Gentleman's Magazine* makes high claims for its debate of May 25, 1742, on the bill for indemnifying evidence relating to Walpole.[41] At the end of the debate the magazine affirms, "The aforementioned Lords were all who spoke in this Debate." At the beginning is a long paragraph denouncing "an account of this Debate ... already published." (The *London Magazine* reported the debate in the issues of July, August, and September; the *Gentleman's Magazine,* in the issues of October, November, and December, 1742). The rival magazine is chided for reporting only six speakers instead of ten, and especially for making Chesterfield answer Hardwicke and not Hardwicke, Chesterfield. Indeed, Secker's *Journal* does show Johnson to have been much closer to fact than Gordon was. But Secker[42] names *eleven* speakers (the speech omitted by Johnson is that of Berkeley of Stratton), and does not record a second speech by Argyle, reported—or made up—by Johnson. Aside from these discrepancies, however, the order of speakers is the same in the two accounts; in the *London Magazine* three of the six speeches are out of correct sequence. Johnson, then, was in no sense dependent on the account earlier published. He worked with a fairly accurate list of speakers, and evidence within the speeches indicates that he worked also with some accurate notations of statements and arguments.

We can mention here only a few of the similarities of detail. Carteret, the first speaker, uses in Johnson's debate three separate Latin phrases quoted also by Secker. According to Secker, Hervey argued that the bill might have dangerous consequences not intended by its promoters.

If any person can interweave a confession of his own crime with an accusation of the person mentioned in the Bill, he is safe, provided any question leads at all to such a confession. So that to confess his own guilt would be all a man would aim at in his answer. "Did Lord Orford give 5 guineas at such an election?" "Yes, for I saw the man take it and I murdered him."⁴³

A parallel passage from Johnson's Hervey not only indicates that some witness must have passed this point on to the compilers, but also illustrates Johnson's tendency to add an ironic twist and—it must be admitted—to dull the edge of a dramatic argument by thickening it with words.

A Man Whom the Consciousness of Murder has for some Time kept in continual Terrors, may clear himself forever, by alleging, that he was commissioned by the Eral of *Ofrord* to engage, with any certain Sum, the Vote or Interest of the murdered Person; that he took the Opportunity of a Solitary Place to offer him the Bribe, and prevail upon him to comply with his Proposals, but that finding him obstinate and perverse, filled with Prejudices against a wise and just Administration, and inclined to Obstruct the Measures of the Government, he for some time expostulated with him, and being provoked by his contumelious Representations of the State of Affairs, he could no longer restrain the Ardour of his Loyalty, but thought it proper to remove from the World a Man so much inclined to spread Sedition among the People, and that therefore finding the Place convenient, he suddenly rush'd upon him and cut his Throat."

In Johnson's speech of the Duke of Argyle we find phrases that correspond closely with those found in Secker. Secker has: "The public hath a right to the evidence of every individual of the society. And yet no man can be bound to accuse himself."⁴⁵ In Johnson's version, "a Maxim of indubitable certainty" is *"that the Publick has a Claim to every Man's Evidence,"* and it is equally true that *"no Man is obliged to accuse himself."*⁴⁶ Is it possible that by the italics Johnson intends to indicate that the phrases are quotations?⁴⁷

The *Gentleman's Magazine* echoes Chesterfield's phrase, *cor-*

pus suspicionis, recorded by Secker. Hardwicke's response produces the following parallel. Secker has it: *"Corpus suspicionis* is a new term, it is the body of a shadow: That is the foundation of the bill."[48] Johnson's version is:

I very well understand what is meant by *Corpus Delecti,* and so does every other Lord, it is universally known to mean the *Body of an Offence;* but as to the words *Corpus Suspicionis,* I do not comprehend what they mean. It is an Expression indeed which I never before heard, and can signify in my Apprehension, nothing more than the *Body of a Shadow,* the Substance of something which is itself Nothing.[49]

We cannot call the Lilliputian version of the debate authentic. The parallels between Johnson and Secker are isolated phenomena. If we look for a parallel line of argument running through a whole speech we are disappointed: the order, the proportion, the manner differ. What do the close likenesses and the profound differences tell us of Johnson's raw material? It is probable that someone on the scene took written notes of striking phrases, but was neither thorough enough nor discriminating enough to convey the order and gist of the main arguments. Johnson was never at a loss to spin out the thinnest hints until an elaborate fabric had been produced. Can he have had a hint that was more than the "Substance of something which is itself Nothing" when he built the extensive structure of Lord Talbot's speech? According to Secker, Talbot said, "I rise up only to give time to others to consider how they will carry on the debate."

Johnson's debate of February 1, 1743, which records the controversy in the House of Lords over the retention of the Hanoverian troops, appears to represent a further advance toward accuracy. The sequence of speeches in the *Gentleman's Magazine* corresponds exactly with that found in Secker.[50] The *London Magazine,* as we have come to expect, omits some speeches, but not so many as usual. Like two of those debates already analyzed, this is of double character: a motion of censure on the rejected motion is argued at the end of debate on the main question. The three speeches that comprise the secondary debate and three of the speeches of the main debate do not appear in the *London Magazine*. Again that lack of completeness is curious, for it is quite possible that Johnson's version served as a model; the "Political Club" version is contained in the November and December issues and Appendix, 1743, and Johnson's debate was printed in the *Gentleman's Magazine* of June, July, August, September, and October of the same year. But even if Gordon wrote with Johnson's report in mind, several independent correspondences with Secker point to a separate source of information as well. The *London Magazine,* though not so accurate as Johnson, has a larger number of specific facts. Some of these facts seem not to correspond with facts cited by Secker, and may go back to some other source than the debate itself. Typically, the "Political Club" is generous with its conventional summaries of foreign affairs, and deviates from both Secker and Johnson by arranging a careful pattern of answers and counter-answers carried on from speech to speech.

When we compare the speeches of Johnson's debate on the Hanoverian troops with the record in Secker's *Journal* we are struck by the abundance of similarities. The correspondences that are noted throughout the course of a speech we may attribute to better notes from witnesses and perhaps to a more insistent demand of the public for accuracy. But some speeches reveal only general similarities, and Johnson is still, throughout, the shaping artist. There are almost no verbal parallels. Hervey, by Secker's account, argued: "People cannot employ or dare not trust their money in trade: so they put it in stocks. But this florid look is an unhealthy flushing."[51] The *London Magazine* reports the figure of speech accurately: "Our publick Credit ... is so far from being a Sign of Health, that like the flushings in some Diseases it may perhaps be found to be a Sign of approaching Death."[52] But Johnson, still close to the original, transfigures it: "The Rise of our

The Debates as Fact 117

Stocks, my Lords, is such Proof of Riches, as dropsical Tumors are of Health; it shows not the Circulation but the Stagnation of our Money."[53]

The close correspondence between Secker's and Johnson's versions of this debate make several errors of Johnson more noticeable than they might have been in other, less authentic reports. One such mistake may serve as an example, and remind us that the material with which Johnson worked, though full and reasonably accurate for this debate, was by no means infallible. Bathurst, according to Secker, argued: "Our debts are no reason against endeavoring to save what we have left. When all is at stake we must play for all."[54] Johnson's Bathurst assumes the existence of a different state of affairs. "The Abundance of our Wealth, my Lords, and the Profit of our Commerce are sufficiently Apparent...Another Proof of the Exuberance of our Riches, and the Prosperity of our Commerce..."[55]

The Lilliputian debate on the spirituous liquors bill in the House of Lords is really a series of three debates. The first records the debate of February 22, 1743, at the time of the second reading of the bill; the second, the debate of February 24, when the house "went into committee;" the third, the debate of February 25, after the third reading. Again using Secker's *Journal*[56] as the basis for comparison, we must pronounce Johnson's debate less accurate but more complete than Gordon's.[57] Only on the last day's debate does the sequence of Johnson's speakers exactly parallel that found in Secker. In the report of the first day, one speech is out of proper order, one is missing, and one is added.[58] In Johnson's version of the second day's debate, four speakers do not correspond with Secker's, and one speech is omitted.[59] The *London Magazine* omits three speeches of the first day's debate, but those reported are in correct order.[60] In the account of the second day's proceedings no speech is omitted and only one is out of place up to the time of putting the question that the house be resumed. At that point the *London Magazine* concludes its version, but Johnson proceeds to report five more speeches of that day and an additional five of the next day.

The individual speeches in the three versions reveal close similarities between Secker's account and the reports of the two magazines. In some speeches the correspondences are isolated, not supported by a basic similarity of plan. Sometimes, as in Cholmondeley's speech of the first day, one magazine (here the *Gentleman's Magazine*) is much closer to fact. In others, as in Hervey's first speech, there are close parallels in plan, in detail of argument and citation, even in an occasional phrase, between Secker and *both* the magazine accounts. Still, in Johnson's version, a speech as circumscribed in matter as Hervey's can only be thought of as Johnsonian in its essence. Certainly such a sentence as the following contains more of Johnson than of Hervey: "Before any one of its pernicious Effects is fully dilated a Thousand other[s] appear, the Hydra still shoots out new Heads, and every Head vomits out new Poison to infect Society, and lay the Nation desolate."[61] And the arguments, even if they are Hervey's, are made to find their base in maxims that are Johnson's: "Pride, my Lords, is the Parent and Intrepidity the Fosterer of Resentment ... Laws, My Lords, suppose Reason ... To promote Trust, my Lords, is the apparent Tendency of all Laws."

Two speeches of this debate as they are recorded in Secker's *Journal* are of special interest. One is a speech of Secker himself (that is, the Bishop of Oxford) preserved in greater detail than is usual with the journal keeper; the other, the speech of Chesterfield, the special tone of which seems to emerge from Secker's notes. The *London Magazine's* Bishop of Oxford is rather closer to the original than is Johnson's, with more parallels in individual details, in the use of statistics, in words. Secker preserves his own description of "great gin-shops with places behind them for stowing drunken men and women promiscuously."[62] The *London Magazine* apes the last phrase when it speaks of the "back shop or Cellar ... where those that got drunk were

The Debates as Fact

thrown, Men and Women promiscuously together."[63] Johnson has them "Backrooms and secret Places...Receptacles of those who had drank till they had lost their Reason and their Limbs[;] there they were crowded together till they recovered Strength sufficient to go away, or drink more."[64] No verbal echo in this last, but note how similar is the concept in all three versions. In parallel statements, the differences are often as revealing as the similarities. Secker records this passage from his own speech: "Besides, as one melancholy part of the evil is the destruction of young children, a very small quantity will do this. Two were killed with each a spoonful, but last week. [Dr. Wilson.]"[65] The corresponding sentence of Johnson is: "For such is the Quality of these Spirits that they are sometimes fatal to those who indiscreetly venture upon them without Caution and whose stomachs have not been prepared for large Draughts by proper Gradations of Intemperence; a single spoonful has been found sufficient to hurry two Children to the Grave."[66] Certainly the good bishop was incapable of the delicate irony of "proper Gradations of Intemperence."

Chesterfield's speech is characterized in Secker's notes by good-humored sarcasm. The tone is typified by the statement (not paralleled in the magazine), "This liquor hath abolished the old, good-natured, lethargic English drunkenness." Johnson seems unable to sustain the light touch and to convey this tone. Note, in the following parallel passages, the degree to which Johnson has weighted the humor with words. Secker:

How would such a preamble as this look, "Whereas for certain reasons us thereunto moving, we think it proper that the people of England should be drunk for this year."[67]

Johnson:

I shall humbly propose, that it shall be introduced in this Manner: Whereas the Designs of the present Ministry, whatever they are, cannot be executed without a great Number of Mercenaries, which Mercenaries cannot be hired without Money; and whereas the present Disposition of this Nation to Drunkenness inclines us to believe, that they will pay more chearfully for the undisturbed Enjoyment of distilled Liquors than for any other Concession that can be made by the Government, be it enacted by the King's most excellent Majesty, that no Man shall hereafter be denied the Right of being drunk on the following Conditions.[68]

All the debates of the second group, as we have divided them, have been compared as whole debates with both reliable and nonreliable evidence. It cannot have escaped notice that all the debates of the group record proceedings in the House of Lords, that all the reliable evidence is in Secker's *Journal* and the nonreliable, as always, in the *London Magazine*.

In the third group—debates of Johnson which have counterparts in the other magazine but for which authentic records are incomplete—all report happenings in the House of Commons. The reason, obviously, is that the House of Commons had no Secker. That deficiency is particularly unfortunate because the magazines' versions of debates in Commons, with one exception, exhibit far greater differences than do their versions of debates in the Lords.

Taking up the debates of this group in chronological order, as before, we discover that the exception just noted must be considered first. Johnson's debate of February 24, 1741, on the quartering of soldiers is, in outline, similar to the versions of the *London Magazine*. That magazine gives speeches to three members not in Johnson's report (Harley, Branstone, and Ryder); the *Gentleman's Magazine* has two speakers (Gybbon and Cocks) not found in the other.[69] Johnson goes on to report the proceedings of February 26 and 27 concerning the bill, but the *London Magazine* completes its account at the end of the first day. For that one day the *London Magazine* report contains more speeches (by one), and the speeches themselves are much longer. The speeches common to both magazines have some superficial,

The Debates as Fact 121

though little genuine, likeness. In both versions Yonge cites two difficulties arising from the ambiguity of the existing law, but these citations are reversed and are free of verbal similarities. We are tempted to think that the *Gentleman's Magazine* used the other publication as a model here, for, although in some speeches there is no similarity between the two versions, in others a single point of the *London Magazine* account seems to have been swelled out to become the whole speech of the *Gentleman's Magazine*. Most of the Lilliputian speeches are cramped in size; nowhere does the debate expand in true Johnsonian fashion.

The debate of March 9, 1742, is quite another matter. The subject, Lord Limerick's motion, "That a Committee be appointed to Enquire into the Conduct of Affairs at Home and Abroad during the last Twenty Years,"[70] gave Johnson an opportunity to demonstrate his agility and enthusiasm in attacking and defending Walpole and to discourse on public affairs in general. We have but a brief authentic record of this debate, but from it we learn at least the names of the principal speakers. "The motion ... was made by Lord Limerick, and seconded by Sir John St. Albin [*sic*]: Pitt, Lyttleton, sir John Cotton, and Phillips, were the chief who spoke for it. Mr. Pelham, sir William Yonge, Wynnington, the Attorney General [i.e., Mr. Dudley Ryder], Coke and Lord Hartington against it."[71] The *Gentleman's Magazine* includes from this list of twelve speakers, seven, and gives speeches to six others not on the list. The *London Magazine*, with a total of nine speakers, reports five that are on the authentic list. There is almost no correspondence in sequence between the two magazine accounts. (Both place the speeches of the motion maker and the seconder correctly.) The speeches common to both have few parallels. Johnson tends toward general statement, the *London Magazine* toward facts and historical survey. If Johnson had read the *London Magazine* report, which preceded his own by six months, he must have forgotten or ignored it.

On March 23 of the same year a similar motion was argued.

Again Limerick made the motion, this time for a committee to inquire into affairs for the last ten years; whereas the former motion had failed by two votes, the new one was carried by a vote of 252 to 245. Authentic references to this debate by three contemporaries have been printed.[72] From them we learn of six of the speakers: Limerick, St. Aubyn (who again made the seconding speech), Pulteney, Horace Walpole (the letter writer—his first speech in Parliament), Pitt, and Ellis. Johnson's account includes speeches by four of these (Limerick, St. Aubyn, Pitt, and Pulteney) and three others. The *London Magazine* reports three of these speeches and two others. (In that magazine St. Aubyn is reported to have seconded, but no speech is printed.) Only two speeches (Limerick's and Pitt's) appear in both magazines, and the two versions bear little except a general resemblance. There is a touch of the authentic in the *London Magazine* version of Pitt's speech, where reference is made to the previous speech of the young Walpole. Horace himself in a letter[73] records a compliment by Pitt on his own maiden effort, which in form, however, has little resemblance to the passage in the magazine. The *London Magazine* prints a version of Walpole's speech, but Walpole himself is witness to the fact that it "was entirely false."[74] Oddly enough, Gordon fails to report the speech of Pulteney that seems to have made the strongest impression on the three contemporary witnesses. In Johnson's version of Pulteney's speech, one point, made in the last sentence, is founded on an actual utterance attested to by all three: Pulteney asserts he will not sit on the secret committee because his own past remarks may give suspicion that he is motivated by personal rancor.

For the last debate of the third group—the debate in Commons on retaining the Hanoverian troops in British pay—no authentic witnesses can be found outside the magazines. But internal evidence suggests the probability that each version[75] contains two authentic speeches contributed by the speakers themselves. One speech is shared by the magazines. At the end of the "Political

The Debates as Fact 123

Club" section of the *London Magazine* of June, 1743,[76] is the speech of John St. Aubyn, prefaced by the following: "The speech of *L. Sergius Fidenas,* in Answer to that made by *L. Valerius Flaccus* in the Beginning of this Debate, which we gave in our last, coming too late to be inserted in its proper Place, we shall give it as follows." Certainly the statement indicates that St. Aubyn had presented the magazine with a copy of his own speech. The fact that Johnson reprints the speech of the *London Magazine* convinces us that he considered it an authentic record.

The other probably authentic speech in the *London Magazine,* that of Sir John Phillips, is added in the issue of November, 1743[77] (the debate had been brought to an end in July), and is prefaced by a remark similar to that used before Aubyn's speech. Johnson, for some reason, neither reprints this nor gives another version of Phillips' speech. In his account, between the speeches of Nugent and Grenville is inserted the note: "See Lord P–c–v–l's Speech, Vol. XIII, p. 184."[78] Nearly a year previously the speech had been printed as "Lord P—l's Speech for Hanover Forces,"[79] and again we suppose it to have been contributed by the speaker. Strictly speaking, in spite of the citation in the Lilliputian narrative, the speech itself is not a part of Johnson's *Debates* and should not have been included in Johnson's *Works*— as it was—without such a notation. The *London Magazine* does not use the Percival speech. For the rest, there is little resemblance between the two magazine reports. Johnson has eleven speakers (including Percival), Gordon seven. Only four of these appear in the casts of both magazines, and the four exhibit no significant parallels.

We have been able to compare these four debates with parallel magazine reports, but have been unable to verify them by reference to comprehensive authentic accounts. Now we turn to that group of *Debates in the Senate of Lilliput,* designated here the fourth group, for which we have no *London Magazine* equivalents but of which we possess authentic evidence. Of the three members of the group, one is not strictly speaking a debate. Perhaps that one should be disposed of first, out of chronological order.

In the *Gentleman's Magazine* for July, 1742, at the conclusion of the "Debate on the Clinabs Address in Favour of the Q. of *Hungruland*" and preceding the "Debate in the House of Hurgoes on the Emperor's Speech to the new Senate" is inserted an exchange of speeches identified in the table of contents as "The Forms used in the Choice of President of the Clinabs." This records part of the proceedings of the opening session of Commons, December 1, 1741. Although placed under the running title "Debates *in the Senate of* Lilliput," we cannot say that the ceremony there reported constitutes a debate, and perhaps the strongest evidence that it was not so thought of is the fact that a record of the entire ritual, including the speeches, is printed in the entry of that date in the *Journals of the House of Commons*.[80] The only "debate," then, of which we have an official record and the only Commons "debate" of which we have adequate authentic evidence is not a debate at all.

Still, it is interesting to compare the two records. The same three speakers figure in both. Pelham moves that Arthur Onslow be called to the chair. Clutterbuck seconds. And Onslow first protests and then gives a short speech of thanks. It is hard to estimate the similarities of the speeches themselves. Both are made up of conventional compliments and conventional protestations of inadequacy, but there are no verbal parallels. The *Gentleman's Magazine* reports the "forms" themselves with reasonable accuracy, but the Lilliputian trappings give a touch of grotesqueness. After the seconding speech, *"the whole Assembly cried out, with a general Acclamation,* Olswon, Olswon." "Olswon" first protested at his seat, was led to the chair, there protested again, and on the members calling out, *"The* Chair, Chair, Chair" [the *Journal* has "No! No!"], *"he ascended the Step and ... address'd himself to the House."* The whole would not be inappropriate to

The Debates as Fact

Gulliver's Travels. The lack of complete conformity to the *Journal* record (and even the fact of publication under the Lilliputian disguise) assures us that the speeches were not current in printed form; the degree of accuracy and completeness—unusual, as far as we can tell, in a Commons debate—may perhaps be attributed to the relaxing of vigilance against witnesses on the opening day of the session.

For the Lords debate of December 9, 1740, on the state of the army and on a resolution against augmenting it by new regiments, we return to Secker's *Journal*.[81] In this debate Johnson reflects with some accuracy the true sequence of speakers. Though at the end of the debate is printed the notation that other lords spoke, we learn of only two others from Secker's account. Johnson deviates again from the journal keeper by adding two short speeches not recorded by Secker in an exchange between Cholmondeley and Argyle. The addresses in the Johnson report are for the most part similar to the originals as we know them. There are no significant verbal echoes, but Johnson often reproduces arguments recorded by Secker, sometimes in the same order. Secker's record of Argyle's speech, long and finished in form, is probably a transcript of a written copy of the speech perhaps supplied by Argyle. With the general contours of the speech so preserved the Lilliputian version agrees. It even follows closely some of the intricate arguments. But Johnson for some reason fails to match the vigorous irony we find in the speech given us by Secker. As a matter of fact, Johnson throughout this debate disappoints. Perhaps he felt constricted by the necessity of following notes that were fuller than usual.

If that supposition is true, Johnson, by the time he wrote the debate of June 1, 1742,[82] had developed the ability to shape prescribed materials into forms that might display his own peculiar abilities. This debate is as close to Secker[83] as the last, but more Johnsonian. Winchelsea, by both accounts, conducts a clause-by-clause analysis of the bill. The points made in the two versions differ, but the real difference is that Johnson, by inserting a maxim here, a discourse there, manages to produce a unified and finished essay where his original was only a disjointed series of objections. In this debate Johnson is in good, "generalizing" form: "It is well known My Lords, that there is, in a great Part of Mankind, a secret Malignity, which makes one unwilling to contribute to the Advantage of another, even when his own Interest will suffer no Diminution."[84] The familiar concern with human institutions finds its way quite logically into this debate on "trade and navigation." There is no parallel in Secker. Chesterfield observes:

> Nothing my Lords is more necessary to the Legislature than the Affection and Esteem of the People [;] all Government consists in the Authority of the *Few* over the *Many,* and Authority, therefore, can be founded only on Opinion, and must always fall to the Ground, when that which supports it is taken away.[85]

The last group is made up of debates for which we have only incomplete records, usually of individual speeches. The first of these, Johnson's account of the Commons debate on augmenting the forces by raising new regiments,[86] is confusing because it is admittedly an amalgam of two separate debates: those of December 4 and December 11, 1740. In addition to these two, there was another debate on the question on December 10; unfortunately, it is impossible to fix the dates of the two authentic speeches on augmentation that are preserved to us.[87] In any case, the speech of Horatio Walpole (Sir Robert's brother) has no counterpart in Johnson's account and therefore cannot be given comparative study. The authentic address of Lord Gage now extant has only tenuous points of contact with the speech Johnson reports, but we cannot be sure that Gage gave only one speech in the series of debates. We learn from a contemporary letter[88] that General Wade spoke on December 10, Pulteney and Sir Robert Walpole on the eleventh. Dodington "opened the opposition"—in which debate we cannot be sure. Of these four, Johnson includes

The Debates as Fact   127

speeches by Pulteney and Wade. The very fact that the debate makes no pretense of reporting a single day's proceedings—it is said of the two original debates that "Mr. Gulliver *has throw[n] them into one"*—makes us suspect the reliability of the report.

From a short passage in Egmont's *Diary*,[89] we learn of a hot exchange between Pulteney and Admiral Norris in the debate on the motion that His Majesty cause to be laid before the house certain letters of instruction to Admiral Haddock.[90] Pulteney, according to Egmont, said that Norris "had nothing with his fleet." Sir John Norris took the remark as a personal reflection and answered "in great warmth." But Pulteney replied that he meant no reflection. Johnson reports the same series of speeches in a way that does not violate the Earl of Egmont's account. But we cannot compare any but these three short speeches.

Johnson reports a series of debates on the seamen's bill (January 27 to March 23, 1741).[91] We have an authentic speech, Lord Gage's,[92] but again it does not carry a date. In Johnson's series, Gage is given two short speeches neither of which is a near relation to the real one. The debate contains the reply of Pitt to Horatio Walpole that begins:

> Sir,
> The atrocious Crime of being a young Man, which the honourable Gentleman has with such Spirit and Decency charged upon me, I shall neither attempt to palliate, nor deny, but content myself with wishing that I may be one of those whose Follies may cease with their Youth, and not of that Number, who are ignorant in spite of Experience.[93]

Coxe challenges the reliability of both Walpole's speech and Pitt's reply in Johnson's version.[94] His evidence rests on an "anecdote communicated by the late lord Sydney from the authority of his father, who was present." Walpole " 'lamented that, having been so long in business, he found that such young men were so much better informed in political matters than himself; he had, however, one consolation, which was, that he had a son not twenty years old, and he had the satisfaction to hope that he was as much wiser than them, as they were than his father.' Mr. Pitt got up with great warmth, beginning with these words: 'With the greatest reverence to the grey hair of the honourable Gentleman!' Mr. Walpole pulled off his wig, and shewed his head covered with grey hair; which occasioned a general laughter, in which Mr. Pitt joined, and all warmth immediately subsided." A letter from the younger Horace Walpole confirms the outlines of the anecdote and also, unfortunately for Coxe's theory, gives it a date—November 21, 1745.[95] Johnson's account of the "warmth" between the youthful and the aging orator had then been long in print, and was to become—perhaps had already become—the most famous passage in the *Debates*. We have no evidence for its authenticity.[96]

The Commons debate of December 8, 1741, on the address of thanks for the king's speech is the last for which collateral evidence has been unearthed.[97] A letter from John Orlebar to the Rev. Henry Etough[98] gives us some clues on the outline of the debate. Somerset introduced an amendment seconded by Shippen, but that motion was dropped "upon Sir Robert Walpole's coming into another amendment, proposed by Mr. P—y, who declared against dividing; and observed with a witticism, that dividing was not the way to multiply." Pulteney and Sir Robert are said each to have spoken two or three times. In Johnson's version Pulteney speaks once and Walpole twice, and the debate is free of this and of another of Pulteney's quoted "witticisms"; otherwise it corresponds to the outlines suggested in Orlebar's letter. Horace Walpole in a letter to Mann[99] records some of his father's remarks. Neither of Johnson's speeches attributed to Walpole reflects the gist of this record except at one point: Walpole's proposal that if another should move for a day to examine the state of the nation he would second it.

It is difficult to state in general terms the results of the comparative study as a whole. Perhaps no unqualified statement can be made about the nature of the entire collection of *Debates in*

The Debates as Fact 129

the Senate of Lilliput. Each debate, even each speech, reflects a different sort and degree of accuracy in reporting, of originality in conception. Certainly, for some of these debates Cave's agents brought away from the house "the subjects of discussion, the names of the speakers, the side they took, the order in which they rose"—to go back to Murphy's statement. However, the list of names was often deficient, the order of the speakers confused, the subjects of discussion imperfectly preserved. Many of the speeches have been established as products of Johnson's mind alone. Occasionally the record was full; notes brought to Johnson preserved at times the line of argument in individual speeches and perhaps some striking phrases. Still, the "compiler" was more than that. He could shape a collection of miscellaneous arguments into a unified essay; he could transform a conventional figure of speech into one more powerful and exact. I think that Johnson can, without question, be called not simply the reporter but the *author* of all the *Debates.*

Johnson, as a matter of fact, seems to have taken pride in the originality of his version. We may guess, because verbal echoes are rare (rarer, for example, than in the *London Magazine*), that he often took pains to alter phrases communicated to him until they became his own. Certainly he avoided the temptation of letting the *London Magazine's* "Proceedings of the Political Club" influence his *Debates.* It was evidently a matter of first importance that the *Gentleman's Magazine's* reports be fuller and more accurate than those of the rival, and free of echoing phrases that might suggest dependence on what was ordinarily the earlier printed version. We have seen that the Lilliputian account was generally more complete and more correct, at least in its broader outline. The *London Magazine* usually has more details, but often they do not correspond with those in our original records, and we may surmise that the writer took over from pamphlets and periodicals facts that would give an illusion of accuracy. A favorite device in the *London Magazine* is the elaborate survey of foreign negotiations, a subject on which Gordon must have been particularly well informed.

We have been able to find no evidence of intentional bias in the reporting of arguments. Indeed, Johnson sometimes gives more space to the supporters of Walpole than was necessary in view of the facts. He seems in these *Debates* to have taken joy in searching out and developing arguments that might support other convictions than his own. There was in him still, perhaps, something of the boy who "used always to choose the wrong side of a debate, because most ingenious things, that is to say, most new things, could be said upon it."[100] In the presentation of arguments there is undoubtedly more heat and vehemence in the speakers who represent Johnson's own views and perhaps this may be considered bias against the "Whig Dogs." But it must be kept in mind that these were men of the opposition and that violence was more appropriate to their speech. We may indeed feel that Johnson, by characteristic methods of shaping arguments and choosing emphases, does unconsciously reveal, not his precise political beliefs, but the dominant concerns of his thought: "the people," liberty, representative government—large questions of individual and public morality.

CHAPTER IV

THE DEBATES AS ART: THEIR PLACE IN THE LITERARY CAREER OF SAMUEL JOHNSON

THE *Debates in the Senate of Lilliput,* in accord with their position as poor relations in a large family, have never been given due attention as legitimate connections of Johnson the writer. Other examples of his writings have been examined under the light of criticism, turned this way and that for a fuller view, grouped one with another for a better perspective. The *Debates,* if they have contributed a lively anecdote to the Johnson legend, seem hardly to exist as a work of literature. Yet in sheer bulk the work looms largest of all (only the *Rambler* and the *Lives of the Poets* approaching it), and certainly no other large work can be said to occupy a more crucial position in the early development of Johnson as a writer of prose. The reasons for the critics' neglect have already been advanced: the delay in discovering that the *Debates* were Johnson's, the confusion of the reports with fact, the assumption that the work was mere journalism. If the evidence brought forward in the foregoing pages makes possible a clearer view of the *Debates,* these considerations need no longer stand in our way. The *Debates* can be given serious study as a creative work.

It would be inconsiderate not to mention two writers who have made observations on the literary qualities of the *Debates.* Hawkins alone among the eighteenth-century biographers of Johnson gives evidence of having read them. To them he devotes a number of pages[1] (more, for example, than to the *Rambler*) and speaks of them with more enthusiasm than has any other writer. He makes claims for Johnson's "system of debate" which G. B.

---

[1] For notes to chapter iv see pages 163–166.

Hill, the sole important modern commentator, does not allow. Hill's critical observations are contained within a single paragraph.[2] His generalities are penetrating and on the whole sound, but he does not always support them with evidence, and they cannot stand without qualification.

Hawkins and Hill both discuss the work in relation to a literary type. The *Debates* purport to be "debates"; that fact arouses expectations in the reader. Johnson's means of fulfilling those expectations can tell us much about the working of his creative mind in this formative stage. If we look upon the one line of inquiry as being concerned in large part with the matter of the *Debates,* the other confines itself to the manner, or texture, of the writing. The prose style of Samuel Johnson has been thought important enough to provide the subject for a book and for a number of articles as well. Yet no wholehearted attempt has been made to examine the style in its early stages. In the *Debates* there is sufficient material to reveal a comprehensive view of Johnsonian prose ten years before the *Rambler*. Though it is true that both matter and manner were somewhat restricted by the nature of the work, we can, by observing his methods within the limits imposed on him, learn much about Johnson's early habits of conception and of expression.

The Debates as "Debates"

Behind Hawkins' praise of Johnson's "system of debate" for the variety and persuasiveness of its speeches and for its manner of differentiating the various speakers, and behind Hill's assertion that "they do not read like speeches that had ever been spoken," but "like a series of leading articles on both sides of the question ... all written by the same man," lies the assumption, not overtly expressed by either author, that it is pertinent to look in the *Debates* for debate-like qualities. Behind that lies the further assumption, borne out by the investigation just completed, that the *Debates* are, in a measure, products of the imagination. What are

The Debates as Art

the qualities we expect in an imaginatively conceived debate in Parliament? Those which distinguish the debate are primarily dramatic qualities. We look for the play of argument and counterargument, of charge and countercharge, for a clear conception of character, for differentiation of thought and expression among the debaters, for a persuasiveness directed toward a particular audience, and for the telling details that give the illusion of reality. How does Johnson, one of the least dramatically inclined of authors, fulfill these expectations?

"Of debating he knew nothing... there is little of 'the tart reply'; there is indeed scarcely any examination of an adversary's arguments. So general are the speeches that the order in which they are given might very often without inconvenience be changed." So Hill insists. Yet the most famous passage in Johnson's *Debates,* the exchange between the elder Horace Walpole and Pitt in the debate on the seamen's bill, is notable chiefly for Pitt's "tart reply."[3] It seems significant that the best-known speech in the work is also the tartest. Other retorts may be less vehement, but Pitt's is not unique in its tone of personal invective. In the same debate (the previous day's session) Yonge accuses Lyttelton of having drawn a false parallel.

To draw Parallels, Sir, where there is no Resemblance, and to accuse by Insinuations where there is no Shadow of a Crime, to raise Outcries when no Injury is attempted, and to deny a real Necessity because it was once pretended for a bad Purpose, is surely not to advance the publick Service, which can only be promoted by just Reasonings and calm Reflections, not by Sophistry and Satire, by Insinuations without Ground, and by Instances beside the Purpose.

To which Lyttelton replies:

Sir, true Zeal for the Service of the Publick is never discovered by collusive Subterfuges and malicious Representations: a Mind attentive to the common Good, would hardly, on an Occasion like this, have been at Leisure to pervert a harmless Illustration and extract Disaffection from a casual Remark... [He] that is above the Practice of little Arts, or the Motions of petty Malice, does not easily imagine them incident to another.[4]

In another debate Admiral Norris directs himself to Pulteney.

> ... nor can you, Sir, who have thus contemptuously treated me, allege any Thing against me that may justify your Neglect of Decency: That you have transgressed the Rules of Decency is the softest Censure that your Behavior admits, and I think it may with equal Propriety be asserted, that you have broken the Laws of Justice.[5]

Heathcote to Fox on another day:

> But to this Gentleman, Sir, whom I am now answering, Arguments can be of very little Importance, because, by his own Confession, he is retained as a mere Machine, to speak at the Direction of another, and to utter Sentiments which he never conceived, and which his Hesitation and abrupt Conclusion shews him to admit with very little Examination.

And Heathcote goes on to answer such assertions "as require Confutation."[6]

There is, indeed, sometimes a strong sense of argumentative interchange even when there is no "tart reply." The answer may be dressed in lavish courtesy.

> Sir, if Zeal were any Security against Error, I should not willingly oppose the Hon. Gentleman who has now declared his Sentiments: and declared them with such Ardour as can hardly be produced but by Sincerity....
>
> But I am too well acquainted with his Candor to imagine, that he expects his Assertions to be any farther regarded than they convince; or that he desires to debar others from the same Freedom of Reason which he has himself used. I shall therefore proceed to examine his Opinion, and to show the Reasons by which I am induced to differ from him.[7]

A lengthy exchange of argument between two members is not unusual. So Lord Cholmondeley in the debate on the state of the army is twice interrupted by the Duke of Argyle and twice replies to him.[8] Clearly, Johnson's speeches were by no means intended as set pieces without relation to one another. Notice should be taken of the emphasis placed on the notion of "answer" and "reply," when Johnson—or some writer associated with him on the *Gentleman's Magazine*—accuses the rival periodical of altering the proper sequence of speeches in its report of a debate: "the noble Person understood by the name of *Piso* did not answer *Caecilius*; ... *Caecilius* replied to *Piso* as well as to two other noble Persons. ... What Confusion such an Error must make in a Learned and Political Argument, we need not inform our Readers."[9]

And yet, in spite of numerous examples that tend to an opposite conclusion, the majority of speeches are isolated, not dramatically related. Too often the speech is invested with but the illusion of a connection with the previous utterance. The following is a typical opening: "My Lords, the Manner in which the noble Lord who spoke last expresses his Sentiments never fails to give Pleasure, even where his Arguments produce no Conviction; and his Eloquence always receives its praise, though it may sometimes disappoint of its more important Effects."[10] But, typically, the speech proceeds with no further mention of the previous speaker or his arguments. Even more often the oration begins by referring not to a debater or his arguments but to the question itself, and in the most general terms: "My Lords, I am convinced that this Bill is very far from being either absurd or useless."[11] And numerous speakers open with a maxim that might apply to a number of subjects and turn but gradually, and then generally, to the question at hand: "Sir, it is a standing Maxim, both in private Life and publick Transactions, that no Man can obtain great Advantages, who is afraid of petty Inconveniences."[12]

But we must recollect the limitations within which the *Debates* were conceived. Though always, in a measure, imaginative, they had usually some basis in fact, and were taken by the public as "reports," not as dramatic diversions. Does the weakness of progression and connection reflect the parliamentary practice of the time? The reader, who will have gained some sense of the "real" parliamentary debate from the authentic accounts that have already been studied, will no doubt agree with that eighteenth-century member of Parliament who remarked, "None of Johnson's were at all like real debates."[13] For example, Secker's notes of the debate on the motion to remove Walpole reveal a natural movement from the beginning orations, formal and comprehensive, to a series of interchanges on individual points. Gesture and tone of voice, not conveyed by Secker's hurried words, must have heightened the forensic interplay. But Johnson, in his version of the debate on the main question, tends to treat each speech as a unit, to give each a theme and a carefully turned beginning and end. His treatment of the minor debate on the second motion of the day is of different character; there are not only answers and counteranswers but a tart reply. Here the speeches are, in the nature of the debate, comparatively short, and Johnson, when he writes a succession of short speeches, tends to treat it as a series. It is significant that the tart reply is not an invention of Johnson's dramatic fancy but was inspired by fact. Cave's agent no doubt passed on word that in the course of the debate Talbot had boiled over and had been called to order. But how much less of dramatic life in Johnson's long paragraphs than in Secker's brief note: *"Talbot. By the eternal G—, I will defend my cause everywhere—!"*[14]

Nevertheless, even where Johnson is master of the hot retort or the lively interchange, we look for something more before acknowledging the achievement of dramatic life or the illusion of reality. The speeches must seem to emerge from men. The success of the exchange between Walpole and Pitt may be partly attributed to differentiation of character. If the speakers are but pasteboard figures, there is at least no danger of mistaking them. They represent different human qualities and conditions: aged dignity and youthful ardor. Hawkins praised Johnson for his art, throughout the *Debates,* of giving "different colours to the several speeches."[15] He cites the person high in the government

The Debates as Art

who "declared, that by the style alone of the speeches in the debates, he could generally assign them to the persons who made them,"[16] and himself professes to be able to distinguish between "the deep-mouthed rancour of Pulteney" and "the yelping pertinacity of Pitt."[17] Hill, without bothering to mention Hawkins' opinion, takes the opposite view: "They are commonly formed of general statements which suit any one speaker just as well as any other." And, with an air of finality, "His parliamentary speakers have scarcely more variety than the characters in *Irene*."[18]

The reader of all the speeches is inclined to record an impression close to Hill's: they are spoken—if they may be said to give an oral effect—by one man, Johnson. But can we summarily dismiss the opinion of Hawkins, backed up as it is by explanation and example? He quotes in full the speech of Hardwicke against the motion to remove Walpole and the speech of Chesterfield against the spirituous liquors bill and points out the differences: in the one, "wisdom, gravity, and experience," the style "nervous," "matter weighty," and "arguments convincing"; in the other, "the glare of false rhetoric, specious reasoning, an affectation of wit, and a disposition to trifle with subjects the most interesting."[19] And certainly to glance through the speeches is to see that the difference is great.

Now it will be remembered that we have in Secker's manuscript fairly extended authentic records of both speeches. We need only read them to be convinced that the actual differences were far greater. Johnson's version of Chesterfield's speech is close to fact in certain points and phrases, and yet much of the singularity of Chesterfield's tone, conveyed in Secker's artless notes, is lost by Johnson. The verbal weight that he piles on Chesterfield brings that speaker closer to Hardwicke and his "weighty matter."

In short, we feel a lack of variety in Johnson's speeches because of the uniformity of the language. All is reduced to the common denominator of Johnsonian style, but if we accept as a convention, and so discount, the peculiarities of language, we become aware of variety among the speakers, even of rudimentary characterization. We need not draw the conclusion, suggested by the foregoing citation of Chesterfield's speech, that the variety always stems from fact and can be traced to the notes that were Johnson's raw material. We have seen that the peculiar ironic tone of Sandys in the Commons debate on the motion was Johnson's invention. And how different that is from the calm, methodical tone Johnson gives to Fox's refutation!

Hill offers, as combined explanation and proof of the lack of variety in the speeches (according to his view), the statement that Johnson "could not have acquired any knowledge of the style and the peculiarities of the different members."[20] But surely one cannot accept this without qualification. Even if Johnson had never been within either house (and according to Murphy he *had* been in the Commons once), he was in constant communication with the men who were attending and gathering notes, and certainly he could have learned much about the members as men if that aspect of the debates had interested him. In the spring of 1740 the *Gentleman's Magazine*, in place of a debate for its March issue, published the first installment of an account of the "Characters of the Lilliputian Senate." In this and the following article (in the May issue), brief sketches were given of the personal and forensic traits of the important speakers of both houses. Johnson probably did not write the essays—the style is not his—but they no doubt passed through his editorial hands. The magazine, then, was conscious of the desirability of distinguishing the speakers; Johnson, had he been interested, might have learned something of their characteristics. But, perhaps most important, if Johnson's inclination and literary purpose had demanded it he would have conveyed a far livelier sense of the speakers as different men, even if he had had no notion of their genuine traits of character.

The Debates as Art 139

In the dramatic situation that constitutes the debate, the audience as well as the speaker has a character. Do Johnson's speeches seem to be directed toward a particular audience? Hawkins claims that he can distinguish the characteristic qualities of the debates of each house: "Dignity in the one; Freedom of Expression" in the other.[21] Again the ornaments of language which overlie the *Debates,* irrespective of the house in which they purport to take place, stand in the way of our perception of the qualities that Hawkins sees. He is probably in a sense correct. The "Freedom of Expression" is exemplified by the "tart replies," generally found only in the debates of the popular house. The intense sarcasm of the motion maker, Sandys, has no counterpart in the debates of the Lords. But there is so much dignity running through all the debates that we are hard put to discover any heightening of that quality in the speeches of the upper house. We cannot escape the conclusion that the audience on which Johnson kept his eye most steadily was the whole reading public of England. Some of the speeches seem peculiarly ill adapted to winning over a parliamentary audience[22] but well suited to setting before a large magazine audience the two extremes of a nationally absorbing issue and the relations of that issue to universal moral truths.

To convey the illusion of reality we need, in addition to realistic conflict between realistic characters, the carefully chosen detail. That Johnson has no inclination to supply the detail has been shown. Throughout our comparison of Johnson's *Debates* with authentic accounts, we have seen him sometimes rejecting detail, often using it, but always subordinating it to the general principle. The point need not be further labored. Hill has expressed it well: "His was an imagination which supplied him with the general far more readily than with the particular." And, by raising the name of Defoe, Hill impresses on us the peculiar nature of Johnson's *Debates:* "Had Defoe been the composer, he would have scattered over each speech the most ingenious and probable matters of detail, but Defoe and Johnson were wide as the poles asunder."[23]

Our conclusion must be that the *Debates* lack the qualities that we expect of imaginatively re-created parliamentary controversy. Though an occasional dramatic spark flashes out—the skirmish between Walpole and Pitt comes first to mind—it is not sustained, or integrated in a total dramatic situation.[24] It is plain that the original purpose of the periodical debate report was not to entertain readers with lively parliamentary scenes but to inform them of the issues before their legislature. By the time Johnson had assumed the position of writer of debates, a primitively dramatic method of reporting was being developed.[25] But Johnson was a man of ability and we should be disappointed to find him accepting the limitations of the form as he found it. Defoe, as Hill has suggested, would have pushed the debate report farther in the direction of imaginative and dramatic re-creation. That Johnson did not do so demonstrates again that his genius and his literary purposes lay in another quarter. He did not move toward the "debate" as we understand it, and so we have found it necessary here to put much emphasis on what the *Debates* are *not*. We must now, by making explicit the implications of our examination, try to say what the *Debates are*.

We should begin by turning our attention from the whole debate to the individual address. It is plain that Johnson's contemporaries took the speeches rather than the debates as the artistic units. His orations are compared to those of Demosthenes and Cicero;[26] debates as wholes are ignored. If a debate lacks inner movement, if it ends abruptly without any other resolution than the bare report of a vote, its speeches will always be found to have finish and cohesion. But they are not really speeches: they lack essential oral quality; the conceptions are too complex; the surface is too polished. We should perhaps look upon them as essays.

What sort of essays are they? Each examines a question from

a single point of view and presents that point of view in its strongest, most persuasive light. The position is then reversed and the opposite side explored. Johnson cannot stand back and place before our view others who speak. He must himself participate, take both sides. This is Johnson in his element. He was, all his life, a "talker for victory," even from his boyhood, when he always took the wrong side of a debate.[27] "Exulting in his intellectual strength and dexterity, he could, when he pleased, be the greatest sophist that ever contended in the lists of declamation; and, from a spirit of contradiction, and a delight in shewing his powers, he would often maintain the wrong side with equal warmth and ingenuity."[28] The essays which are the speeches of the *Debates* foreshadow the Johnsonian conversation that Boswell was to record many years later. No doubt Johnson's apprentice work on the *Gentleman's Magazine* served to strengthen the natural inclination toward conversational debate and to develop the latent forensic skill.[29] Boswell probably forgot the *Debates* when he wrote that Johnson never argued for the "wrong" side in print, because he was "too consciencious to make error permanent and pernicious by deliberately writing it."[30] But we do not feel that it was pernicious for Johnson, in spite of his violent opposition to the Whig position, to put that position into convincing permanent form.

The "argument for victory" is only one aspect of the Lilliputian "speeches." We can, at this distance, read the *Debates* with little consciousness of "side." We feel that the emphasis is not on the arguments themselves but on the great questions which embrace those arguments. Johnson always brings the particular within the frame of the general and so gives the *Debates* universality.[31] If we look for the real subjects of these essays (or speeches—and I refer now to the extended examples that are most typical because most individualistically Johnsonian) we find not politics but morals. The *Debates* might be described as a collection of writings, superficially political pamphlets, but in a deeper sense moral essays.

JOHNSONIAN STYLE AND THE DEBATES

Although the style of the *Debates* has inevitably cropped up as an important consideration in determining their peculiar literary nature, we have reserved the fuller study for separate treatment. But it must be admitted that to separate an element we call "style" from a body of writing is a purely artificial expedient. We cannot in reality divorce meaning from the words and phrases that express it. Style is not something apart, "something superficial, a kind of scum,"[32] but a way of looking at a body of writing.[33] Still, it is a fruitful way of looking, one that has been a favorite in the past and can give us a clearer insight into the artistic whole of a work. This aspect of Johnson's literary labors created a stir from the beginning. "A large party pronounced the style perfect, so absolutely perfect that it would be impossible for the writer himself to alter a single word for the better. Another party, not less numerous, vehemently accused him of having corrupted the purity of the English tongue."[34]

Because of its pronounced individuality, Johnsonian style has received much attention. The fullest and best study yet made on the subject is by W. K. Wimsatt. That scholar, however, has found it necessary to give the *Debates* but glancing attention. "Johnson's style ... had its first opportunity in the *Rambler*,"[35] he says. But what of the more than one thousand pages of the *Debates in the Senate of Lilliput* written ten years before? Wimsatt speaks in passing of the prose of that work as "uninteresting" and "puffy," "that of Johnson expressing other men's opinions, without the moral conviction and spirit of the *Ramblers*"[36]—a judgment based on a partial misconception of the nature of the work. Our purpose here is to subject the *Debates* to the sort of scrutiny applied by Wimsatt to the major works. The qualities that he finds peculiar to the Johnsonian style will be sought and the continuity of the style as it is reflected in the *Debates* will be examined. Wimsatt names three major rhetorical

The Debates as Art

topics that have special relevance to the Johnsonian style: parallelism, antithesis, and abstract and philosophic diction. There are, in addition, two of less importance: inversion and chiasmus.[37] The presence of Johnsonian traits in the prose of the *Debates* will be examined in relation to these topics.

Wimsatt speaks of the "implicitly expressive parallel," in which "like syntactic positions are filled by words of like weight or emphasis."[38] In its simplest form such a parallel has but a single word in each parallel position:

Avarice or Ambition.[39]

The parallel is said to be multiplied when the number of "elements" or "members" is increased. Thus, the following has two elements in two members:

Known Crimes or attested Facts.[40]

Four elements in two members:

every Motive combines to make it the Duty, and every Argument concurs to prove it the Privilege.[41]

Two elements in three members:

a Zeal for publick Happiness, an Ardour for Liberty, or Tenderness for the People.[42]

Manifestly, such multiplication of parallel is not achieved without conscious effort by the writer nor accepted without immediate notice by the reader. If much used, it becomes an obvious stylistic trait, and so Johnson has ever been remarked for the parallelism and balance of his phrases.

These examples of extended parallel, all from the *Debates*, are typical. In estimating the prominence of this feature of style, example can be supported by statistics. A passage from the first thousand words of Carteret's speech on removing Walpole contains fifteen implicit parallels of two or more elements—or, to put the finding in the terms of Wimsatt's book, has a quotient (that is, incidence per hundred words) of 1.5.[43] This is not appreciably lower than the quotient of a comparable passage from a political essay of Johnson's maturity (1775), *Taxation No Tyranny:* 1.6.[44] The initial speech of Hervey on the spirituous liquors bill, one of the last written by Johnson, as Carteret's was one of the first, gives a quotient of 1.6,[45] and we may thus assume a stability in this respect throughout the period of the *Debates*. These figures become striking when we count the parallels in a passage of similar nature from the last pre-Johnsonian debate.[46] The quotient is much lower: 0.4. A passage from an early pre-Johnsonian debate, one which may have been revised by Johnson,[47] yields an equivalent quotient: 0.5. But the narrative that introduces to Lilliputian disguise of the *Debates* ("Appendix to Capt. Lemuel Gulliver's Account") has a quotient that is well within the range of narrative passages of known works of Johnson's maturity: 0.7.[48] A passage from a post-Johnsonian debate—one of those written, presumably, by Hawkesworth, "Johnson's closest imitator"[49]—has a quotient of 0.9.[50]

Numbers by no means tell the whole story. They give us no clue to the prevalence of such parallels as these:

It contains such a Concatenation of Enormities, teems with so vast a Number of Mischiefs, and therefore produces, in those minds that attend to its Nature, and persue its Consequences, such endless Variety of Arguments against it, that the Memory is perplexed, the Imagination crowded, and Utterance overburthened.[51]

... that they discharge the Duty of Commanders in a Manner more likely to preserve Dignity and encrease Reverence, that they discover, on all Occasions, a Sense of Honour and Dread of Disgrace, which are not easily to be found in a Mind contracted by a mean Education, and depressed by long Habits of Subjection.[52]

Neither the debate standing immediately before Johnson's nor that coming after can produce examples that compare with these. In the former debate, the phrase "Guardian of the Prince's Honour, and the People's Liberties" represents the extreme of

The Debates as Art 145

extension, and the purpose of the parallel should be noted. The terms express two distinct ideas (increase "range," as Wimsatt would have it). Johnson, however, tends to pile up parallels around the aspects of a single concept: memory perplexed, imagination crowded, utterance overburdened. Some of Hawkesworth's parallels are of the Johnsonian kind, but none are so intricately elaborated. Several parallels in the "Appendix to Capt. Lemuel Gulliver's Account" have the mark of Johnson upon them:

Happy had it been for Mankind, had so noble and instructive a Subject been cultivated and adorn'd by the Genius of LEMUEL GULLIVER, a Genius equally sublime and extensive, acute and sagacious, worthy to display the Policy of the most refined, and celebrate the Atchievements of the most warlike Nation.[53]

Heavy antithesis is another quality that has traditionally been seen as a characteristic of Johnson's prose. In a sense it is parallelism in reverse. Antithesis is a "contrast of ideas expressed by parallelism of strongly contrasted words."[54] Since "the negative defines the positive," a complex affirmation is apt to require complex negation. Therefore, we should expect much antithesis in Johnson, and when we read him we have a strong impression of its presence. The impression is confirmed by a statistical study, but not so dramatically as was our impression of balance or parallelism. When we count the clear antitheses in the Carteret speech previously examined, the result is a quotient of 1.8,[55] a fairly high count, but not so high as that of *Taxation No Tyranny*: 2.0. Just as there is wide range in the frequency of antithesis in Johnson's mature writings, so there is in the *Debates*. The quotient of the Hervey speech before noted is 1.4—still high, higher for example than the figure of 0.9 for the last pre-Johnson Lilliputian debate and still higher than the 0.8 of the earlier debate, probably revised by Johnson. The Hawkesworth passage previously studied yields a quotient of 1.0, the "Appendix to Capt. Lemuel Gulliver's Account," 0.8.[56]

Again, to define the peculiar nature of Johnson's antitheses we must read rather than count. His tendency, as with parallel, is to extend the antithesis by elaboration. The following typical examples from the *Debates* will clarify our view of his method:

...not abetted by the personal Malevolence of particular Men, but enforced by the Voice of the People....[57]

...will not be practiced here with the same Efficiency, though they should happen to be attempted with the same Confidence—[58]

...of the same Man in the Vigour of Youth and the Frigidity of old Age, in the Flush of Health and the Languor of Disease, of the same Man newly risen from Rest and Plenty, and debilitated with Hunger and Fatigue.[59]

Such distinctive antitheses are not to be found, for example, in the debate written just before Johnson's assumption of authorship. Though many antitheses are present, they do not impress us because they are not distinctively elaborated:

...the most general, yet dutiful Terms.

...not as the Words of the Sovereign himself, but of his Minister.[60]

The speech of Pulteney printed in July, 1738, which has been under consideration, contains a Johnsonian antithesis—not an elaborate one to be sure—that may be attributable to his editorial hand: "Instead Sir, of precipitating us into a War, this Bill must hasten on a Peace."[61] Johnson's prose, then, of the period of the *Debates* is of a piece with his maturer writings not only in richness of antithesis but in richness of a peculiar sort of antithesis.

A third major peculiarity of Johnson's style, one immediately apparent, is the distinctiveness of diction. Wimsatt notes two qualities that set Johnson's prose vocabulary apart: the tendency toward general and abstract words and toward "philosophic" words. The first cannot be revealingly studied numerically, for there is no clear-cut distinction between a general and a particular word; all depends on the meaning of the word in its context. It

The Debates as Art

is therefore enough to note again Johnson's inclination to generalize and to make abstract. But examples will clarify the tendency in terms of diction. The word "dragg'd" in the following passage is made abstract by context and, because of its normally concrete and particular associations, emphasizes the abstractness and the generality of the other words, especially the nouns: "He is dragg'd to Tyranny and Hardships, he is punished for endeavoring to avoid them, and involves in the same Misery with himself any Friend whom Charity or Gratitude shall prompt to protect him."[62] "Johnson's most abnormal employment" of the abstract noun in place of another part of speech is the linking of noun to noun by the preposition "of."[63] The *Debates* are full of this unusual form, and it is often emphasized by multiplication.

... increase the Gratification of Luxury and enlarge the Prospects of Ambition.[64]

... Weariness of Labor, Satiety of Profit, or Fear of Oppression.[65]

Philosophic words are "general or abstract words which have a scientific or philosophic flavor."[66] Johnson's use of such words in the *Debates* is the one aspect of their style that has heretofore been extensively examined. Wimsatt, in his *Philosophic Words*, concludes that the major part of such words entered Johnson's vocabulary as an accompaniment of his labors on the dictionary. Thus the *Rambler* is far richer in them than is the work written ten years earlier. Specifically, of the 380 important philosophic words of the *Rambler*, only 69 appear in the *Debates*.[67] That the tendency toward the use of such words existed at the time of the *Debates* is demonstrated by the 69 and by an additional 17 not appearing in the *Rambler*. Examples of words used in the earlier work are: adscititious, equipoise, inclination ("inclinations to the Balance of Power"), palliative.[68] Wimsatt calls attention to this "medico-moral passage" in Lord Hervey's speech on spirituous liquors.

...these Liquors, my Lords, Liquors of which the Strength is heighten'd by Distillation, have a natural Tendency to inflame the Blood, to consume the vital Juices, destroy the Force of the Vessels, contract the Nerves...they not only disorder the Mind for a time, but by a frequent Use precipitate old Age, exasperate Diseases, and multiply and encrease all the Infirmities to which the Body of Man is liable.[69]

The tendency to general or abstract diction is extremely strong in the *Debates,* but the special form of the tendency, the use of philosophic words, has not arrived at its full development.

Two minor features of style may be briefly noted: inversion and chiasmus. Inversion is natural to our language, but becomes noticeable when idiom is strained.

To the Principle laid down by those noble Lords, I have no Objection.[70]

That any Lord should be unwilling to concur in the customary Expressions of Thankfulness and Duty to his Majesty, or in Acknowledgment of that Regard for this Assembly with which he asks our Assistance and Advice, I am unwilling to suspect.[71]

Even on those who have hardened themselves in Opposition to their own Consciences, by a long Course of implicite Approbation and unlimited Submission, Reason is not always without Effect.[72]

Typically, Johnson calls attention to his inversions by separating the elements widely. Our impression is that the *Debates* are as strong in nonidiomatic inversion as any of the later works. Because of difficulties of distinction and definition, it is impossible to test the impression mathematically.

Chiasmus is a sort of inversion that is found occasionally in Johnson and stands out because of its singularity. It is a rhetorical figure, and may be looked at as a pair of expressions in reverse order: "1—2:2'—1'," as Wimsatt puts it.[73] It will be sufficient to quote an example (an example of antithesis, as well) from the *Debates.*

The Debates as Art

...those who could not be terrify'd (1) have been caressed (2) and those whose Understanding enabled them to discover the Tendency of false Caresses (2'), have been harassed with Menaces and Hardships (1').[74]

The style, then, of the *Debates in the Senate of Lilliput*—the earliest work of Johnson large enough for extended study—is strongly marked by distinctively Johnsonian features. If the manner has less than its highest polish—a parallel, perhaps, blurred by an extra modifier in one of the elements—none of these traits except philosophic diction appears to have become intensified with time. But our eyes have been so fixed on style that we have temporarily lost sight of the larger view. The three Johnsonian peculiarities that we have found characteristic of the prose of the *Debates* are an integral part of the broader aspects of meaning that have already been observed. Obviously, the use of abstract and general words is the reflection of a meaning that subordinates detail to the universal principle. The extension of parallels leads inevitably to the overlapping of meaning: closely related words cluster around general concepts, and the matter, with the manner, becomes weighty. And the habit of antithesis is an echo of the mind that is constantly shifting position, striving for a clearer notion of what *is* by determining what is *not*.

To say that the style of the *Debates* is consistent with that of the well-known examples of Johnson's prose is but to repeat that they fit into the pattern of Johnson's theory and practice of writing. The function of the artist is to serve as "the interpreter of Nature and legislator of Mankind." "He must divest himself of the prejudices of his age or country; he must consider right and wrong in their abstracted and invariable state; he must disregard present laws and opinions, and rise to general and transcendental truths, which will always be the same."[75] So Johnson finds Shakespeare admirable for his "just representations of general nature," prefers Richardson's characters of nature to Fielding's characters of manners, declares *Hudibras* to be "every day less intelligible and less striking" because "the manners being founded on opinions, are temporary and local."

The use of the abstract, the general, the antithetical style is one means of lifting a work above the particular, of giving universal application. As Johnson, in his single attempt at the drama proper, deliberately suppresses dramatic realism in order to gain universality, so in the *Debates* he attempts to give timelessness to what might have been nothing more than hack work, not by bringing up the sights and sounds of an actual debate, but by relating the proceedings, in appropriate language, to great, general truths. The *Debates,* consistent with Johnson's literary ideals (and so with the neoclassical ideals themselves), take a secure place among his writings as a genuine and characteristic creative work.

NOTES AND BIBLIOGRAPHY

NOTES TO INTRODUCTION

[1] There is an unpublished work which more nearly parallels the proportions of the present study. A dissertation by Medford Evans, "Johnson's Debates in Parliament," came to my attention as my own work was nearing completion. The copy examined by me is undated. It is assigned the date 1933 in the only reference found—*Horace Walpole's Correspondence* (New Haven, 1937–), XIII (1948), p. 12, note 78—but is unlisted in *Doctoral Dissertations Accepted by American Universities* (New York, 1934), covering the period 1933–1934, or in subsequent volumes of the same compilation. A number of my "discoveries," independently made, were found to have been made by Evans some years before. However, though some of the conclusions reached by us run along parallel lines, the method of reaching them is very different.

[2] *Boswell's Life of Johnson*, ed. G. B. Hill (Oxford, 1887), I, 501–512. Appendix A is reprinted without alteration in L. F. Powell's revision (Oxford, 1934). Those who have written about the *Debates* after Hill have adapted his work, but, so far as it pertains to Johnson, have extended it only slightly: Michael MacDonagh, *The Reporters' Gallery* (London, n.d.), pp. 118–167; C. L. Carlson, *The First Magazine* (Providence, 1938), pp. 83–109; Edward A. Bloom, "Samuel Johnson as Journalist" (unpublished dissertation, 1947), pp. 89–104. Some historians have been concerned with the reliability of the debate reports in this period. In writing of Johnson they also have leaned heavily on Hill: Paul J. Mantoux, *Notes sur les Comptes rendus de séances du Parlement anglais au XVIIIe siècle conservés aux archives du Ministère des Affaires étrangères* (Paris, 1906), pp. 2–35; Basil Williams, *The Life of William Pitt, Earl of Chatham* (London, 1913), II, Appendix A; A. J. Turberville, *The House of Lords in the XVIIIth Century* (Oxford, 1927), the second appendix; Mary Ransome, "The Reliability of Contemporary Reporting of the Debates of the House of Commons, 1727–1741," *Bulletin of the Institute of Historical Research*, XIX (May, 1942), 67–79.

NOTES TO CHAPTER I

[1] I am indebted to Michael MacDonagh's *The Reporters' Gallery* (London, n.d.) for pointing out Addison's mention of Dyer. MacDonagh's book, a popularization not well documented and not dependable, is the sole general history of parliamentary reporting. Debate reporting in the seventeenth century has been extensively studied, notably in the introduction to Wallace Notestein and Frances Relf, *Commons Debates for 1629* (Minneapolis, 1921). Several articles and books concerning the press are helpful for the earlier period: H. R. Fox Bourne, *English Newspapers* (London, 1887); J. D. Williams [i.e., J. G. Muddiman], *A History of English Journalism to the Foundation of the Gazette* (London, 1902); W. M. Clyde, "Parliament and the Press, 1740–3," *The Library*, Series 4, XIII (March, 1933), 339–424. I have found all the foregoing helpful in writing a summary of debate reporting before the era of the periodicals, and have been guided by them to some of the original sources. A documented account of debate reporting as practiced by the periodicals in the first half of the eighteenth century was felt to be necessary in order to provide background for Johnson's activities. In gathering material for this study I found valuable clues in "The Autobiography of Sylvanus Urban," *Gentleman's Magazine*, CCI (November, 1856), 531–538, and in MacDonagh. Mary Ransome, "The Reliability of Contemporary Reporting of the Debates of the House of Commons, 1727–1741," *Bulletin of the Institute of Historical Research*, XIX (May, 1942), 67–79; Lawrence Hanson, *Government and the Press, 1695–1763* (Oxford, 1936), pp. 73–83; and C. L. Carlson, *The First Magazine* (Providence, 1938), were found helpful for some

phases of the account. F. S. Siebert, *Freedom of the Press in England, 1476–1776* (Urbana, 1952), published after this chapter was written, gives a full account of the restrictions on parliamentary reporting. G. B. Hill's work, *Boswell's Life of Johnson* (Oxford, 1887; rev. L. F. Powell, 1934–1950), Vol. I, Appendix A, was found to be by far the most complete account of Johnson's part in the tradition. Cited hereafter as *Life*.

[2] Addison meant, no doubt, to make fun of Sir Harry for his extreme Toryism, for "Dyer's Letter" was rabidly partisan.

[3] MacDonagh, *op. cit.*, p. 90.

[4] Guy Eden, *The Parliament Book* (London, 1949), p. 149.

[5] *Ibid.*, p. 147; W. J. Brown, *Everybody's Guide to Parliament* (London, 1946), p. 122.

[6] *Journals of the House of Commons*, XI, 192. Cited hereafter as *C.J.*

[7] *Ibid.*, p. 193.

[8] *Ibid.*, p. 439.

[9] Luttrell, *Relation of State Affairs*, III, 542, as quoted in MacDonagh, *op. cit.*

[10] *Journals of the House of Lords*, XVI, 391. Cited hereafter as *L.J.*

[11] Josef Redlich, *The Procedure of the House of Commons* (London, 1908), I, 26.

[12] *Ibid.*, II, 34.

[13] *Ibid.*, p. 36.

[14] MacDonagh does not give the source of his statement. *Op. cit.*, p. 103.

[15] *C.J.*, I, 885.

[16] *Ibid.*, II, 12.

[17] *Ibid.*, p. 42.

[18] Bourne, *op. cit.*, I, 9.

[19] Notestein and Relf show that the official *Diurnals* began as unauthorized publications, and that licensing was found to be the easiest method of controlling them. *Op. cit.*, p. xlix. For the fullest published account of the complex history of parliamentary reporting during the Revolution and Commonwealth, see Siebert, *op. cit.*, pp. 202–233.

[20] H. H. Bellot, "Parliamentary Printing, 1660–1837," *Bulletin of the Institute of Historical Research*, XI (November, 1933), 86. The *Votes and Proceedings* were augmented and printed as *Journals of the House of Commons*, beginning in 1742, but the *Journals* were not brought up to date for twenty years. The Lords did not print *Votes* or their equivalent until 1824. *Journals of the House of Lords* began publication in 1777 and were not brought up to date until 1830.

[21] *C.J.*, XX, 29.

[22] I do not mean that there was not some disinterested reporting of the news at the time but that disinterested accounts of debates were unusual.

[23] Abel Boyer was born in France in 1667. The biographical facts given here are from the *Dictionary of National Biography*. Hereafter cited as *D.N.B.*

[24] *L.J.*, XIX, 243–253.

[25] *The Political State of Great Britain*, XI (April, 1716), 429 ff.

[26] *C.J.*, XXI, 85, 104, 108, 119, 127.

[27] *Ibid.*, p. 238.

[28] *Life*, I, 502.

[29] *Cobbett's Parliamentary History of England* (London, 1812), X, 807.

[30] *The Historical Register* continued until 1738, but after 1720 dropped from the title page the line "Published at the Expence of the Sun Fire-Office," and presumably was not connected with the organization thereafter.

[31] Ransome, *op. cit.*, p. 68.

[32] *Gentleman's Magazine*, I, 48. Cited hereafter as *G.M.*

[33] *Ibid.*, II, 864.

[34] *Ibid.*, p. 886.

[35] Carlson, *op. cit.*, p. 92 n.

[36] Ransome, *op. cit.*, p. 68.

Notes
155

[37] *G.M.*, V, 777; VI, 365, 405, 447.

[38] John Nichols, *Literary Anecdotes of the Eighteenth Century* (London, 1812), V, 40 ff.

[39] *Ibid.* Both letters are quoted in *Life*, I, 151.

[40] *The Political State of Great Britain*, LIV (September, 1737), 285.

[41] *G.M.*, VII, 830.

[42] The king's answer was printed in the April issue, "Historical Chronicle," *ibid.*, VIII, p. 217.

[43] *C.J.*, XXIII, 148.

[44] Ransome, *op. cit.*, quotes this.

[45] A letter dated February 13, 1738, from the French ambassador in London to his Foreign Office indicates that, although access to the house became strictly limited in that year, orders had not been so rigidly observed in the past: "The compliance by which we were enabled to procure them [the debates] in the days of M. de Chavigny and M. de Bussy [i.e., 1731–1737] is now absolutely forbidden, owing to the strict orders given this year to let nobody in when they are transacting business." Paul J. Mantoux, "French Reports of British Parliamentary Debates in the Eighteenth Century," *American Historical Review*, XII (January, 1907), 256. The letter is given at greater length in its original French in Mantoux, *Notes sur les Comptes rendus des séances du Parlement anglais au XVIIIe siècle ...* (Paris, 1906), p. 59.

[46] Quoted by Ransome, *op. cit.*

[47] *Ibid.*, p. 70.

[48] *Life*, I, 106–107.

[49] *Ibid.*, p. 135.

[50] John Hawkins, *The Life of Dr. Samuel Johnson* (London, 1787), p. 45.

[51] *Life*, I, 112. Johnson's position seems to have been that of general literary handy man. The Rev. John Hussey wrote in his copy of the *Life*, "Johnson told me that he was employed by Cave, as *editor* of the *Gentleman's Magazine* from 1738 to 1745—and that he took it about the middle of the former year and relinquished it about the middle of the latter." *Life*, I, 532.

[52] *G.M.*, VII, 156.

[53] *London Magazine*, VII, 237 ff.

[54] *G.M.*, VIII, 283 ff. The title was soon reduced to *Debates in the Senate of Lilliput*.

[55] *G.M.*, CCI (December, 1856), 668. Information concerning Guthrie is given in the text and notes of *Life*, I, 116 ff.

[56] *Life*, p. 117.

[57] *Ibid.*, p. 502.

[58] I shall test this attribution by the analysis of style in chap. iv.

[59] I have seen only one key to the "Club" of the *London Magazine*, that printed on the back of a handbill or advertisement issued in March, 1742. When the "Political Club" was reprinted in the *Scots Magazine*, the title page of each volume after the first incorporated a key on its reverse.

[60] The descriptions are taken from the index for 1739.

[61] *Life*, I, 510.

[62] I am indebted to Professor James L. Clifford for calling this to my attention. The advertisement was printed in the *London Evening Post* for July 8–10, 1740.

[63] This handbill was found, in one copy, conveniently bound into a March, 1742, issue of the *Gentleman's Magazine!*

[64] *G.M.*, XII, 512.

[65] Hawkins, *op. cit.*, p. 136. Hawkins' statement about the magazine's circulation may be an exaggeration. In 1746 Cave boasted a monthly sale of 3,000 copies. See Carlson, *op. cit.*, pp. 62–63.

[66] *G.M.*, XII, 136.

⁶⁷ *Ibid.*, XIII, 59. I have been unable to substantiate these claims. I can discover no trace of the *Etat politic*, and the similarity of the title to that of the familiar *Political State* suggests that it may have been the product of imagination.

⁶⁸ *Life*, I, 112.

⁶⁹ Murphy probably follows Boswell and so is not a reliable source on this point. Thomas Tyers, "Biographical Sketch," *G.M.*, LVI, indicates that the *Debates* were "begun in 1740"; the account is pre-Boswell (printed in December, 1784) and hence independent.

⁷⁰ *Life*, I, 150.

⁷¹ From Nichols, *Literary Anecdotes...*, reprinted in *Johnsonian Miscellanies*, ed. G. B. Hill (Oxford, 1897), II, 412.

⁷² Hawkins, *op. cit.*, p. 96.

⁷³ All original authorities agree on the hasty composition of the *Debates*: Hawkins, *op. cit.*, p. 99; *Life*, IV, 408; Nichols, *G.M.*, LVI, 891. Nichols says that Johnson wrote an average of three columns of the *Debates* in an hour. "They were written at those seasons when he was able to raise his imagination to such a pitch of fervor as bordered upon enthusiasm," says Hawkins. He would at those times shut himself in a room at St. John's Gate and would let no one approach but Cave's boy or the compositor. As fast as he composed it, "he tumbled [it] out the door" (Hawkins). This certainly sounds like the meeting of a publication deadline.

⁷⁴ The fact that the installments of most of the debates end at the bottom of a page lends color to this possibility.

⁷⁵ Hawkins, *op. cit.*, p. 132. Hawkins evidently refers to the time of publication (November, 1743—February, 1744).

⁷⁶ *Ibid.*, p. 132. "The Autobiography of Sylvanus Urban" denies that Hawkesworth was the author of the resumed *Debates*, but does not give any authority for the denial.

⁷⁷ *Life*, I, 252.

⁷⁸ *Ibid.*, p. 505. He develops his belief from Boswell's statement, "As soon as he found that the speeches were thought genuine, he determined that he would write no more of them" (p. 152).

⁷⁹ *Ibid.*, p. 118.

⁸⁰ *Ibid.*, p. 136.

⁸¹ *Ibid.*, p. 118.

⁸² A. L. Reade, *Johnsonian Gleanings* (London, 1933), Part VI, pp. 96–122.

⁸³ Such a conjecture assumes that it was Johnson's custom to write the *Debates* just before publication. If they were prepared soon after the occurrence of the events, they would have been in Cave's hands before Johnson left London.

⁸⁴ Unfortunately, a stylistic analysis designed to fix responsibility and extent of revision is hardly possible where we do not have the original versions. I shall, however, in chap. iv examine an earlier debate for evidence of authorship by Johnson.

⁸⁵ Hawkins, *op. cit.*, p. 122.

⁸⁶ *Johnsonian Miscellanies*, I, 379.

⁸⁷ *Life*, I, 118.

⁸⁸ So Nichols reports in *Literary Anecdotes*, reprinted in *Johnsonian Miscellanies*, II, 412.

⁸⁹ *Johnsonian Miscellanies*, I, 379.

⁹⁰ Hawkins, *op. cit.*, p. 95.

⁹¹ *Ibid*.

⁹² Cave's difficulties with the House of Lords will be more fully described hereafter. *L.J.*, XXVII, 107–108.

⁹³ The following exchange of letters (found by Professor Clifford in the British Museum and copied by him from the originals) reveals something of Cave's news-gathering

Notes 157

methods and of reactions to them. The first letter is written by Cave to Thomas Birch, from St. John's Gate, July 3, 1744 (MS 4302):

"Good Sir

You will see what stupid, low abominable stuff is put upon your noble & learned Friend's Character in ye London Mag. Such as I should quite reject, and endeavour something better towards doing justice to ye character. But as I cannot expect to attain my desire in that Respect, it would be a great satisfaction to me, as well as an Honour to our Work to have the favour of ye Genuine speech. It is a Method that several have been pleased to take, as I could shew, but think myself under a Restraint. I shall say so far that I have had some by a third hand, wch I understood well enough to come from ye first, others by Penny Post, & others by ye Speakers themselves, who have been pleased to visit St. John's Gate, & shew particular marks of their being pleased. With regard to secrecy, I have been too scrupulous, as in Dr. Broome's Case. As to ye service of ye Public I think it an unquestionable Point, and as ye Case now is a Piece of Justice due to themselves, to rescue their Reputation from a Load, w^{ch}, if it should have no effect in this age, may in some future.

"You may well know which will be ye most proper way to prevent this Consequence, wch when I had ye favour of your Company, you indeed seemed to apprehend, & I need now only repeat that I shall be extremely ready & glad to be ye Instrument."

On July 7, 1744, Birch wrote to Philip Yorke (Add. MS 35,396):

"Have you seen what an illustrious Figure you make among the Orators in the London Magazine for last Month? Cave wrote to me on tuesday last, to complain of the Stupidity & Impudence of his Rival, in presuming to pass such a Jargon upon the Public under your Name; & to represent his own Moderation, in not offering to personate you so much to your Disadvantage. But at the same time he intimated to me, how glad he should be to do you Justice. [He quotes a long section from Cave's letter above] ... You see the only Method perhaps you have to obviate the progress of so injurious a Forgery, which will otherwise descend to posterity, & be incorporated in the Histories of the Ralphs & Guthries."

Yorke replied to Birch on July 8 (Add. MS 35,396):

"Cave's Request is an impertinent one—the boast he makes of communications from speakers of ye first Class, a very inartificial bam to procure the genuine Copy of a speech from an orator of the lowest; & ye whole intended for nothing else than that he may parade in the magazine with an abuse upon his Rivals & a Puff upon his own Superior Correspondence."

Birch wrote again to Yorke from London on July 21:

"Your Brother has shewn me your Letter, wherein you desire my Assistance in procuring the publication of your Remonstrance against the Forgeries of the Magazines. I wish I could find out a Method of doing this both for your Sake & that of the public. But the whole Body of the Printers & Booksellers are so tender of each other's Interest, where their own is not concern'd, & the Publishers of the Magazines have so large a Share in the Daily & Weekly Papers, that I know it to be absolutely in vain to attempt it, but am seriously of Opinion with you, that their Insolence deserves the Interposition of Parliament."

[94] The discussion of Johnson's activities in reporting contemporary debates for the *Gentleman's Magazine* should not be concluded without noting his account, published in 1741 (Boswell is responsible for the attribution; the account is derived from Anchitell Grey's notes), of "A Debate between the Committee of the House of Commons in 1657, and O. Cromwell, upon the Humble Petition and Advice of the Parliament by which he was desired to assume the Title of King." *G.M.*, XI, 93-100, 148-154. An undated letter from Johnson to Cave, placed by Boswell in the year 1742 but evidently

written after August 1, 1743, refers to "our historical design," a project which would "give the most complete account of Parliamentary proceedings that can be contrived." This, no doubt, refers to the work later (?) announced in "The Proposals for Publishing the Debates of the House of Commons, From the Year 1667 to the Year 1694. Collected by The Honourable Anchitell Grey, Esq." *G.M.*, XV (1745), 135-136.

[95] *L.J.*, XXVII, 94, 100, 101, 107-109.

[96] *Parliamentary History of England*, Vol. XIII, Preface.

[97] An extended account of this altercation between Commons and the press may be found in MacDonagh, *op. cit.*, pp. 186-264.

[98] Bourne, *op. cit.*, I, 214.

[99] *The Historical Register*, of course, was a quarterly publication, but its reports were derived from the monthly *Political State*.

NOTES TO CHAPTER II

[1] From Arthur Murphy's "Essay on the Life and Genius of Samuel Johnson, LL.D.," *Johnsonian Miscellanies*, ed. G. B. Hill (Oxford, 1897), I, 378-379. John Hawkins, *The Life of Dr. Samuel Johnson* (London, 1787), pp. 125-128, has a different account of the revelation: "We are further told of a person in a high office under the government, who being at breakfast at a gentleman's chambers in Gray's inn, Johnson being also there, declared, that by the style alone of the speeches in the debates, he could severally assign them to the persons by whom they were delivered. Johnson, upon hearing this, could not refrain from undeceiving him, by confessing that himself was the author of them all."

[2] Philip Francis' *Demosthenes* was published in 1757-1758, and he suggests by his words, if Murphy reports him correctly, that the work had been long finished. Francis became very ill in 1767, was paralyzed after 1771, and died in 1773. Murphy, of course, writes from memory in 1792. In one detail we are sure he is wrong: Johnson did not live in Exeter Street while working on the *Debates*.

[3] *Journals of the House of Lords*, XXVII, 107. Hereafter cited as *L.J.*

[4] The preface is printed in Allen T. Hazen, *Samuel Johnson's Prefaces and Dedications* (New Haven, 1937), pp. 128-131.

[5] So Nichols reports in *Literary Anecdotes*, reprinted in *Johnsonian Miscellanies*, I, 379.

[6] Hawkins, *op. cit.*, p. 129. Hawkins asserts that Johnson, while Smollett was writing his *History*, "cautioned him not to rely on the debates," for "they were, excepting as to general import, the work of his own imagination." If Smollett received the warning, he did not heed it.

[7] *Thraliana*, ed. K. C. Balderston (Oxford, 1942), I, 204.

[8] *The Letters of Horace Walpole*, ed. Mrs. Paget Toynbee (Oxford, 1903-1905), XIV, 438.

[9] W. P. Courtney and D. Nichol Smith, *A Bibliography of Samuel Johnson* (Oxford, 1915). This has not been revised (the edition of 1925 being simply a reissue with added plates), but there is a "supplement" by R. W. Chapman and Allen T. Hazen, "Johnsonian Bibliography," in *Oxford Bibliographical Society Proceedings*, V (1938), Part III, 119-166.

[10] In the set, so made up, that I examined, the second series was begun with a title page that was an exact duplicate of that of the first volume of the consecutive series: *History and Proceedings ... from the Restoration to the Present Time*, Vol. I. The correct title page, according to H. H. Bellot ("General Collections of Reports of Parliamentary Debates for the Period since 1660," *Bulletin of the Institute of Historical Research*, X, 173), reads: *The History and Proceedings of the House of Commons ... from the Death of Queen Anne*.

[11] The information about Chandler, including the quotation from Gent, has been taken from the article in the *D.N.B.*

[12] *Gentleman's Magazine* (hereafter cited as *G.M.*), XII, 395; Timberland, VIII, 17.

[13] *G.M.*, XII, 398; Timberland, VIII, 21.

[14] The volume we have designated Timberland, VIII, must have been very quickly compiled. The last installment of the spirituous liquors debate was printed in the February number (issued March 1), 1744, of *G.M.*, XIV, 59-64. If we are to trust the date on Timberland's title page (1743), it must have been published by Lady Day (March 25), 1743/1744.

[15] *L.J.*, XXV, 610.

[16] *Ibid.*, p. 615.

[17] Bellot, *op. cit.*, p. 173.

[18] The volume introduces itself as "a Volume of the same Price, bound in the same Manner." There is no evidence that it is an authorized continuation.

[19] *Bibliography of British History: The Eighteenth Century*, eds. Stanley Pargellis and D. J. Medley (Oxford, 1951), p. 56.

[20] I have seen only Volumes XIX and XX of what is apparently the second Dublin edition (no place of publication or publisher named, dated 1743) and the *Impartial History* of Cowse. There may, in addition, have been debates of Johnson, reporting events of the 1742-1743 session, in the later volumes of the second Dublin edition which I have been unable to trace. See Appendix 2, p. 220.

[21] *Boswell's Life of Johnson*, ed. G. B. Hill (Oxford, 1887); rev. L. F. Powell (Oxford, 1934), III, 351. Hill points out that either Boswell or Johnson makes an error here. Three speeches were printed in Chesterfield's *Miscellaneous Works*. Only the last two were Johnson's. The editor of Chesterfield (I, 228) says that the first is in "the strong nervous style of Demosthenes, the two latter in the witty, ironical manner of Tully." The speeches continued to be printed in editions of the works of Chesterfield well into the next century.

[22] *G.M.*, LIV, 891.

[23] See article in the *D.N.B.*

[24] From the obituary notice in *G.M.*, LXXXV (June, 1815), quoted in the *D.N.B.*

[25] Chapman and Hazen, *op. cit.*, p. 164.

[26] Curiously enough, the "mistranslation" has brought down a charge of carelessness on Johnson that has persisted even within the past twenty-five years. A. J. Turberville, *The House of Lords in the XVIIIth Century* (Oxford, 1927), Appendix B, cites three instances in which Johnson attributes a Chesterfield speech to Carteret. Reference to *Cobbett's Parliamentary History of England* (London, 1812) shows that Turberville took this information from three footnotes in Volume XII of that work: "In the Collection of Dr. Johnson's Debates, this speech is erroneously attributed to Lord Carteret." And how did Wright (the editor of the *Parliamentary History*) make his error? Is it possible that he was working with a copy, at his side, of the Stockdale edition, which he vigorously despised? Two of the speeches had already been printed as Chesterfield's in his *Works*.

[27] *G.M.*, XII, 341; Stockdale, XII, 371.

[28] *G.M.*, XI, 677; Stockdale, XII, 672.

[29] *G.M.*, XII, 691; Stockdale, XII, 63.

[30] *G.M.*, XII, 228; Stockdale, XII, 2.

[31] William Coxe, *Memoirs of the Life and Administration of Sir Robert Walpole* (London, 1798), I, xx-xxii.

[32] John Almon, *Anecdotes of the Life of the Right Hon. William Pitt, Earl of Chatham* (London, 1791). The speeches are printed in the sixth edition (London, 1797), that seen by me, in I, 50-124.

[33] See the article on Wright in the *D.N.B.*

[34] One of the nineteenth-century works which makes most extensive use of Johnson is Francis Thackerey, *A History of the Rt. Hon. William Pitt* (London, 1827).

[35] Basil Williams, *The Life of William Pitt, Earl of Chatham* (London, 1913), Vol. II, Appendix A. Paul J. Mantoux, *Notes sur les Comptes rendus de séances du Parlement anglais au XVIII⁰ siècle* ... (Paris, 1906).

[36] See, for example, *Select British Eloquence*, ed. Chauncey A. Goodrich (New York, 1875), pp. 43, 46, 78, 82, 83 (speeches of Johnson attributed to Pulteney, Chesterfield, Pitt); *The World's Best Orations*, ed. David J. Brewer (St. Louis, 1899), X, 3716 (the familiar exchange between Walpole—here made Sir Robert instead of Horace—and Pitt).

[37] *Famous Speeches*, ed. Herbert Paul (Boston, 1911), pp. 431-454.

[38] *Johnson, Prose and Poetry*, ed. Mona Wilson (London, 1950).

NOTES TO CHAPTER III

[1] *Johnsonian Miscellanies*, ed. G. B. Hill (Oxford, 1897), I, 379.

[2] This statement does not take into account the unpublished dissertation of Medford Evans (Yale University, *ca.* 1933). Evans compares the Secker notes (only) with a number of Johnsonian debates and assigns each speech a grade (A, B, C) for "accuracy." His purposes and conclusions are rather different from mine.

[3] *Boswell's Life of Johnson*, ed. G. B. Hill (Oxford, 1887); rev. L. F. Powell (Oxford, 1934), I, 501-512; Michael MacDonagh, *The Reporters' Gallery* (London, n. d.), chaps. xvi, xvii, xviii.

[4] *Bulletin of the Institute of Historical Research*, XIX (May, 1942), 67-79.

[5] Miss Ransome cites Shippen and Wager as speakers in Johnson's debate. It is therefore obvious that she has not worked with the original magazine texts, but has used only Cobbett's *Parliamentary History of England* (cited hereafter as *Parliamentary History*), which reprints these two short speeches, taken from Chandler, as part of Johnson's account.

[6] The manuscript is described on the fourth (unnumbered) page of the *Parliamentary History*, Vol. IX. The manuscript is now in the British Museum. For the account of this debate see XI, 1047 ff.

[7] Other brief references to the debate are to be found, but Secker's account is so much fuller than any other that it is unnecessary to make use of them.

[8] The monthly issues of the two magazines were published at the same time—during this period, at the first of the month following the date of the magazine (e.g., the January issue was published on February 1). C. L. Carlson, *The First Magazine* (Providence, 1938), p. 78.

[9] The "[Carteret]" is printed thus in the *Parliamentary History*. I assume that it has been added by the editors.

[10] For the sake of uniformity between the two accounts, I have counted the columns as they appear in the *Parliamentary History*.

[11] Letter of Thomas Carte to James Stuart. Philip Henry Stanhope, *History of England from the Peace of Utrecht to the Peace of Versailles* (London, 1858), III, Appendix, p. iv.

[12] Letter of the Rev. Etough to the Rev. Dr. Burch (containing Walpole's "narrative of the motion"). William Coxe, *Memoirs of the Life and Administration of Sir Robert Walpole* (London, 1798), III, 562.

[13] *Ibid.*

[14] *Ibid.*

[15] Account of the Hon. Philip Yorke to the "Club" at Cambridge. Philip C. Yorke, *The Life and Correspondence of Philip Yorke Earl of Hardwicke* (Cambridge, 1913), I, 252.

[16] *Ibid.* See also the letter of John Orlebar to Henry Etough. Coxe, *op. cit.*, III, 563. Harley's speech is mentioned also in *Manuscripts of the Earl of Egmont: Diary of Viscount Percival* (London, 1920-1923), III, 192.

Notes

[17] Yorke, *op. cit.*, I, 252. Chandler, after reprinting parts of Johnson's report in his Addenda to XIII, 222, adds a very short quotation from Shippen and another from Wager, the sources of neither of which can be traced. Both are printed as part of Johnson's debate, *Parliamentary History*, XI, 1374-1375.

[18] Letter of Orlebar to Etough. Coxe, *op. cit.*, III, 563.

[19] See note 17, above, and Walpole's reference to Wager in the authentic record of his speech.

[20] Bussy à Amelot, 27 fev. et 9 mars 1741. "Archives du Ministère des Affaires étrangères, Correspondance d'Angleterre," CDXI, 151, 203. Quoted in Paul Vaucher, *Robert Walpole et la politique de Fleury* (Paris, 1924), p. 361.

[21] One does not know whether to accept Coxe's statement: "The principal speakers in favour of the motion were Pulteney, Bootle, Fazakerly, Pitt, and Lyttleton." He does not give the source of his information, but we know he had access to "Walpole's Parliamentary Memorandums."

[22] Etough to Burch. Coxe, *op. cit.*, III, 563.

[23] The account is given in the letter in the French Foreign Office cited above.

[24] *Journals of the House of Commons* records the reading of journals of the former sessions concerning these very same members.

[25] Stanhope, *op. cit.*, III, Appendix, p. iv.

[26] These are printed in Coxe, *op. cit.*, III, 559-561. In the account of the speech in the main narrative of his work (I, 645-652), Coxe draws mainly from Fox and Chandler. Occasional phrases, not drawn from Fox or either of the magazines, may have their source either in "Walpole's Parliamentary Memorandums" or may be have been invented by Coxe.

[27] Since Coxe apparently leaves unfilled here the spaces left by Fox when he took the notes, we are given some hope that the whole text has not been heavily "edited."

[28] This does not include the discussion of the Convention treated under domestic affairs.

[29] A summary earlier in the speech mentions other accusations but does not elaborate them.

[30] Coxe, *op. cit.*, I, 653.

[31] *Ibid.*, p. 657.

[32] Coxe's treatment of Sandys' speech shows how he worked in putting together a speech from a number of accounts. See note 26.

[33] Coxe states in his preface that he made use of the *Gentleman's Magazine* in writing his book on Sir Robert Walpole.

[34] *A Review of the Late Motion for an Address to his Majesty against a Certain Great Minister and the Reasons for it ... by a Member of Parliament* (London, 1741).

[35] These references may have caused Coxe to give this part of the *London Magazine* account greater credence.

[36] There are only two verbal differences, apart from the adaptation to Lilliputian terms in the *Gentleman's Magazine*.

[37] Secker's account is printed in *Parliamentary History*, XII, 223 ff.

[38] *Ibid.*, p. 224.

[39] *Gentleman's Magazine*, XII, 351. Hereafter cited as *G.M.*

[40] *Ibid.*, p. 348.

[41] Several witnesses brought before the secret committee investigating Walpole's conduct had refused to answer questions because answers "might tend to accuse themselves." To obtain answers, therefore, the House of Commons passed a bill that would indemnify persons who should produce evidence relating to Walpole. The debate under discussion reports the proceedings on the occasion of the second reading of the bill in the house.

[42] *Parliamentary History*, XII, 643 ff.

[43] *Ibid.*, p. 646.
[44] *G.M.*, XII, 523.
[45] *Parliamentary History*, XII, 648.
[46] *G.M.*, XII, 570.
[47] A note at the end of Johnson's report states that the "former Part" of the Lords' protest was drawn from the speech of the Duke of Argyle and "the latter Part," from that of Lord Chesterfield. Actually, there is little relation between the protest and those two speeches either in Secker or in Johnson, but the protest does contain these phrases concerning evidence and self-accusation which are labeled an "uncontroverted Maxim." The form of Johnson's "Maxim" is closer to that contained in the protest than to that in Secker's account. The *London Magazine* does not include the "Maxim," though the protest was published in the July issue of that magazine, concurrently with the debate. In its version of the debate the *London Magazine* appears to make use of facts contained in the protest, except for the phrases cited. Johnson seems to avoid it.
[48] *Parliamentary History*, XII, 652.
[49] *G.M.*, XII, 567.
[50] *Parliamentary History*, XII, 1058 ff.
[51] *Ibid.*, p. 1063.
[52] *London Magazine*, XII, 558. Hereafter cited as *L.M.*
[53] *G.M.*, XIII, 406.
[54] *Parliamentary History*, XII, 1063.
[55] *G.M.*, XIII, 405.
[56] *Parliamentary History*, XII, 1294 ff.
[57] The *Gentleman's Magazine* printed its version in the November and December issues and Supplement, 1743, and the January and February issues, 1744: *G.M.*, XIII and XIV. The *London Magazine* printed its account in the October and November issues and Appendix, 1743, and the January and February issues, 1744: *L.M.*, XII and XIII.
[58] Carteret's speech is out of order, Bathurst's second speech missing, a speech for Delawar added.
[59] Talbot is omitted. Hervey is substituted for Lonsdale, Cholmondeley for Ilay, Oxford for Sandwich, Bath for Bathurst. The *Parliamentary History* obscures two of these errors by silently changing the names before two speeches from Lonsdale to Hervey and from Oxford to Sandwich.
[60] Newcastle's speech and the second speeches of Bathurst and Lonsdale are omitted.
[61] *G.M.*, XII, 565.
[62] *Parliamentary History*, XII, 1294.
[63] *L.M.*, XII, 478.
[64] *G.M.*, XIII, 581.
[65] *Parliamentary History*, XII, 1297.
[66] *G.M.*, XIII, 621.
[67] *Parliamentary History*, XII, 1299.
[68] *G.M.*, XIII, 627.
[69] The *Parliamentary History* has made the magazines appear to agree even more closely by assigning the *London Magazine's* Harley speech to Gybbon, its Ryder speech to Cocks. The *London Magazine* reported the debate in the Appendix, 1741, and the January and February issues, 1742: *L.M.*, XI. The *Gentleman's Magazine* followed in March and April, 1742: *G.M.*, XII. No authentic evidence of the debate has been found.
[70] Johnson's version was printed in May, June, and July, 1743: *G.M.*, XIII. Gordon's report was published some months earlier, in the December issue and Appendix, 1742: *L.M.*, XI.
[71] Letter from Orlebar to Etough. Coxe, *op. cit.*, III, 595.
[72] Letter from Walpole to Mann. *The Letters of Horace Walpole*, ed. Mrs. Paget Toynbee (Oxford, 1903–1905), I, 199–203. "From the Secker Manuscript," *Parliamentary*

History, XII, 586. *Manuscripts of the Earl of Egmont: Diary of Viscount Percival* (London, 1920–1923), III, 263.

[73] *The Letters of Horace Walpole*, p. 202.

[74] "Short Notes of My Life," *ibid.*, p. xxxvi. Walpole reproduces his speech in full in a letter to Mann, pp. 199–203.

[75] That is, if we look on Percival's speech as being part of Johnson's report. The *Gentleman's Magazine* printed the debate in February and March, 1744: *G.M.*, XIV. The *London Magazine* published its version in May, June, July, and November, 1743: *L.M.*, XII. The debate itself took place on December 10, 1742.

[76] *L.M.*, XII, 284.

[77] *Ibid.*, p. 535.

[78] *G.M.*, XIV, 123.

[79] *Ibid.*, XIII, 184.

[80] *Journals of the House of Commons*, XXIV, 7.

[81] *Parliamentary History*, XI, 894 ff.

[82] The debate was on the trade and navigation bill. Johnson's report was printed in the December issue and Supplement, 1742: *G.M.*, XII.

[83] *Parliamentary History*, XII, 754 ff. Johnson has all the speeches in the sequence reported by Secker, but gives second and third speeches by Winchelsea not mentioned in the *Journal*.

[84] *G.M.*, XII, 666.

[85] *Ibid.*, p. 668.

[86] *Ibid.*, XII, Supplement, 1742; and XIII, January, 1743.

[87] Horatio Walpole's in William Coxe, *Memoirs of Horatio, Lord Walpole* (London, 1808), II, 3. Lord Gage's, printed as "L—d G—E's Speech against Augmentation of the Troops," *L.M.*, X, 285 ff., and evidently contributed.

[88] Letter from Orlebar to Etough. William Coxe, *Memoirs of the Life and Administration of Sir Robert Walpole*, III, 558.

[89] *Manuscripts of the Earl of Egmont: Diary of Viscount Percival* (London, 1920–1923), III, 183.

[90] The debate took place on January 26, 1741. Johnson's report was printed in the *Gentleman's Magazine*, February, 1742: *G.M.*, XII, 59–65.

[91] Printed in September, October, and November, 1741: *G.M.*, XI.

[92] Again an apparently authentic version was contributed: "Lord G—E's Speech against the Seamen's Bill, 1741," July, 1741: *L.M.*, X.

[93] *G.M.*, XI, 569.

[94] Coxe, *Memoirs of Horatio, Lord Walpole*, II, 184.

[95] *The Letters of Horace Walpole*, II, 154.

[96] A short debate in the *London Magazine* on a "clause" in the seamen's bill does not coincide either in speakers or in argument with any part of the *Gentleman's Magazine* series. It is difficult to make a comparative study because one does not know what should be compared.

[97] The debate was printed in September and October, 1742: *G.M.*, XII.

[98] Coxe, *Memoirs of . . . Robert Walpole*, III, 581.

[99] *The Letters of Horace Walpole*, I, 138.

[100] *Boswell's Life of Johnson*, I, 441.

NOTES TO CHAPTER IV

[1] John Hawkins, *The Life of Dr. Samuel Johnson* (London, 1787), pp. 94–132.

[2] *Boswell's Life of Johnson*, ed. G. B. Hill (Oxford, 1887), rev. L. F. Powell (Oxford, 1934–1950), I, 506. Hereafter cited as *Life*.

[3] The duel between Walpole and Pitt may be found in the extract from the debate on the seamen's bill reproduced in Appendix 1.
[4] *Gentleman's Magazine*, XI, 525–526. Hereafter cited as *G.M.*
[5] *Ibid.*, XII, 63.
[6] *Ibid.*, XIII, 17.
[7] *Ibid.*, XIV, 70.
[8] *Ibid.*, XI, 624–625.
[9] *Ibid.*, p. 512.
[10] *Ibid.*, p. 408.
[11] *Ibid.*, p. 672.
[12] *Ibid.*, p. 692.
[13] So said Henry Flood. *Life*, II, 139.
[14] *Cobbett's Parliamentary History of England* (London, 1812), XI, 1050.
[15] Hawkins, *op. cit.*, p. 124.
[16] *Ibid.*, p. 126.
[17] *Ibid.*, p. 100; also pp. 128–129.
[18] *Life*, I, 506.
[19] Hawkins, *op. cit.*, p. 100. Hawkins may well have been inclined to read into the speeches his personal judgment of the members.
[20] *Life*, I, 506.
[21] Hawkins, *op. cit.*, pp. 99–100.
[22] The reader is referred to the earlier discussion of this in connection with Sandys' speech (chap. iii) introducing the motion to remove Walpole.
[23] *Life*, I, 506.
[24] The reader will note, in the Walpole-Pitt exchange, the lack of dramatic connection between Pitt's first speech and Walpole's response, the weakness in the resolution of the quarrel, and the abruptness with which the session is brought to an end.
[25] The *London Magazine* was more concerned with linking the speeches than was the *Gentleman's Magazine*, but the method was artificial. Cf. chap. iii.
[26] It is difficult to prove that Johnson modeled his speeches solely on ancient oratory, as Hill states. It is true that, if we examine their "disposition," we find that many of the speeches conform to the structure required by ancient rhetoric: they are divisible into exordium, narration, argument, and peroration. See R. L. Irwin, "The Classical Speech Divisions," *Quarterly Journal of Speech*, XXV (April, 1939). Johnson's emphasis on the general reflects the practice of the classical rhetoricians. See Quintilian's *Institutio Oratoria* on "general" or "indefinite" questions, Book III, v. But the rules of rhetoric were so ingrained in the habits of speaking and writing in Johnson's period that it is difficult to distinguish conscious imitation of ancient models. Johnson's life-long interest in rhetoric is pointed out by W. E. Moore, "Samuel Johnson on Rhetoric," *Quarterly Journal of Speech*, XXX (April, 1944).
[27] *Life*, I, 441.
[28] *Ibid.*, IV, 429. For other references to Johnson's "talking for Victory" see *ibid.*, II, 105, 238; III, 23–24, 80; IV, 111, 192; *Johnsonian Miscellanies*, ed. G. B. Hill (Oxford, 1897), I, 450–452.
[29] Is it fancy to see the "Sirs" that punctuate a phrase in the mature conversation of Johnson as a development of the "Sirs" that were a convention of the Commons debate?
[30] *Life*, IV, 429.
[31] Evidence for this contention has been given at length in chap. iii and need not be repeated.
[32] W. K. Wimsatt, *The Prose Style of Samuel Johnson* (New Haven, 1941), p. 1. The introduction is a summary of the concept of style as "detail of meaning."
[33] Wimsatt attempts a definition *(ibid.*, pp. 11, 63): "the last and most detailed elaboration of meaning."

Notes

[34] Thomas Babington Macaulay in *Encyclopaedia Britannica*, 11th ed. (Cambridge, 1911), XV, 466–467.

[35] Wimsatt, *op. cit.*, p. 133.

[36] *Ibid.*, p. 83. In a later book, *Philosophic Words* (New Haven, 1948), Wimsatt examines a single aspect of the style of the *Debates* more thoroughly.

[37] Wimsatt, *The Prose Style of Samuel Johnson*, p. 67.

[38] *Ibid.*, p. 18. "What is implicit is the support which the resemblance of form between A and B gives to the resemblance of meaning."

[39] *G.M.*, XIII, 339.

[40] *Ibid.*, XI, 352.

[41] *Ibid.*, p. 339.

[42] *Ibid.*, XIII, 128.

[43] *Ibid.*, XI, 339 ff.

[44] Samuel Johnson, *Works* (Oxford, 1825), VI, 224. Wimsatt, in a similar count, has found the following quotients: *Life of Pope*, 1.94; *Rambler* No. 2, 1.60; *Idler* No. 10, 1.09. These are appreciably higher than figures for Hazlitt and Addison. He rightly emphasizes that such a count requires judgments of fine distinctions and that another tabulator might arrive at a different figure. He has counted the first 1,500 words of the Carteret speech and arrived at a figure very close to mine: 1.47. Thus his quotients are probably comparable with mine. I have used passages of 1,000 words.

[45] *G.M.*, XIII, 564 ff.

[46] *Ibid.*, XI, 243 ff.

[47] *Ibid.*, VIII, 332 ff.

[48] *Ibid.*, pp. 283 ff.

[49] *Life*, I, 252.

[50] *G.M.*, XIV, 235 ff.

[51] *Ibid.*, XIII, 565.

[52] *Ibid.*, p. 5.

[53] *Ibid.*, p. 283.

[54] H. W. Fowler, *The Concise Oxford Dictionary* (Oxford, 1929). Quoted by Wimsatt, *The Prose Style of Samuel Johnson*, p. 38.

[55] Wimsatt's findings are: *Life of Pope*, 2.06; *Rambler* No. 2, 1.87; *Idler* No. 6, 1.00. Hazlitt's range is from 0.53 to 1.94 and Addison's from 0.92 to 1.90.

[56] It should be emphasized here that I have, following Wimsatt, chosen, for counting, passages distinctively Johnsonian, those with a typical expository matter. Passages of other sorts have very low quotients both of parallelism and antithesis. For example, a passage giving a narrative of foreign affairs in the Carteret speech has a quotient of 0.3. Therefore the quotient of 0.8 for the narrative of Gulliver's nephew is not low. I should say that the statistical study gives strong support to the theory that Johnson had a hand in the piece.

[57] *G.M.*, XI, 339.

[58] *Ibid.*, XIII, 564.

[59] *Ibid.*, p. 11. I have simplified my discussion by disregarding Wimsatt's classification of types of extended antithesis.

[60] *Ibid.*, XI, 243. The evidence is clearly against the attribution of this debate to Johnson.

[61] *Ibid.*, VIII, 332.

[62] *Ibid.*, XI, 454.

[63] See Wimsatt, *The Prose Style of Samuel Johnson*, p. 57.

[64] *G.M.*, XI, 340.

[65] *Ibid.*, p. 452.

[66] Wimsatt, *The Prose Style of Samuel Johnson*, p. 59. For a fuller treatment see *Philosophic Words*.

[67] Wimsatt, *Philosophic Words*, p. 124.
[68] *Ibid.*, pp. 124–145.
[69] *G.M.*, XIII, 567.
[70] *Ibid.*, XI, 417.
[71] *Ibid.*, XII, 453.
[72] *Ibid.*, XIII, 349.
[73] Wimsatt, *The Prose Style of Samuel Johnson*, p. 71.
[74] *G.M.*, XIII, 71.
[75] *The History of Rasselas,* ed. R. W. Chapman (Oxford, 1927), chap. x, p. 50.

BIBLIOGRAPHY

Appendix 2, used in conjunction with chapters i and ii, provides a bibliography of the *Debates* themselves. The following list includes other works cited.

JOHNSON AND HIS WORKS

Bloom, Edward A. "Samuel Johnson as Journalist." Unpublished dissertation, University of Illinois, 1947.
Boswell's Life of Johnson, ed. George Birkbeck Hill. Oxford, 1887. Rev. L. F. Powell. 6 vols. Oxford, 1934–1950.
Chapman, R. W., and Allen T. Hazen. "Johnsonian Bibliography," *Oxford Bibliographical Society Proceedings,* Vol. V (1938), Part III, pp. 119–166.
Courtney, W. P., and D. Nichol Smith. *A Bibliography of Samuel Johnson.* Oxford, 1915. Reissued with plates, Oxford, 1925.
Evans, Medford. "Johnson's Debates in Parliament." Unpublished dissertation, Yale University, 1933 [?].
Hawkins, John. *The Life of Dr. Samuel Johnson.* 2d ed. London, 1787.
Hazen, Allen T. *Samuel Johnson's Prefaces and Dedications.* New Haven, 1937.
Johnson, Samuel. *The History of Rasselas,* ed. R. W. Chapman. Oxford, 1927.
———. *The Works of Samuel Johnson.* 11 vols. Oxford, 1825.
Johnson, Prose and Poetry, ed. Mona Wilson. London, 1950.
Johnsonian Miscellanies, ed. George Birkbeck Hill. 2 vols. Oxford, 1897.
Macaulay, Thomas Babington. "Samuel Johnson," *Encyclopaedia Britannica.* 11th ed. Cambridge, 1911.
Moore, W. E. "Samuel Johnson on Rhetoric," *Quarterly Journal of Speech,* XXX (April, 1944), 165–168.
Reade, A. L. *Johnsonian Gleanings.* Part VI. London, 1933.
Thraliana, ed. K. C. Balderston, 2 vols. Oxford, 1942.
Wimsatt, W. K. *Philosophic Words.* New Haven, 1948.
———. *The Prose Style of Samuel Johnson.* New Haven, 1941.

SOURCES FOR THE HISTORY OF DEBATE REPORTING

"The Autobiography of Sylvanus Urban," *Gentleman's Magazine,* CCI (November, December, 1856), 531–538, 667–677.
Bellot, H. H. "General Collections of Reports of Parliamentary Debates for the Period since 1660," *Bulletin of the Institute of Historical Research,* X (February, 1933), 171–177.
———. "Parliamentary Printing, 1660–1837," *ibid.,* XI (November, 1933), 85–98.
Bibliography of British History: The Eighteenth Century, eds. Stanley Pargellis and D. J. Medley. Oxford, 1951.
Bourne, H. R. Fox. *English Newspapers.* 2 vols. London, 1887.
Brown, W. J. *Everybody's Guide to Parliament.* London, 1946.
Carlson, C. L. *The First Magazine.* Providence, 1938.
Clyde, W. M. "Parliament and the Press, 1740–3," *The Library,* Series 4, XIII (March, 1933), 339–424.
Eden, Guy. *The Parliament Book.* London, 1949.
The Gentleman's Magazine: or, Trader's Monthly Intelligencer (The Gentleman's Magazine: or, Monthly Intelligencer, Vols. II–V; *The Gentlemans' Magazine and Historical Chronicle,* Vols. VI–XVI), Vols. I–XVI. London, 1731–1746.
Hanson, Lawrence. *Government and the Press, 1695–1763.* Oxford, 1936.

The Historical Register. 23 vols. London, 1716–1738.
Journals of the House of Commons. Vols. I–XXIV. N.p., n.d.
Journals of the House of Lords. Vols. I–XXVII. N.p., n.d.
The London Magazine, or, Gentleman's Monthly Intelligencer. Vols. I–XXVI. London, 1732–1757.
MacDonagh, Michael. *The Reporters' Gallery.* London, n.d.
Mantoux, Paul J. "French Reports of British Parliamentary Debates in the Eighteenth Century," *American Historical Review,* XII (January, 1907), 244–269.
———. *Notes sur les Comptes rendus de séances du Parlement anglais au XVIIIe siècle conservés aux archives du Ministère des Affaires étrangères.* Paris, 1906.
Nichols, John. *Literary Anecdotes of the Eighteenth Century.* 9 vols. London, 1812–1815.
Notestein, Wallace, and Frances Relf. *Commons Debates for 1629.* Minneapolis, 1921.
The Political State of Great Britain. 58 vols. London, 1711–1740.
Ransome, Mary. "The Reliability of Contemporary Reporting of the Debates of the House of Commons, 1727–1741," *Bulletin of the Institute of Historical Research,* XIX (May, 1942), 67–79.
Redlich, Josef. *The Procedure of the House of Commons.* 3 vols. London, 1908.
Siebert, F. S. *Freedom of the Press in England, 1476–1776.* Urbana, 1952.
Turberville, A. J. *The House of Lords in the XVIIIth Century.* Oxford, 1927.
Williams, Basil. *The Life of William Pitt, Earl of Chatham.* 2 vols. London, 1913.
Williams, J. D. (J. G. Muddiman). *A History of English Journalism to the Foundation of the Gazette.* London, 1902.

SOURCES OF CONTEMPORARY DEBATE REPORTS (NONPERIODICAL)

Cobbett's Parliamentary History of England. Vols. XI, XII. London, 1812.
Coxe, William. *Memoirs of Horatio, Lord Walpole.* 2d ed. 2 vols. London, 1808.
———. *Memoirs of the Life and Administration of Sir Robert Walpole.* 3 vols. London, 1798.
Perceval, John, 1st earl of Egmont. *Manuscripts of the Earl of Egmont: Diary of Viscount Percival.* 3 vols. London, 1920–1923.
A Review of the Late Motion for an Address to his Majesty against a Certain Great Minister and the Reasons for it ... by a Member of Parliament. London, 1741.
Stanhope, Philip Henry, 5th earl (Lord Mahon). *History of England from the Peace of Utrecht to the Peace of Versailles.* 5th ed. 7 vols. London, 1858.
Vaucher, Paul. *Robert Walpole et la politique de Fleury.* Paris, 1924.
Walpole, Horace, 4th earl of Orford. *The Letters of Horace Walpole,* ed. Mrs. Paget Toynbee. 16 vols. Oxford, 1903–1905. *Supplement,* ed. Paget Toynbee. 3 vols. Oxford, 1918–1925.
Yorke, Philip C. *The Life and Correspondence of Philip Yorke Earl of Hardwicke.* 3 vols. Cambridge, 1913.

OTHER WORKS CITED

Almon, John. *Anecdotes of the Life of the Right Hon. William Pitt, Earl of Chatham.* 6th ed. 3 vols. London, 1797.
Chesterfield, Philip Dormer Stanhope, 4th earl of. *Miscellaneous Works.* 2d ed. 4 vols. London, 1779.
Famous Speeches, ed. Herbert Paul. Boston, 1911.
Irwin, R. L. "The Classical Speech Divisions," *Quarterly Journal of Speech,* XXV (April, 1939), 212–213.
Select British Eloquence, ed. Chauncey A. Goodrich. New York, 1875.
Thackerey, Francis. *A History of the Rt. Hon. William Pitt.* 2 vols. London, 1827.
The World's Best Orations, ed. David J. Brewer. 10 vols. St. Louis, 1899.

APPENDIX 1

THIS appendix comprises three specimens of the text. The first two are not certainly by Johnson, but they serve the function here of clarifying the "Lilliputian" nature of the *Debates*. In order that the reader of the study may sample, without undue labor, one of the debates proper in the original form, I have included an extended extract from the debate on the seamen's bill which contains the celebrated answer of Pitt to the elder Horace Walpole.

The "Appendix to Capt. Lemuel Gulliver's Account" introduced to the readers of the *Gentleman's Magazine* the Lilliputian disguise in which the parliamentary accounts of that magazine were dressed during the years of Johnson's connection. It has been asserted to be of Johnson's authorship by no less an authority than G. B. Hill, but the attribution must be based on evidence of the style alone. An analysis of the style (see chap. iv) indicates that Johnson at least had a hand in its revision and may well have composed it.

The passage, which has never been reprinted, appeared in the *Gentleman's Magazine,* VIII (June, 1738), 283–287. It should be noted that those page numbers are in brackets and are duplicated (without brackets) later in the same issue, an indication that the Lilliputian content of the magazine was got up and inserted at the last minute. No attempt has been made to modernize or normalize spelling and punctuation, but typographical errors have been corrected and such changes are indicated by footnotes. The text of the other specimens has been prepared in the same way. The title is derived from the entry concerning the piece in the table of contents on the cover of the magazine.

APPENDIX
TO CAPT. LEMUEL GULLIVER'S ACCOUNT OF THE FAMOUS EMPIRE OF LILLIPUT

The Publick several Years ago received a great deal of Entertainment and Instruction from Capt. *Gulliver's* elaborate and curious Account of the newly discovered Empire of LILLIPUT;[1] a Relation, which (however rejected at its first Appearance, by some, as incredible, and criticis'd by others, as partial or ostentatious) has, with the Success almost always attendant on Probity and Truth, triumphed over all Opposition, gain'd Belief from the most obstinate Incredulity, and established a Reputation in the World, which can fear no Diminution, nor admit of any Increase.

It is much to be regretted, that the ingenious Traveller was diverted from his Design of compleating a full and accurate Description of that unknown Country; by bringing down its History from the earliest Ages, explaining the Laws and Customs of the Inhabitants, and delineating the Works of Art, and Productions of Nature, peculiar to that Soil and People. Happy had it been for Mankind, had so noble and instructive a Subject been cultivated and adorn'd by the Genius of LEMUEL GULLIVER, a Genius equally sublime and extensive, acute and sagacious, worthy to display the Policy of the most refined, and celebrate the Atchievements of the most warlike Nation. Then might the Legislators of *Lilliput* have been produced as Rivals in Fame to *Numa* or *Lycurgus;* and its Heroes have shone with no less Lustre than *Cadmus* and *Theseus.*

---

[1] LILLIPUT] LILIPUT

Appendix 1

Felix tanto Argumento Ingenium, felix tanto Ingenio Argumentum![2]

But as the Hope conceived by the Publick of seeing this immense Undertaking successfully compleated, has been frustrated by Indolence, Business, or perhaps by the unexpected Stroke of sudden Death; we doubt not but our Readers will be much pleased with an Appendix to Capt. GULLIVER's Account, which we received last Month, and which the late Resolution of the House of Commons, whereby we are forbidden to insert any Account of the Proceedings of the *British Parliament,* gives us an Opportunity of communicating in their Room.

Some Years after the Publication of Capt. GULLIVER's Discoveries, in the midst of the Clamour raised against them by Ignorance, Misapprehension, and Malice, a Grandson of the Captain, fired with Resentment at the Indignities offered to his Ancestor's Character, by Men, who, without the least Regard to his celebrated Veracity, dared to charge his Relation with no less than premeditated, deliberate Falshood, resolved, as the most effectual Method of vindicating his Memory, to undertake a Voyage to *Lilliput,* that he might be able at his Return to confirm his Grandfather's Reports by ocular Testimony, and for ever silence those Aspersions, which were, in his Opinion, founded on nothing but extreme Ignorance of both Geography and human Nature.

This Voyage, by the Assistance of some Charts and Observations which he found amongst his Grandfather's Papers, he successfully performed in the Ship named the *Confidence,* and met, upon his discovering his Name and Family, with such a Reception at the Court of *Lilliput,* as sufficiently shewed that the Memory of the *ManMountain* was far from being obliterated among them; and that Time had in *Lilliput* the Effect which it is observ'd to have on our Side of the Globe, of preserving and

---

[2] The epigram cannot be traced through the *Thesaurus Linguae Latinae* and may well be Johnson's invention.

increasing a Reputation built on great and illustrious Actions, and of dissipating the Whispers of Malice and Calumnies of Faction. The Accusations brought against the Captain by his Enemies were cleared up, or forgot; and the Grandson, at his Arrival, found the Preservation of MILDENDO from the Flames, and the Conquest of the formidable Navy of *Blefuscu,* the Subject of Epic Poems, and annual Orations, the old Man's constant Topic of Discourse, and the Example by which their Youth were animated to Fidelity, Presence of Mind, and military Prowess.

The hospitable and generous Reception he found in the Country, gave him Opportunities of informing himself more fully of the State of that Part of the World; for which he came prepared by his Grandfather's Conversation, and a tolerable Knowledge of the *Lilliputian* Tongue, attain'd by the Help of a Grammar and a Vocabulary, which, with other Writings in that Language, Captain GULLIVER had left behind him.

Enabled by these concurrent Advantages to make a speedy Progress in his Enquiries, he returned at the End of 3 Years, not with a Cargo of Gold, or Silk, or Diamonds, but with Histories, Memoirs, Tracts, Speeches, Treaties, Debates, Letters and Instructions, which will be a sufficient Compensation to Mankind for the Loss they have sustained by the Negligence or untimely Death of Capt. GULLIVER; and establish'd a Correspondence between *Lilliput* and the *English* Colonies in the *East-Indies,* by which all the valuable Writings published there, and all historical and political Novelties, are to be annually transmitted to him.

This Gentleman, notwithstanding that Veneration for his Grandfather which engaged him to take so long and tedious a Voyage, upon no other Motive than a Desire of obliging the World to do Justice to his Character, has given the highest Testimonies that Truth is yet dearer to him than the Reputation of his Family, and that no mistaken Piety can prevail upon him to palliate the Mistakes, or conceal the Errors which were the

Appendix 1

necessary Effects of Capt. GULLIVER's short Stay, difficult Situation, formidable Appearance, and perplex'd Affairs.

The ready Access to the great Men of *Lilliput,* and Familiarity with the Emperor himself, which the traditional Regard paid to his Grandfather's Merit procured him, rendered it easy for him to make greater Discoveries in three Days, than Capt. *Gulliver* had been able to do during his whole Stay. He was particularly surprized in his first Conference with the Emperor, to hear him mention many States and Empires beside those of *Lilliput* and *Blefuscu;* and, upon observing that in his Grandfather's Account no other Nations are taken Notice of, he was told with great Condescension by his Majesty, that there had been lately discovered, in an old Repository of Archives, an Edict of those Times, absolutely forbidding, under the Pain and Penalty of Death, any Person or Persons to give the *Man-Mountain* the least Information relating to the State of any other Country; lest his Ambition might prompt him to seize upon some defenseless Part, either of his *Lilliputian* Majesty's Dominions, or of some weak Prince, or petty State, and to erect an absolute Dominion, which might in time perhaps become formidable to the State of *Lilliput* itself. Nor do I believe, said his Majesty, that your Ancestor would have heard the Name of *Blefuscu,* had not the Necessities of State obliged the Court unwillingly to discover it; and even in that Emergence of Affairs, they gave him so imperfect an Account, that he has represented *Blefuscu* as an Island; whereas it is a very large Empire on the Continent, confining on other Empires, Kingdoms, and States, of which I'll order my Geographer to communicate to you an accurate Description.

He had immediately recourse to the Royal Professor of Geography, and found upon Inspection, that the Maps of *Lilliput* and *Blefuscu,* and the neighbouring Islands, Kingdoms and Empires, were a perfect Epitome of the Map of Europe, and that these petty Regions, with their Dependencies, constitute a

Resemblance or Compendium of our great World, just as the Model of a Building contains all the Parts in the same Disposition as the principal Design.

This Observation engaged him closely to his Geographical Studies, and the farther he advanced, the more he was convinced of the Justness of the Notion he had conceived of a World in Miniature, inhabited by this Pigmy Race—In it he found all the four Parts of our Earth represented by correspondent Countries, excepting that the *Lilliputian* World is not Spherical, but must be considered as bearing the Form which the Ancients attributed to our own. Neither need I acquaint the Mathematical Reader, that being enlightened by our Sun, it does not admit of any Diversity of Zones, or Climates, but bears an exact Analogy to our Earth in its Lands and Seas, Chains of Mountains, Tracts of Desarts, and Diversity of Nations.

The People of *Degulia,* or the *Lilliputian Europe,* which Name is derived from DEGUL, *illustrious,* (a Word now obsolete, and only known to Antiquaries and Etymologists) are, above those of the other Parts of the World, famous for Arts, Arms, and Navigation, and, in consequence of this Superiority, have made Conquests, and settled Colonies in very distant Regions, the Inhabitants of which they look upon as barbarous, tho' in Simplicity of Manners, Probity, and Temperance superior to themselves; and seem to think that they have a Right to treat them as Passion, Interest or Caprice shall direct, without much Regard to the Rules of Justice or Humanity; they have carried this imaginary Sovereignty so far, that they have sometimes proceeded to Rapine, Bloodshed and Desolation. If you endeavour to examine the Foundation of this Authority, they neither produce any Grant from a superior Jurisdiction, nor plead the Consent of the People whom they govern in this tyrannical Manner; but either threaten you with Punishment for abridging the Emperor's Sovereignty, or pity your Stupidity, or tell you in positive Terms, that *Power is right.* Some indeed pretend to a

Appendix 1

Grant from a Pontiff, to whom, as they happen to be inclined, they sometimes pay an absolute Submission, and as often deny common Respect; but this Grant is not worth Examination, the Pontiff from whom it is derived, being equally at a loss to fix his own Authority upon any solid Ground; so that at best the *Degulians* Claim to these Settlements, is like the Mahometan World, which rests upon an Elephant, which is supported by a Stone, which is supported by nothing.

It is observable, that their Conquests and Acquisitions in *Columbia,* (which is the *Lilliputian* Name for the Country that answers our *America,*) have very little contributed to the Power of those Nations, which have, to obtain them, broke thro' all the Ties of human Nature. They have indeed added Extent to their Territories, and procured new Titles for their Princes, but at the same time have exhausted their Mother Country of its Inhabitants, and subjected themselves to a thousand Insults, by possessing vast Tracts of Land, which are too spacious to be constantly garrison'd, and too remote to be occasionally and duly supply'd.

Even *Iberia,* a Country at the Southwest Point of *Degulia,* whose Inhabitants were the first Discoverers of *Columbia,* tho' she boasts herself Mistress of the richest and most fertile part of that Quarter of the World, which she secured to herself by the most dreadful Massacres and Devastations, has not yet, in all the Gold she has imported, received an Equivalent for the Numbers of her Natives sent out to people those Kingdoms her Sword has wasted; so that the whole Advantage of her mighty Conquests, is Bulk without Strength, and Pride without Power.

It must be observed to the Honour of the *Lilliputians,* who have in all Ages been famous for their Politicks, that they have the Art of civilizing their remote Dominions without doing much Injury to their Native Country; for when any of their People have forfeited the Rights of Society, by Robberies, Seditions, or any other Crimes, which make it not safe to suffer them to live, and yet are esteemed scarce heinous enough to be punished with Death, they send them to some distant Colony for a certain Number of Years proportionate to their Crimes. Of these Mr. *Gulliver,* during his Stay, saw ten thousand convey'd from the Prisons of *Mildendo* in close Lighters to Ships that lay at Anchor in the River to carry them to Columbia, where they were disposed among the Inhabitants, undoubtedly very much to the Propagation of Knowledge and Virtue, and no less to the Honour of their native Country.

Another Inconvenience of these new Claims, is, that they are a constant Source of Discord and Debate among the *Degulian* Powers, some of which are perpetually disputing their Titles to Countries, which neither has a Right to, and which sometimes are defended by the Natives against both. There not long since arose a Quarrel of this Kind, between the *Lilliputians* and *Iberians,* who contested the Limits of their *Columbian* (or *American*) Acquisitions. The *Lilliputians,* contrary to the ancient Genius of that martial People, made very liberal Concessions, such as rather drew upon them the Imputation of Cowardice, than procured them the Praise of Moderation; but the *Iberians,* insatiable in their Ambition, resolved to insist on nothing less than the absolute uninterrupted Possession of that whole Quarter of the World. In pursuance of this Resolution they seiz'd, upon various Pretences, all the *Lilliputian* Shipping that ventured or were drove near their Shores in the *Columbian* Seas, confiscated their Lading, and imprisoned, tortured, and starved their Seamen. The *Lilliputians* were patient under all these insults for a long time, but being at length awakened by frequent Injuries, were making, at Mr. *Gulliver*'s Departure, Preparations for War; the Event of which is not yet come to his Knowledge.

Our Author having satisfied his Curiosity, with regard to the Geography of this petty World, began to enquire more nearly into the Constitution and Laws of *Lilliput:* But how great was his Suprize, when he found it so nearly to resemble our own! The Executive Power being lodged wholly in the Emperor; as the Legislative is in the Emperor, the House of *Hurgos,* or Lords, whose Honours and Privileges are Hereditary, and the House of *Clinabs,* or Commons, Representatives elect of the Body of the People, whose Assemblies are continued by several Sessions and Adjournments, or Prorogations, for the space of seven *Moons,* after which their Authority determines, and Writs are issued for new Elections.

Mr GULLIVER, astonish'd at this wonderful Conformity between the Constitution of *England* and *Lilliput,* consulted *Flibo Quibus,* the *Royal Historiographer,* upon that Subject, who gave him the following Account:

' 'Tis now, according to the best Chronologers, more than 392 'Moons since the Arrival of your illustrious Ancestor *Quinbus 'Flestrin,* or the *ManMountain* upon the Confines of *Lilliput,* 'where he performed those Atchievements still recorded in our 'Histories, and celebrated by our Poets; but alas! he was at last 'disgraced and banished by the Effects of the most undeserved 'Calumny and Malice.

'After his Departure, the People, who had been irritated 'against him by false Reports, finding the same evil Measures that 'were imputed to his Advice still pursued, and all the Calamities 'still subsisting which had been describ'd as the Effects of his Stay 'amongst them, were on the sudden, not only convinc'd of his 'Innocence, but so exasperated against his Enemies by the Re-'membrance of his Wisdom, Clemency, and Valour, that they 'surrounded the Royal Palace, and demanded the Heads of the '*Man-Mountain's* Accusers. The Ministers, according to Custom, 'ran for Shelter to the Royal Authority; but far from appeasing 'the People by that Artifice, they involved their Master in the 'common Destruction.

'The People having set fire to the Palace, and buried the whole 'Royal Family in its Ruins, placed one *Mulgo Malvin,* who had

'been Secretary to the *Man-Mountain,* upon the Throne of
'Lilliput. This Man new-modelled the Form of Government,
'according to the Plan which his Master had delivered to him,
'and affirm'd to be an exact Account of the *British* Constitution.

'Our Government (continued the *Lilliputian*) has in some
'Particulars varied from its Original. The *Clinabs* were at first
'elected every Moon, but now continue in Office 7 Moons; to
'which Alteration many attribute the present Venality and De-
'pendency discovered in their Assemblies. They were likewise
'anciently paid by the People they represented for their Attend-
'ance on the Publick Business; but of late it is more common for
'the *Clinabs* to pay the People for admitting them to attend. Our
'Ancestors, in ancient Times, had some Regard to the moral
'Character of the Person sent to represent them in their national
'Assemblies, and would have shewn some Degree of Resentment,
'or Indignation, had their Votes been asked for a Murderer, an
'Adulterer, a known Oppressor, an hireling Evidence, an At-
'torney, a Gamester, or a Pimp. They demanded likewise in those
'who stood Candidates for the Power of making Laws, some
'Knowledge of the Laws already made; but now neither the most
'flagrant Immorality, nor the grossest Ignorance, are, amongst
'some Electors, any Objections to the Character of a Man who
'solicits Voices with Gold in his Hand.'

Such was the Answer of the learned *Lilliputian,* which incited
Mr GULLIVER to pursue his Search into their Laws, Customs, and
History; if haply he might discover, since human Nature gener-
ally operates alike in all Parts of the World, by what Means the
Government of *Lilliput,* which had been once establish'd on so
excellent a Plan, became so miserably degenerate; while the
Government of *Britain,* its Original, maintained inviolate the
Purity and Vigour of its primitive Constitution.

As we propose to publish every Month such Part of Mr
GULLIVER's Papers as shall seem most proper to bring our Readers
acquainted with the History and present State of *Lilliput,* we

Appendix 1

have chosen for this half Year's Entertainment, the DEBATES of the *Lilliputian* Senate, and shall begin with a very important one upon Occasion of the *Iberian* Depredations already mentioned, and the Measures to be pursued for Redress, which Debate, as indeed all others on such high Affairs, was carried on with the greatest Eloquence and Spirit, in the 4th Session of the 8th Senate (or Parliament) of *Magna Lilliputia,* held at †*Belfaborac* in the 11th Moon of the Reign of the Emperor GORGENTI the Second.

† A City at the West End of Mildendo. [Footnote in the original text.]

The following was printed on the last page of the Supplement for 1738, *Gentleman's Magazine,* Volume VIII. Several annual installments of the same nature were issued. By 1741 the specimen of *Anagrammata Rediviva* was simply a list of Lilliputian terms and names with their equivalents. The present piece, however, appears to be the announcement of such a list, to be distributed as a handbill separate from the magazine. One phrase has a markedly Johnsonian sound: "the Nature of the Undertaking, the Usefulness of the Art, and the Reasonableness of the Conditions."

In a few Days will be publish'd
PROPOSALS for printing by Subscription
ANAGRAMMATA REDIVIVA,
OR
THE ART OF COMPOSING AND RESOLVING ANAGRAMS
Compiled after Fifty Seven Years Study, Labour, Enquiry,
and Experience
By a Professor of Universal Learning, and a Descendent of the Renown'd Cabalist Rabbi Levi Ben Iarchi

I. The Work will consist of 50 large Octavo Volumes printed in the same Manner with the Specimen annexed to the Proposals.

II. The Price to Subscribers will be 20 Guineas, half to be paid at the Time of Subscription, and half at the Delivery of a perfect Sett in Sheets.

III. A small Number will be printed in Quarto for those who are desirous to add their own Observations, at 35 Guineas.

IV. As the Work is of an extraordinary Nature, and carried on wholly at the Author's Expence, he assures his Subscribers, that he will immediately after Publication double the Price, with regard to the Copies not subscrib'd for; a Method which ought constantly to be observ'd, that the unjustly Suspicious, and the Discouragers of all useful Proposals by Subscription may be deservedly punish'd with Disappointment of Expence.

I have by me 9 large Folio *Manuscripts,* alphabetically digested on this Subject.

As soon as the ingenious Mr *Gulliver* appear'd in the *Gentleman's Magazine,* I immediately fell to Work and digested the names of the *Clinabs,* the *Hurgoes,* &c. there mention'd into my Work, and by an infinite Labour, found that there are many Descendants of our *English* Families in *Lilliput.*

I hope that no *Englishman* will be offended at his Relation to this diminutive Race; for it is plain, from several Monuments of Antiquity, that we have fallen as much below the Bulk of the first Descendants of *Brutus,* as the Natives of *Lilliput* below ours, and I flatter myself that the Specimen will make any farther Apology unnecessary, and shew, at once, the Nature of the Undertaking, the Usefulness of the Art, and the Reasonableness of the Conditions.

The Rudiments of the Art being explained in all Modern Languages, Proposals are deliver'd and Subscriptions taken in by the Booksellers of

Mildendo, Belfaborac, Broslit, Roffen, Edina, Odfrox and *Guntar* in *Lilliput.*

London, Westminster, Bristol, Rochester, Edinburgh, Oxford and *Cambr.* in *Britain.*

Mardit and *Sebfule* in *Iberia. Madrid, Seville* and *Salamanca* in *Spain.*

Ultralt, Munstru, Romenia in *Degulia.*

Utrecht, Munster, Rome, and most other Cities in *Europe.*

Receipts may also be had properly sign'd, of the Residents or Agents from

Allemanu, Blefuscu, Belchia, Hungruland, Dancram, Swecte, Mausqeeta, Laurnia, Lusitnia, Koranbec, Itlascu and *Poldraud.*

Germany, France, Holland, Hungary, Denmark, Sweden, Muscovy, Lorrain, Portugal, Turkey, Italy and *Poland.*

Likewise of most Matters of Ships trading to

Ierne, Ghineac, Zhamengol, Iberionola, Cabu, Bardosba, Gorgentia, Capemchy, Jutacan, and other Places in *Columbia* or the *Idnies.*

Ireland, Guinea, Jamaica, Hispaniola, Cuba, Barbadoes, Georgia, Campeachy, Jucatan, and other Places in *America* or the *Indies.*

The debate on the Seamen's bill was published in the September, October, and November, 1741, issues of the *Gentleman's Magazine,* Volume XI, and was second to be published of those wholly Johnson's. Though the magazine refers to it as a single "Remarkable *Debate,*" it is made clear that the proceedings of several sessions are reflected. The first of these is the debate on the occasion of the first reading of the bill, January 27, 1741. This is followed by a series of debates on individual clauses and amendments running from March 2 to 13. The present extract is the latter portion of the report of the session of March 4, beginning with the speech of Pitt, which brings on, belatedly, the attack by Horace Walpole, which in turn brings on the famous counterattack by Pitt.

We have no important authentic record of the debate. The bill itself was designed to meet the problem of a serious shortage of sailors, who were needed in manning the fleet in the war against Spain. In April, 1740, only "twenty of the thirty vessels reserved to guard the Channel were manned." (I. S. Leadam, *The Political History of England,* IX, 364.) The expedient of an embargo on all shipping was tried, but with little success. The purpose of the bill was to establish a register of all seafaring men. A similar bill had been proposed the previous year but the opposition had managed to defeat it. This time the bill passed by a majority of 153 to 79.

The part of the debate from which this is an extract (*Gentleman's Magazine,* XI, 562–571) reports proceedings on the day of considering the clause: "That no Merchants, or Bodies Corporate or Politic, shall hire Sailors at higher Wages than Thirty-five Shillings for the Month, on Pain of forfeiting the treble Value of the Sum so agreed for; which Law was to commence after Fifteen Days, and continue to be agreed on by the House." (*Gentleman's Magazine,* XI, 529.)

The title "Remarkable Debate..." is taken from the cover of the magazine. The names of the speakers have been supplied in brackets after their Lilliputian designations.

REMARKABLE DEBATE
IN THE HOUSE OF CLINABS
ON THE BILL FOR ENCOURAGING SEAMEN
AND MANNING THE FLEET
(An Extract)

The Urg; Ptit [Pitt] *spoke to the following Purport.*
S I R,

It is common for those to have the greatest Regard to their own Interest who discover the least for that of others. I do not, therefore, despair of recalling the Advocates of this Bill from the Prosecution of their favourite Measures by Arguments of greater Efficacy than those which are founded on Reason and Justice.

Nothing, Sir, is more evident, than that some Degree of Reputation is absolutely necessary to Men who have any Concern in the Administration of a Government like ours; they must either secure the Fidelity of their Adherents by the Assistance of Wisdom, or of Virtue; their Enemies must either be awed by their Honesty, or terrified by their Cunning. Mere artless Bribery will never gain a sufficient Majority to set them entirely free from Apprehensions of Censure. To different Tempers different Motives must be applied: Some, who place their Felicity in being accounted Wise, are in very little Care to preserve the Character of Honesty; others may be persuaded to join in Measures which they easily discover to be weak and ill-concerted, because they are convinced that the Authors of them are not corrupt but mistaken, and are unwilling that any Man should be punished for natural Defects or casual Ignorance.

I cannot say, Sir, which of these Motives influence the Advocates for the Bill before us; a Bill in which such Cruelties are proposed as are yet unknown among the most savage Nations, such as Slavery has not yet borne, or Tyranny invented, such as cannot be heard without Resentment, nor thought of without Horror.

It is, Sir, perhaps, not unfortunate, that one more Expedient has been added rather ridiculous than shocking, and that these Tyrants of the Administration, who amuse themselves with oppressing their Fellow Subjects, who add without Reluctance one Hardship to another, invade the Liberty of those whom they have already overborn with Taxes, first plunder and then imprison, who take all Opportunities of Heightening the publick Distresses, and make the Miseries of War the Instruments of new Oppressions, are too ignorant to be formidable, and owe their Power not to their Abilities, but to casual Prosperity, or to the Influence of Money.

The other Clauses of this Bill complicated at once with Cruelty and Folly, have been treated with becoming Indignation; but this may be considered with less Ardour of Resentment, and fewer Emotions of Zeal, because, tho' perhaps equally iniquitous, it will do no Harm; for a Law that can never be executed can never be felt.

That it will consume the Manufacture of Paper and swell the Books of Statutes, is all the Good or Hurt that can be hoped or fear'd from a Law like this; a Law which fixes what is in its own Nature mutable, which prescribes Rules to the Seasons and Limits to the Wind.

I am too well acquainted, Sir, with the Disposition of its two chief Supporters, to mention the Contempt with which this Law will be treated by Posterity, for they have already shewn abundantly their Disregard of succeeding Generations; but I will remind them, that they are now venturing their whole Interest at once, and hope they will recollect before it is too late that those who believe them to intend the Happiness of their Country will never be confirmed in their Opinion by open Cruelty and notorious Oppression; and that those who have only their own

Interest in View, will be afraid of adhering to those Leaders, however old and practiced in Expedients, however strengthen'd by Corruption, or elated with Power, who have no reason to hope for Success from either their Virtue or Abilities.

The Urg; Brusttath [Bathurst] *next spoke to this Effect.*
S I R,

The Clause now under our Consideration is so inconsiderately drawn up, that it is impossible to read it in the most cursory Manner, without discovering the Necessity of numerous Amendments; no malicious Subtilities or artful Deductions are required in raising Objections to this Part of the Bill, they croud upon us without being sought, and instead of exercising our Sagacity, weary our Attention.

The first Error, or rather one Part of a general and complicated Error, is the Computation of Time not by Days but by Kalendar Months, which, as they are not equal one to another, may embarrass the Account between the Sailors and those that employ them. In all Contracts of a short Duration, the Time is to be reckoned by Weeks and Days, by certain and regular Periods, which has been so constantly the Practice of the sea-faring Men, that perhaps many of them do not know the Meaning of a Kalendar Month: This indeed is a Neglect of no great Importance, because no Man can be deprived by it of more than the Wages due for the Labour of a few Days, but the other Part of this Clause is more seriously to be consider'd, as it threatens the Sailors with greater Injuries. For it is to be enacted, that all Contracts made for more Wages than are here allowed shall be totally void.

It cannot be denied to be possible, and in my Opinion it is very likely, that many Contracts will be made without the Knowledge of this Law, and consequently without any Design of violating it; but Ignorance, inevitable Ignorance, tho' it is a valid excuse for every other Man, is no Plea for the unhappy Sailor; he must suffer, tho' innocent, the Penalty of a Crime; must undergo Dan-

Appendix 1

ger, Hardships, and Labour, without a Recompence, and at the End of a successful Voyage, after having enriched his Country by his Industry, return Home to a necessitous Family without being able to relieve them.

It is scarcely necessary, Sir, to raise any more Objections to a Clause in which nothing is Right; but to shew how its Imperfections multiply upon the slightest Consideration, I take the Opportunity to observe that there is no Provision made for regulating the Voyages performed in less Time than a Month, so that the greatest Part of the Abuses, which have been represented as the Occasion of this Clause, are yet without Remedy, and only those Sailors who venture far, and are exposed to the greatest Dangers, are restrain'd from receiving an adequate Reward.

Thus much, Sir, I have said upon the Supposition, that a Regulation of the Sailors Wages is either necessary or just, a Supposition of which I am very far from discovering the Truth. That it is just to oppress the most useful of our Fellow-Subjects, to load those Men with peculiar Hardships to whom we owe the Plenty that we enjoy, the Power that yet remains in the Nation, and which neither the Folly nor the Cowardice of Ministers have yet been able to destroy, and the Security in which we now sit and hold our Consultations; that it is just to lessen our Payments at a Time when we increase the Labour of those who are hired, and to expose Men to Danger without Recompence, will not easily be proved even by those who are most accustomed to Paradoxes, and are ready to undertake the Proof of any position which it is their Interest to find true.

Nor is it much more easy to shew the Necessity of this Expedient in our present State, in which it appears from the Title of the Bill, that our chief Endeavour should be the Increase and Encouragement of Sailors, and, I suppose, it has not often been discover'd, that by taking away the Profits of a Profession greater Numbers have been allured to it.

The high Wages, Sir, paid by Merchants are the chief Incitements that prevail upon the Ambitious, the Necessitous, or the Avaritious, to forsake the Ease and Security of the Land, to leave easy Trades, and healthful Employments, and expose themselves to an Element where they are not certain of an Hour's Safety. The Service of the Merchants is the Nursery in which Seamen are trained up for his Majesty's Navies, and from thence we must, in Time of Danger, expect those Forces by which alone we can be protected.

If, therefore, it is necessary to encourage Sailors, it is necessary to reject all Measures that may terrify or disgust them; and as their Numbers must depend upon our Trade, let us not embarrass the Merchants with any other Difficulties than those which are inseparable from War, and which very little Care has been hitherto taken to alleviate.

The Urg; Heagh [Hay] *replied.*

S I R,

The Objections which have been urged with so much Ardour, and display'd with such Power of Eloquence, are not, in my Opinion, formidable enough to discourage us from prosecuting our Measures; some of them may be perhaps readily answered, and the rest easily removed.

The Computation of Time, as it now stands, is allow'd not to produce any formidable Evil, and therefore did not require so rhetorical a Censure, the Inconveniency of Kalendar Months may easily be removed by a little Candour in the contracting Parties, or that the Objection may not be repeated to the Interruption of the Debate, Weeks or Days may be substituted, and the usual reckoning of the Sailors be still continued.

That some Contracts may be annulled, and Inconveniencies or Delays of Payment arise, is too evident to be questioned; but in that Case the Sailor may have his Remedy provided, and be enabled to obtain by an easy Process, what he shall be judg'd to *have deserved;* for it must be allow'd reasonable, that every Man who

Appendix 1

labours in honest and useful Employments, should receive the Reward of his Diligence and Fidelity.

Thus, Sir, may the Clause, however[1] loudly censured and violently opposed, be made useful and equitable, and the publick Service advanced without Injury to Individuals.

Sir Rub. Walelop [Robert Walpole] *next rose and spoke as follows.*

S I R,

Every Law which extends its Influence to great Numbers in various Relations and Circumstances must produce some Consequences that were never foreseen or intended and is to be censured or applauded as the general Advantages or Inconveniencies are found to preponderate. Of this kind is the Law before us, a Law enforced by the Necessity of our Affairs and drawn up with no other Intention than to secure the publick Happiness and produce that Success which every Man's Interest must prompt him to desire.

If in the Execution of this Law, Sir, some Inconveniencies should arise, they are to be remedied as fast as they are discovered, or if not capable of a Remedy to be patiently born in Consideration of the general Advantage.

That some temporary Disturbances may be produced is not improbable; the Discontent of the Sailors may for a short Time rise high, and our Trade be suspended by their Obstinacy; but Obstinacy however determined must yield to Hunger, and when no higher Wages can be obtained they will cheerfully accept of those which are here allowed them. Short Voyages indeed are not comprehended in the Clause and therefore the Sailors will engage in them upon their own Terms, but this Objection can be of no weight with those that oppose the Clause, because, if it is unjust to limit the Wages of the Sailors, it is just to leave those Voyages without Restriction; and those that think the Expedient

---

[1] however] however,

here proposed equitable and rational, may perhaps be willing to make some Concessions to those who are of a different Opinion.

That the Bill will not remove every Obstacle to Success; nor add Weight to one Part of the Balance without making the other lighter; that it will not supply the Navy without incommoding the Merchants in some degree; that it may be sometimes evaded by Cunning, and sometimes abused by Malice, and that at last it will be less efficacious than is desired, may perhaps be proved; but it has not yet been proved that any other Measures are more eligible, or that we are not to promote the publick Service as far as we are able, though our Endeavours may not produce Effects equal to our Wishes.

The Hurgolet Branard [Barnard] *then spoke to this Effect:*
S I R,
I know not by what Fatality it is that Nothing can be urged in Defence of the Clause before us which does not tend to discover its Weakness and Inefficacy. The warmest Patrons of this Expedient are impelled by the mere Force of Conviction to such Concessions as invalidate all their Arguments, and leave their Opponents no Necessity of replying.

If short Voyages are not comprehended in this Provision what are we now controverting? what but the Expedience of a Law that will never be executed? The Sailors, however they are contemned by those who think them only worthy to be treated like Beasts of Burthen, are not yet so stupid but that they can easily find out, that to serve a Fortnight for greater Wages is more eligible than to toil a Month for less; and as the numerous Equipments that have been lately made have not left many more Sailors in the Service of the Merchants than may be employ'd in the Coasting Trade, those who traffick to remoter parts must shut up their Books and wait till the Expiration of this Act, for an Opportunity of renewing their Commerce.

Appendix 1

To regulate the Wages for one Voyage, and to leave another without Limitation in time of Scarcity of Seamen, is absolutely to prohibit that Trade which is so restrained, and is doubtless a more effectual Embargo than has been yet invented.

Let any Man but suppose that the East *Idnian* Company were obliged to give only half the Wages that other Traders allow, and consider how that part of our Commerce could be carried on; would not their Goods rot in their Warehouses, and their Ships lie forever in the Harbour? Would not the Sailors refuse to contract with them? or desert them after a Contract, upon the first prospect of more advantageous Employment?

But it is not requisite to multiply Arguments in a Question which may not only be decided without long Examination but in which we may determine our Conclusions by the Experience of our Ancestors. Scarcely any right or wrong Measures are without a Precedent, and amongst others this Expedient has been tried by the Wisdom of former times, a Law was once made for limiting the Wages of Tailors, and that it is totally ineffectual we are all convinced. Experience is a very safe Guide in political Enquiries, and often discovers what the most enlightened Reason failed to foresee.

Let us therefore improve the Errors of our Ancestors to our own Advantage, and whilst we neglect to imitate their Virtues, let us at least forbear to repeat their Follies.[a]

Macgya Peerur [Perry] *Urg; spoke to this Purport.*
S I R,

There is one Objection more which my Acquaintance with foreign Trade impresses too strongly upon my mind to suffer me to conceal it.

It is well known that the Condition of a Seaman subjects him to the Necessity of spending a great part of his Life at a Distance from his native Country, in places where he can neither hear of our Designs nor be instructed in our Laws, and therefore it is

---

[a] follies.] follies,

evident that no Law ought to affect him before a certain Period of Time in which he may reasonably be supposed to have been informed of it. For every Man ought to have it in his power to avoid Punishment, and to suffer only for Negligence or Obstinacy.

It is quite unnecessary, Sir, to observe to this Assembly, that there are now, as at all times, great Numbers of Sailors in every part of the World, and that they at least equally deserve our Regard with those who are under the more immediate Influence of the Government.

These Seamen have already contracted for the price of their Labour, and the Recompense of their[3] Hazards, nor can we, in my Opinion, without manifest Injustice, dissolve a Contract founded upon Equity, and confirmed by Law.

It is, Sir, an undisputed Principle of Government, that no Persons should be punished without a Crime; but is it no Punishment to deprive a Man of what is due to him by a legal Stipulation, the Condition of which is on his part honestly fulfilled?

Nothing, Sir, can be imagined more calamitous than the Disappointment to which this Law Subjects the unhappy Men who are now promoting the Interest[4] of their Country in distant Places amidst Dangers and Hardships, in unhealthy Climates and barbarous Nations, where they comfort themselves under the Fatigues of Labour and the Miseries of Sickness, with the Prospect of the Sum which they shall gain for the Relief of their Families, and the Respite which their Wages will enable them to Enjoy; but upon their Return they find their Hopes blasted and their Contracts dissolved by a Law made in their Absence.

No human Being, I think can coolly and deliberately inflict a Hardship like this, and therefore I doubt not but those who have by Inadvertency given Room for this Objection will either remove it by an Amendment, or what is, in my Opinion, more eligible, reject the Clause as inexpedient, useless, and unjust.

---

[3] their Hazards,] their, Hazards,
[4] Interest] Interesl

The Hurgolen Yegon [Yonge] *spoke next, to this Effect.*
SIR,

This Debate has been protracted, not by any Difficulties arising from the Nature of the Questions which have been the Subject of it, but by a Neglect with which almost all the Opponents of the Bill may be justly charged, the Neglect of distinguishing between Measures eligible in themselves, and Measures preferable to Consequences which are apprehended from particular Conjunctures; between Laws made only to advance the publick Happiness and Expedients of which the Benefit is merely occasional, and of which the sole Intention is to avert some national Calamity, and which are to cease with the Necessity that produced them.

Such are the Measures, Sir, which are now intended; Measures, which in Days of Ease, Security, and Prosperity, it would be the highest Degree of Weakness to propose, but of which I cannot see the Absurdity in Times of Danger and Distress. Such Laws are the Medicines of a State, Useless and Nauseous in Health, but preferable to a lingering Disease, or to a miserable Death.

Even those Measures, Sir, which have been mentioned as most grossly absurd, and represented as parallel to the Provision made in this Clause only to expose it to Contempt and Ridicule, may in particular Circumstances be rational and just. To settle the Price of Corn in the Time of a Famine, may become the wisest State, and Multitudes might in Time of publick Misery, by the Benefit of temporary[5] Laws, be preserved from Destruction. Even those Masts, to which with a prosperous Gale, the Ship owes its Usefulness and its Speed, are often cut down by the Sailors in the Fury of a Storm.

With regard to the Ships which are now in distant Places, whither no Knowledge of this Law can possibly be convey'd, it cannot be denied that their Crews ought to be secured from Injury by some particular Exception; for tho' it is evident in Com-

---
[5] temporary] temporray

petitions between public and private Interest, which ought to be preferred, yet we ought to remember that no unnecessary Injury is to be done to Individuals, even while we are providing for the Safety of the Nation.

The Urg; Fakazerly [Fazakerly] *spoke to this Effect.*
S I R,
Tho' I cannot be supposed to have much Acquaintance with Naval Affairs, and therefore may not perhaps discover the full Force of the Arguments that have been urged in Favour of the Clause now under Consideration, yet I cannot but think myself under an indispensible Obligation to examine it as far as I am able, and to make use of the Knowledge which I have acquired, however inferior to that of others.

The Argument, Sir, the only real Argument, which has been produced in Favour of the Restraint of Wages now proposed, appears to me by no Means Conclusive; nor can I believe that the meanest and most ignorant Seaman would, if it were proposed to him, hesitate a Moment for an Answer to it. Let me suppose, Sir, a Merchant urging it as a Charge against a Seaman, that he raises his Demand of Wages in Time of War, would not the Sailor readily reply, That harder Labour required larger Pay? Would he not ask, why the general Practice of Mankind is charged as a Crime upon him only? Enquire, says he, of the Workmen in the Docks, have they not double Wages for double Labour? And is not their Lot safe and easy in Comparison with mine, at once encounter Danger and support Fatigue? carry on War and Commerce at the same Time, to conduct the Ship and oppose the Enemy, and am equally exposed to Captivity and Shipwreck?[6]

---

[6] I have not ventured a correction here, though something is obviously in error. It is difficult to conceive of a typographical mistake, short of the omission of lines, that would be responsible for such scattered confusion. The meaning is obvious: "And is not their Lot safe and easy in comparison with mine, when I at once encounter Danger and support Fatigue? carry on War and Commerce at the same Time,... conduct the Ship and oppose the Enemy, and am equally exposed to Captivity and Shipwreck?"

Appendix 1

That this is in Reality the State of a Sailor in Time of War, I think, Sir, too evident to require Proof; nor do I see what Reply, can be made to the Sailor's artless Expostulation.

I know not why the Sailors alone should serve their Country to their Disadvantage, and be expected to encounter Danger without the Incitement of a Reward.

Nor will any Part of the Hardships of this Clause be alleviated by the Expedient suggested by an honourable Member, who spoke some Time ago, of granting, or allowing, to a Sailor, whose Contract shall be void, what our Courts of Law should adjudge him to deserve, a *Quantum meruit*. For, according to the general Interpretation of our Statutes, it will be determined that he has forfeited his whole Claim by illegal Contract. To instance, Sir, the Statute of Usury. He that stipulates for higher Interest than is allowed, is not able to recover his legal Demand, but irrevocably forfeits the Whole.

Thus, Sir, an unhappy Sailor, who shall innocently transgress this Law, must lose all the Profit of his Voyage, and have nothing to relieve him after his Fatigues, but when he has by his Courage repell'd the Enemy, and by his Skill escaped Storms and Rocks, must suffer yet severer Hardships, in being subject to a Forfeiture where he expected Applause, Comfort, and Recompence.

The Attorney General spoke next to this Purport.
S I R,

The Clause before us cannot, in my Opinion, produce any such dreadful Consequences as the learned Gentleman appears to imagine: However, to remove all Difficulties, I have drawn up an Amendment, which I shall beg leave to propose, That the Contracts which may be affected as the Clause now stands, *shall be void only as to so much of the Wages as shall exceed the Sum to which the House shall agree to reduce the Seamen's Pay;* and as to the Forfeitures, they are not to be levied upon the Sailors, but upon the Merchants, or trading Companies, who employ them, and who are able to pay greater Sums without being involved in Poverty and Distress.

With regards, Sir, to the Reasons for introducing this Clause, they are, in my Judgment, valid and equitable. We have found it necessary to fix the Rate of Money at Interest, and the Rate of Labour in several Cases, and if we do not in this Case, what will be the Consequence? A second Embargo on Commerce, and perhaps a total Stop to all military Preparations. Is it reasonable that any Man should rate his Labour according to the immediate Necessities of those that employ him? Or that he should raise his own Fortune by the publick Calamities? If this has hitherto been a Practice, it is a Practice contrary to the general Happiness of Society, and ought to prevail no longer.

If the Sailor, Sir, is exposed to greater Dangers in Time of War, is not the Merchant's Trade carried on likewise at greater Hazard? Is not the Freight, equally with the Sailors, threatened at once by the Ocean and the Enemy? and is not the Owner's Fortune equally impaired, whether the Ship is dash'd upon a Rock, or seized by a Privateer?

The Merchant, therefore, has as much Reason for paying less Wages in Time of War as the Sailor for demanding more, and nothing remains but that the Legislative Power determine a Medium between their different Interests, with Justice, if possible, at least with Impartiality.

The Prime Minister's Brother, who had stood up Several Times, but was prevented by other Members, spoke next, to this Purport.

S I R,

I was unwilling to interrupt the Course of this Debate while it was carried on with Calmness and Decency, by Men who do not suffer the Ardour of Opposition to cloud their Reason, or transport them to such Expressions as the Dignity of this Assembly does not admit. I have hitherto deferr'd to answer the Gentleman

Appendix 1

who declaimed against the Bill with such Fluency of Rhetoric, and such Vehemence of Gesture, who charged the Advocates for the Expedients now proposed, with having no Regard to any Interest but their own, and with making Laws only to consume Paper, and threatened them with the Defection of their Adherents, and the Loss of their Influence, upon this new Discovery of their Folly, and their Ignorance.

Nor, Sir, do I now answer him for any other purpose than to remind him how little the Clamours of Rage and Petulancy of Invectives, contribute to the Purposes for which this Assembly is called together; how little the Discovery of Truth is promoted, and the Security of the Nation established by pompous Diction, and theatrical Emotions.

Formidable Sounds, and furious Declamations, confident Assertions, and lofty Periods, may affect the young and inexperienced, and perhaps the Gentleman may have contracted his Habits of Oratory by conversing more with those of his own Age, than with such as have had more Opportunities of acquiring Knowledge, and more successful Methods of communicating their Sentiments.

If the Heat of his Temper, Sir, would suffer him to attend to those whose Age and long Acquaintance with Business, give them an indisputable Right to Deference and Superiority, he would learn, in Time, to reason rather than declaim, and to prefer Justness of Argument, and an accurate Knowledge of Facts, to sounding Epithets and splendid Superlatives, which may disturb the Imagination for a Moment, but leave no lasting Impression on the Mind.

He will learn, Sir, that to accuse and prove are very different, and that Reproaches unsupported by Evidence, affect only the Character of him that utters them. Excursions of Fancy, and Flights of Oratory, are indeed pardonable in young Men, but in no other; and it would surely contribute more, even to the Purpose for which some Gentlemen appear to speak, that of depreciating the Conduct of the Administration, to prove the Inconveniences and Injustice of this Bill, than barely to assert them, with whatever Magnificence of Language, or Appearance of Zeal, Honesty, or Compassion.

The Urg; Ptit *replied.*
SIR,
The atrocious Crime of being a young Man, which the honourable Gentleman has with such Spirit and Decency charged upon me, I shall neither attempt to palliate, nor deny, but content myself with wishing that I may be one of those whose Follies may cease with their Youth, and not of that Number, who are ignorant in spite of Experience.

Whether Youth can be imputed to any Man as a Reproach, I will not, Sir, assume the Province of determining; but surely Age may become justly contemptible, if the Opportunities which it brings have past away without Improvement, and Vice appears to prevail when the Passions have subsided. The Wretch that, after having seen the Consequences of a thousand Errors, continues still to blunder, and whose Age has only added Obstinacy to Stupidity, is surely the Object of either Abhorrence or Contempt, and deserves not that his grey Head should secure him from Insults.

Much more, Sir, is he to be abhorr'd, who, as he has advanced in Age, has receded from Virtue, and becomes more wicked with less Temptation; who prostitutes himself for Money which he cannot enjoy, and spends the Remains of his Life in the Ruin of his Country.

But Youth, Sir, is not my only Crime; I have been accused of acting a theatrical Part—A theatrical Part may either imply some Peculiarities of Gesture, or a Dissimulation of my real Sentiments, and an Adoption of the Opinions and Language of another Man.

In the first Sense, Sir, the Charge is too trifling to be confuted,

Appendix 1

and deserves only to be mentioned, that it may be despised. I am at Liberty, like every other Man, to use my own Language; and though I may perhaps have some Ambition to please this Gentleman, I shall not lay myself under any Restraint, nor very sollicitously copy his Diction, or his Mien, however matured by Age, or modelled by Experience.

If any Man shall by charging me with theatrical Behavior imply, that I utter any Sentiments but my own, I shall treat him as a Calumniator, and a Villain;[7] nor shall any Protection shelter him from the Treatment which he deserves. I shall, on such an Occasion, without Scruple, trample upon all those Forms with which Wealth and Dignity intrench themselves, nor shall any Thing but Age restrain my Resentment; Age, which always brings one Privilege, that of being insolent and supercilious without Punishment.

But, with Regard, Sir, to those whom I have offended, I am of Opinion, that if I had acted a borrowed Part, I should have avoided their Censure; the Heat that offended them is the Ardour of Conviction, and that Zeal for the Service of my Country, which neither Hope nor Fear shall influence me to suppress. I will not sit unconcerned while my Liberty is invaded, nor look in Silence upon publick Robbery.—I will exert my Endeavours at whatever Hazard, to repel the Aggressor, and drag the Thief to Justice, whoever may protect them in their Villany, and whoever may partake of their Plunder.—And if the Honourable Gentleman—[8]

---

[7] Villain] Villian

[8] William Coxe, in his *Memoirs of Horatio, Lord Walpole* (London, 1808), II, 184, passes on an anecdote "communicated by the late Lord Sydney from the authority of his father, who was present." Walpole made a disparaging remark about the wisdom of young men and Pitt arose: "With the greatest reverence to the grey hair of the honourable Gentleman!" Walpole "pulled off his wig, and shewed his head covered with grey hair; which occasioned a general laughter, in which Mr. Pitt joined and all warmth immediately subsided." The *Parliamentary History* followed Coxe in connecting the story with the speech here printed and has, in turn, been followed in numerous studies, the latest that of Mary Ransome, who uses the anecdote to demonstrate the lack of accuracy in Johnson's report. But the event recorded by Coxe took place long after Johnson's words were written: November 21, 1745. See *The Letters of Horace Walpole*, II, 154.

Here the Urg; Wintinnong [Winnington] *call'd to Order, and Urg;* Ptit *sitting down, he spoke thus.*

It is necessary, Sir, that the order of this Assembly be observed, and the Debate resumed without personal Altercations. Such Expressions as have been vented on this Occasion, become not an Assembly entrusted with the Liberty and Welfare of their Country. To interrupt the Debate on a Subject so important as that before us, is, in some measure to obstruct the publick Happiness, and violate our Trust: But much more heinous is the Crime of exposing our Determinations to Contempt, and inciting the People to Suspicion or Mutiny, by indecent Reflections, or unjust Insinuations.

I do not, Sir, undertake to decide the Controversy between the two Gentlemen, but must be allowed to observe, that no Diversity of Opinion can justify the Violation of Decency, and the Use of rude and virulent Expressions; Expressions dictated only by Resentment, and uttered without Regard to——

Here the Urg; Ptit *called* to Order, *and said.*

S I R,

If this be to preserve Order, there is no Danger of Indecency from the most licentious Tongue; for what Calumny can be more atrocious, or what Reproach more severe, than that of speaking with Regard to any thing but Truth. Order may sometimes be broken by Passion, or Inadvertency, but will hardly be re-establish'd by Monitors like this, who cannot govern his own Passion, whilst he is restraining the Impetuosity of others.

Happy, Sir, would it be for Mankind, if every one knew his own Province; we should not then see the same Man at once a Criminal and a Judge, nor would this Gentleman assume the Right of dictating to others what he has not learned himself.

That I may return in some Degree the Favour which he intends me, I will advise him never hereafter to exert himself on the Subject of Order; but whenever he finds himself inclined to

Appendix 1

speak on such Occasions, to remember how he has now succeeded, and condemn in Silence what his Censures will never reform.

The Urg; Wintinnong *replied.*
SIR,
As I was hindered by the Gentleman's Ardour and Impetuosity from concluding my Sentence, none but myself can know the Equity or Partiality of my Intentions, and therefore as I cannot justly be condemn'd I ought to be supposed innocent; nor ought he to censure a Fault of which he cannot be certain that it would ever have been committed.

He has indeed exalted himself to a Degree of Authority never yet assumed by any Member of this House, that of condemning others to Silence. I am henceforward, by his inviolable Decree, to sit and hear his Harangues without daring to oppose him. How wide he may extend his Authority, or whom he will proceed to include in the same Sentence I shall not determine; having not yet arrived at the same Degree of Sagacity with himself, nor being able to foreknow what another is going to pronounce.

If, I had given Offence by any improper Sallies of Passion, I ought to have been censured by the concurrent Voice of the Assembly, or have received a Reprimand, Sir, from you to which I should have submitted without Opposition; but I will not be doomed to Silence by one who has no Pretensions to Authority, and whose arbitrary Decisions can only tend to introduce Uproar, Discord and Confusion.

Hynrec Plemahm [Henry Pelham] *Urg; next rose up and spoke to this Effect.*
SIR,
When, in the Ardour of Controversy upon interesting Questions, the Zeal of the Disputants hinders them from a nice Ob-

servation of Decency and Regularity, there is some Indulgence due to the common Weakness of our Nature; nor ought any Gentleman to affix to a negligent Expression a more offensive Sense than is necessarily implied by it.

To search deep, Sir, for Calumnies and Reproaches is no laudable nor beneficial Curiosity; it must always be troublesome to ourselves by alarming us with imaginary Injuries, and may often be unjust to others by charging them with Invectives which they never intended. General Candour and mutual Tenderness will best preserve our own Quiet and support that Dignity which has always been accounted essential to National Debates, and seldom infringed without dangerous Consequences.

Then the Urg; Lettyltno [Lyttelton] *spoke as follows.*
S I R,
No Man can be more zealous for Decency than myself, or more convinced of the Necessity of a methodical Prosecution of the Question before us. I am well convinced how near Indecency and Faction are to one another, and how inevitably Confusion produces Obscurity; but I hope it will always be remembered, that he who first infringes Decency, or deviates from Method, is to answer for all the Consequences that may arise from the Neglect of Senatorial Customs. For it is not to be expected that any Man will bear reproaches without Reply, or that he who wanders from the Question will not be followed in his Digressions and hunted through his Labyrinths.

It cannot, Sir, be denied, that some Insinuations were uttered, injurious to those whose Zeal may sometimes happen to prompt them to warm Declarations, or incite them to passionate Emotions. Whether I am of Importance enough to be included in the Censure, I despise it too much to enquire or consider, but cannot forbear to observe, that Zeal for the Right can never become reproachful, and that no Man can fall into Contempt but those who deserve it.

The Clause was amended and agreed to.

APPENDIX 2

The debates generally accepted as by Johnson are listed in the order of their appearance in the *Gentleman's Magazine*. The Lilliputian content of each number of the magazine is shown, and the position of that section in Stockdale's edition. The dates by which the debates are identified are those given by the *Parliamentary History*, except those of December 4-11, 1740, wrongly given there. The dates in parentheses are the dates Stockdale assigns to the debates.

1741

July
  February 13, 1741. Lords. Removal of Sir Robert Walpole.
    G.M., XI, 339-358.
    Stockdale, XII, 139-169. (Feb. 13, 1741)

August
  February 13, 1741. Lords. Removal of Sir Robert Walpole (concl.).
    G.M., XI, 395-420.
    Stockdale, XII, 169-206.

September
  January 27, 1741. Commons. Seamen's bill (first reading).
    G.M., XI, 451-455.
    Omitted by Stockdale.
  March 2-23, 1741. Commons. Seamen's bill (clauses).
    G.M., XI, 455-473.
    Stockdale, XII, 229-256. (March 2-13, 1741)

October
  March 2-23, 1741. Commons. Seamen's bill (cont.).
    G.M., XI, 507-532.
    Stockdale, XII, 256-294.

November
  March 2-23, 1741. Commons. Seamen's bill (concl.).
    G.M., XI, 561-586.
    Stockdale, XII, 294-333.

December
  December 9, 1740. Lords. State of the army.
    G.M., XI, 617-633.
    Stockdale, XII, 96-120. (Dec. 9, 1740)

Supplement
- December 2–12, 1740. Commons. A seditious paper.
  - G.M., XI, 671–683.
  - Stockdale, XII, 23–40. (Dec. 2–12, 1740)
- December 12, 1740. Commons. Half-pay officers.
  - G.M., XI, 683–686.
  - Stockdale, XII, 121–125. (Dec. 12, 1740)
- February 3, 1741. Commons. The French and Spanish Fleets.
  - G.M., XI, 686–688.
  - Stockdale, XII, 134–138. (Feb. 3, 1741)

1742

January
- February 27, 1741. Commons. Insuring ships.
  - G.M., XII, 3–15.
  - Stockdale, XII, 210–228. (Feb. 27, 1741)

February
- January 26, 1741. Commons. Address for papers.
  - G.M., XII, 59–65.
  - Stockdale, XII, 125–134. (Jan. 24, 1741)
- April 13, 1741. Commons. Queen of Hungary.
  - G.M., XII, 65–75.
  - Stockdale, XII, 376–392. (April 16, 1741)

March
- April 13, 1741. Commons. Queen of Hungary (concl.).
  - G.M., XII, 115–116.
  - Stockdale, XII, 392–394.
- February 24–27, 1741. Commons. Mutiny and desertion.
  - G.M., XII, 117–128.
  - Stockdale, XII, 333–351. (March 13–15, 1741)

April
- February 24–27, 1741. Commons. Mutiny and desertion (concl.).
  - G.M., XII, 171–179.
  - Stockdale, XII, 351–363.
- January 27, 1741. Commons. Cleansing Westminster.
  - G.M., XII, 179–181.
  - Stockdale, XII, 206–209. (Feb. 24, 1741)

May
- November 25, 1740. Commons. Corn bill.
  - G.M., XII, 227–240.
  - Stockdale, XII, 1–21. (Nov. 19–25, 1740)

Appendix 2

June
  November 25, 1740. Commons. Corn bill (concl.).
    G.M., XII, 283–284.
    Stockdale, XII, 21–23.
  April 8, 1741. Commons. Addressing the king.
    G.M., XII, 284–287.
    Stockdale, XII, 363–368. (April 12, 1741)
July
  April 8, 1741. Commons. Addressing the king (concl.).
    G.M., XII, 339–343.
    Stockdale, XII, 368–376.
  December 1, 1741. Commons. Choosing a speaker.
    G.M., XII, 344–346.
    Stockdale, XIII, 1–4. (Dec. 1, 1741)
  December 4, 1741. Lords. The address.
    G.M., XII, 346–352.
    Stockdale, XIII, 4–14. (Dec. 4, 1741)
August
  December 4, 1741. Lords. The address (cont.).
    G.M., XII, 395–418.
    Stockdale, XIII, 15–50.
September
  December 4, 1741. Lords. The address (concl.).
    G.M., XII, 451–458.
    Stockdale, XIII, 50–61.
  December 8, 1741. Commons. The address.
    G.M., XII, 458–471.
    Stockdale, XIII, 61–82. (Dec. 8, 1741)
October
  December 8, 1741. Commons. The address (concl.).
    G.M., XII, 507–511.
    Stockdale, XIII, 82–87.
  May 25, 1742. Lords. Indemnifying evidence.
    G.M., XII, 511–525.
    Stockdale, XIII, 119–141. (May 20, 1741)
November
  May 25, 1742. Lords. Indemnifying evidence (cont.).
    G.M., XII, 555–573.
    Stockdale, XIII, 141–169.

December
  May 25, 1742. Lords. Indemnifying evidence (concl.).
    G.M., XII, 611–616.
    Stockdale, XIII, 169–177.
  June 1, 1742. Lords. Trade and navigation.
    G.M., XII, 617–632.
    Stockdale, XIII, 178–204. (June 1, 1742)
Supplement
  June 1, 1742. Lords. Trade and navigation (concl.).
    G.M., XII, 665–675.
    Stockdale, XIII 204–220.
  December 4–11, 1740. Commons. Raising new regiments.
    G.M., XII, 676–692.
    Stockdale, XII, 41–66. (Dec. 4–11, 1740)

1743

January
  December 4–11, 1740. Commons. Raising new regiments (concl.).
    G.M., XIII, 3–22.
    Stockdale, XII, 66–95.
February
  February 13, 1741. Commons. Removal of Sir Robert Walpole.
    G.M., XIII, 59–74.
    Omitted by Stockdale.
March
  February 13, 1741. Commons. Removal of Sir Robert Walpole (cont.).
    G.M., XII, 115–136.
    Omitted by Stockdale.
April
  February 13, 1741. Commons. Removal of Sir Robert Walpole (concl.).
    G.M., XIII, 171–181.
    Omitted by Stockdale.
May
  November 16, 1742. Lords. Address of thanks.
    G.M., XIII, 227–238.
    Stockdale, XIII, 220–238. (Nov. 16, 1742)
  March 9, 1742. Commons. Public enquiry.
    G.M., XIII, 238–243.
    Stockdale, XIII, 88–95. (March 9, 1742)

Appendix 2

June
  February 1, 1743. Lords. The army.
    G.M., XIII, 283–288.
    Stockdale, XIII, 275–284. (Feb. 1, 1743)
  March 9, 1742. Commons. Public enquiry (cont.).
    G.M., XIII, 289–304.
    Stockdale, XIII, 95–119.

July
  February 1, 1743. Lords. The army (cont.).
    G.M., XIII, 339–344.
    Stockdale, XIII, 284–292.
  March 9, 1742. Commons. Public enquiry (concl.).
    G.M., XIII, 345.
    Omitted by Stockdale.
  March 23, 1742. Commons. Conduct of Orford.
    G.M., XIII, 345–360.
    Omitted by Stockdale.

August
  February 1, 1743. Lords. The army (cont.).
    G.M., XIII, 395–415.
    Stockdale, XIII, 292–323.

September
  February 1, 1743. Lords. The army (cont.).
    G.M., XIII, 451–470.
    Stockdale, XIII, 323–353.

October
  February 1, 1743. Lords. The army (concl.).
    G.M., XIII, 507–528.
    Stockdale, XIII, 353–385.

November
  February 22–25, 1743. Lords. Spirituous liquors.
    G.M., XIII, 563–582.
    Stockdale, XIII, 386–415. (Feb. 21–23, 1743)

December
  February 22–25, 1743. Lords. Spirituous liquors (cont.).
    G.M., XIII, 619–636.
    Stockdale, XIII, 415–441.

Supplement
  February 22–25, 1743. Lords. Spirituous liquors (cont.).
    G.M., XIII, 673–698.
    Stockdale, XIII, 441–480.

1744
January
   February 22–25, 1743. Lords. Spirituous liquors (cont.).
     G.M., XIV, 3–22.
     Stockdale, XIII, 480–509.
February
   February 22–25, 1743. Lords. Spirituous liquors (concl.).
     G.M., XIV, 59–64.
     Stockdale, XIII, 509–516.
   December 10, 1742. Commons. Pay for Hanoverian troops.
     G.M., XIV, 64–77.
     Stockdale, XIII, 238–258. (Dec. 10, 1742)
March
   December 10, 1742. Commons. Pay for Hanoverian troops (concl.).
     G.M., XIV, 119–125.
     Stockdale, XIII, 258–275.

CHRONOLOGICAL LIST OF THE DEBATES BY JOHNSON, WITH THEIR LOCATION IN THE GENTLEMAN'S MAGAZINE

November 25, 1740. Commons. Corn bill.
    May, 1742 (XII, 227–240).
    June, 1742 (XII, 283–284).
December 2–12, 1740. Commons. A seditious paper.
    Supplement, 1741 (XI, 671–683).
December 9, 1740. Lords. State of the army.
    December, 1741 (XI, 617–633).
December 4–11, 1740. Commons. Raising new regiments.
    Supplement, 1742 (XII, 676–692).
    January, 1743 (XIII, 3–22).
December 12, 1740. Commons. Half-pay officers.
    Supplement, 1741 (XI, 683–686).
January 26, 1741. Commons. Address for papers.
    February, 1742 (XII, 59–65).
January 27, 1741. Commons. Cleansing Westminster.
    April, 1742 (XII, 179–181).
January 27, 1741. Commons. First reading. Seamen's bill.
    September, 1741 (XI, 451–455).
February 3, 1741. Commons. The French and Spanish fleets.
    Supplement, 1741 (XI, 686–688).

Appendix 2

February 13, 1741. Lords. Removal of Sir Robert Walpole.
    July, 1741 (XI, 339–358).
    August, 1741 (XI, 395–420).
February 13, 1741. Commons. Removal of Sir Robert Walpole.
    February, 1743 (XIII, 59–74).
    March, 1743 (XIII, 115–136).
    April, 1743 (XIII, 171–181).
February 24–27, 1741. Commons. Mutiny and desertion.
    March, 1742 (XII, 117–128).
    April, 1742 (XII, 171–179).
February 27, 1741. Commons. Insuring ships.
    January, 1742 (XII, 3–15).
March 2–23, 1741. Commons. Seamen's bill.
    September, 1741 (XI, 455–473).
    October, 1741 (XI, 507–532).
    November, 1741 (XI, 561–586).
April 8, 1741. Commons. Addressing the king.
    June, 1742 (XII, 284–287).
    July, 1742 (XII, 339–343).
April 13, 1741. Commons. Queen of Hungary.
    February, 1742 (XII, 65–75).
    March, 1742 (XII, 115–116).
December 1, 1741. Commons. Choosing a speaker.
    July, 1742 (XII, 344–346).
December 4, 1741. Lords. The address.
    July, 1742 (XII, 346–352).
    August, 1742 (XII, 395–418).
    September, 1742 (XII, 451–458).
December 8, 1741. Commons. The address.
    September, 1742 (XII, 458–471).
    October, 1742 (XII, 507–511).
March 9, 1742. Commons. Public enquiry.
    May, 1743 (XIII, 238–243).
    June, 1743 (XIII, 289–304).
    July, 1743 (XIII, 345).
March 23, 1742. Commons. Conduct of Orford.
    July, 1743 (XIII, 345–360).
May 25, 1742. Lords. Indemnifying evidence.
    October, 1742 (XII, 511–525).
    November, 1742 (XII, 555–573).
    December, 1742 (XII, 611–616).

June 1, 1742. Lords. Trade and navigation.
    December, 1742 (XII, 617–632).
    Supplement, 1742 (XII, 665–675).
November 16, 1742. Lords. Address of thanks.
    May, 1743 (XIII, 227–238).
December 10, 1742. Commons. Pay for Hanoverian troops.
    February, 1744 (XIV, 64–77).
    March, 1744 (XIV, 119–125).
February 1, 1743. Lords. The army.
    June, 1743 (XIII, 283–288).
    July, 1743 (XIII, 339–344).
    August, 1743 (XIII, 395–415).
    September, 1743 (XIII, 451–470).
    October, 1743 (XIII, 507–528).
February 22–25, 1743. Lords. Spirituous liquors.
    November, 1743 (XIII, 563–582).
    December, 1743 (XIII, 619–636).
    Supplement, 1743 (XIII, 673–698).
    January, 1744 (XIV, 3–22).
    February, 1744 (XIV, 59–64).

LIST OF THE LILLIPUTIAN CONTENTS OF THE GENTLEMAN'S MAGAZINE PRIOR TO JULY, 1741

Note.—These debates are said to have been revised by Johnson.

1738

June
  Appendix to Capt. Lemuel Gulliver's Account.
    G.M., VIII, 283–287.
  May 8, 1738. Commons. Securing trade to America.
    G.M., VIII, 288–292.
July
  May 8, 1738. Commons. Securing trade to America (concl.).
    G.M., VIII, 331–347.
August
  May 12, 1738. Commons. On order.
    G.M., VIII, 387–392.
  March 3, 1738. Commons. Merchants' petition.
    G.M., VIII, 392–399.

Appendix 2

    March 9, 1738. Lords. Reduction of the army.
      G.M., VIII, 399–407.
September
    March 9, 1738. Lords. Reduction of the army (concl.).
      G.M., VIII, 443–460.
    February 3, 1738. Commons. Reduction of the army.
      G.M., VIII, 460–463.
October
    February 3, 1738. Commons. Reduction of the army (cont.).
      G.M., VIII, 499–520.
November
    February 3, 1738. Commons. Reduction of the army (concl.).
      G.M., VIII, 555–558.
    May 2, 1738. Lords. Spanish depredations.
      G.M., VIII, 558–576.
December
    May 2, 1738. Lords. Spanish depredations (concl.).
      G.M., VIII, 611–627.
    April 25, 1738. Commons. Buttons and button-holes.
      G.M., VIII, 627–632.
Supplement
    April 25, 1738. Commons. Buttons and button-holes (concl.).
      G.M., VIII, 665–668.
    Several short summaries of debates.

1739

January–May
    No debates printed.
June
    February 1, 1739. Lords. Address of thanks.
      G.M., IX, 300–303.
July
    February 1, 1739. Lords. Address of thanks (cont.).
      G.M., IX, 337–357.
August
    February 1, 1739. Lords. Address of thanks (concl.).
      G.M., IX, 391–400.
    February 1, 1739. Commons. Address of thanks.

      G.M., IX, 400–411.

September
   February 1, 1739. Commons. Address of thanks (concl.).
      G.M., IX, 447-448.
   February 8, 1739. Lords. Convention with Spain.
      G.M., IX, 448-454.
   February 23, 1739. Lords. Petitions against the convention.
      G.M., IX, 454-460.
   February 9-12, 1739. Lords. Proceedings against Paul Whitehead.
      G.M., IX, 460-465.
   February 6, 1739. Commons. Papers on the convention.
      G.M., IX, 465-469.
October
   February 6, 1739. Commons. Papers on the convention (cont.).
      G.M., IX, 503-524.
November
   February 6, 1739. Commons. Papers on the convention (concl.).
      G.M., IX, 559-564.
   February 22, 1739. Lords. The Spanish protest.
      G.M., IX, 566-573.
   March 1, 1739. Lords. Convention with Spain.
      G.M., IX, 574-580.
December
   March 1, 1739. Lords. Convention with Spain (cont.).
      G.M., IX, 611-634.
Supplement
   March 1, 1739. Lords. Convention with Spain (concl.).
      G.M., IX, 665-692.
   March 8-9, 1739. Commons. Convention with Spain.
      G.M., IX, 692-698.

1740

January
   May 14, 1739. Lords. King's children's annuity.
      G.M., X, 5-8.
   May 10, 1739. Lords. Treaty with Denmark.
      G.M., X, 8-15.
February
   June 4, 1739. Lords. State of the nation.
      G.M., X, 43-50.

Appendix 2

March
   No debate. "Characters of the principal members of the Senate."
     G.M., X, 99–103.

April
   November 15, 1739. Lords. Address of thanks.
     G.M., X, 155–164.

May
   November 15, 1739. Lords. Address of thanks (cont.).
     G.M., X, 211–227.
   Characters of the principal "Clinabs."
     G.M., X, 227–230.

June
   November 15, 1739. Lords. Address of thanks (concl.).
     G.M., X, 267–269.
   November 15, 1739. Commons. Address of thanks.
     G.M., X, 269–279.
   November 21, 1739. Commons. Navigation in American seas.
     G.M., X, 279–287.

July
   November 21, 1739. Commons. Navigation in American seas (concl.).
     G.M., X, 323–335.
   November 27, 1739. Commons. Raising a body of marines.
     G.M., X, 336–339.

August
   November 27, 1739. Commons. Raising a body of marines (cont.).
     G.M., X, 363–385.

September
   November 27, 1739. Commons. Raising a body of marines (concl.).
     G.M., X, 417–424.
   November 28, 1739. Commons. Number of land forces.
     G.M., X, 425–428.
   November 29, 1739. Commons. Papers relating to the war.
     G.M., X, 428–439.

October
   November 29, 1739. Commons. Papers relating to the war (concl.).
     G.M., X, 475–493.
   December 18, 1739. Commons. Motion for a call of the House.
     G.M., 493–500.

November
  November 16, 1739. Commons. Seamen's bill.
  G.M., X, 530–545.
December
  November 16, 1739. Commons. Seamen's bill (concl.).
  G.M., X, 579–585.
  February 1, 1740. Commons. Navy estimates.
  G.M., X, 585–592.
Supplement
  January 29, 1740. Commons. The Place bill.
  G.M., X, 629–652.

1741

January
  February 5, 1740. Commons. Registering seamen.
  G.M., XI, 2–13.
February
  February 28, 1740. Lords. King's message sent to Commons.
  G.M., XI, 55–71.
March
  March 19, 1740. Lords. Pension bill.
  G.M., XI, 122–137.
April
  March 19, 1740. Lords. Pension bill (concl.).
  G.M., XI, 171–185.
May
  November 18, 1740. Lords. Address of thanks.
  G.M., XI, 243–254.
June
  November 18, 1740. Lords. Address of thanks (concl.).
  G.M., XI, 283–292.

CHRONOLOGICAL LIST OF THE DEBATES BY JOHNSON AS THEY APPEAR IN CHANDLER

November 25, 1740	XII, 338–358.
December 2–12, 1740	XII, 12–27.
December 4–11, 1740	XIII, 127–179 (Addenda).
December 12, 1740	XII, 29–33.
January 26, 1741	XII, 39–47.

Appendix 2

January 27, 1741 (Westminster)	XII, 360–363.
January 27, 1741 (Seamen's bill)	XII, 49–54.
February 3, 1741	XII, 56–60.
February 13, 1741	XIII, 179–222 (Addenda). (Speeches of Sandys, Pelham, Harley, Pulteney, Walpole omitted.)
February 24–27, 1741	XII, 363–392.
February 27, 1741	XII, 180–199.
March 2–23, 1741	XII, 199–312.
April 8, 1741	XII, 441–453.
April 13, 1741	XII, 316–333.
December 1, 1741	XIII, 17–20.
December 8, 1741	XIII, 22–48.
March 9, 1742	XIV, 13–26 (Appendix). (Speeches of Quarendon, Yonge, Lyttelton, Cholmondeley, Mordaunt only.)
March 23, 1742	XIV, 26–40 (Appendix). (Speeches of Limerick, Pitt omitted.)
December 10, 1742	XIV, 99–194. (Combined with *London Magazine* report.)

Chronological List of the Debates by Johnson as They Appear in Timberland

December 9, 1740	VII, 607–630.
February 13, 1741	Omitted except for last part of debate printed in VII, 728–733.
December 4, 1741	VIII, 7–59.
May 25, 1742	VIII, 119–174.
June 1, 1742	VIII, 177–207.
November 16, 1742	VIII, 211–233.
February 1, 1743	VIII, 236–338.
February 22–25, 1743	VIII, 352–479.

List of the Johnson Debates that Appear in Torbuck

Note.—The locations in the second Dublin edition, Vols. XIX and XX, and the *Impartial History,* here designated Cowse. There is a possibility that Johnson's debates of the 1742-1743 session are included in a later volume of the second Dublin edition.

	DUBLIN
November 25, 1740	XIX, 109-138.
December 2-12, 1740	XIX, 148-174.
December 9, 1740	XIX, 350-384.
December 12, 1740	XIX, 386-391.
January 26, 1741	XIX, 391-404.
January 27, 1741 (Westminster)	XIX, 405-409.
January 27, 1741 (Seamen's bill)	XX, 195-201.
February 3, 1741	XIX, 419-425.
February 13, 1741 (Lords)	XIX, 547-554. (Speeches on the second question, only.)
February 24-27, 1741	XX, 162-178. (Debate of the second day, only.)
February 27, 1741	XX, 416-441.
March 2-23, 1741	XX, 202-248, 318-412.
April 8, 1741	XX, 443-459.
April 13, 1741	XX, 461-486.
	COWSE
December 4, 1741	40-66, 81-96. (Speeches of Talbot, Abingdon, Newcastle, Hardwicke, Argyle, Harrington, Islay, Bathurst, Cholmondeley.)
December 8, 1741	99-134.
June 1, 1741	497-542.

Appendix 2

Chronological List of Debates by Johnson as They Appear in the Parliamentary History

November 25, 1740	XI, 845–867.
December 2–12, 1740	XI, 867–894.
December 4–11, 1740	XI, 927–991.
December 9, 1740	XI, 894–927.
December 12, 1740	XI, 991–995.
January 26, 1741	XI, 1001–1010.
January 27, 1741 (Westminster)	XI, 1010–1013.
January 27, 1741 (Seamen's bill)	XII, 26–32.
February 3, 1741	XI, 1035–1040.
February 13, 1741 (Lords)	XI, 1153–1223.
February 13, 1741 (Commons)	XI, 1303–1388.
February 24–27, 1741	XI, 1449–1480.
February 27, 1741	XII, 7–26.
March 2–23, 1741	XII, 32–142.
April 8, 1741	XII, 154–167.
April 13, 1741	XII, 167–185.
December 1, 1741	XII, 214–219.
December 4, 1741	XII, 223–288.
December 8, 1741	XII, 290–319.
March 9, 1742	XII, 496–530.
March 23, 1742	XII, 563–586.
May 25, 1742	XII, 643–733.
June 1, 1742	XII, 753–788.
November 16, 1742	XII, 833–851.
December 10, 1742	XII, 1018–1053.
February 1, 1743	XII, 1058–1189.
February 22–25, 1743	XII, 1293–1439.

INDEX

INDEX

Abingdon, Montagu Bertie, 5th Earl of, 59, 60, 68–69
Addison, Joseph, 1
Address of thanks for His Majesty's speech, debate on, (Commons) 128, (Lords) 111–113
Almon, John, 44, 49
"Anagrammata Rediviva," 20, 183–184
Argyle, John Campbell, 2d Duke of, 13, 59, 60, 72, 73, 113, 114, 125, 134
Army, state of, debate on, 125
Astley, T., 17, 30

Barnard, Sir John, 192–193
Bathurst, Allen, 1st Earl of, 60, 61, 74, 117, 188–190
Birch, Dr. Thomas, 13, 29, 157
Boswell, James, 23–24, 28, 35, 45
Bowes, George, 80, 81
Boyer, Abel, 6–9, 14

Card, Griffith, 3
Carlisle, Henry Howard, Earl of, 74
Carlson, C. L., 12
Carte, Thomas, 83
Carteret, John, Lord, 48, 59–68, 77, 113, 143, 145
Cave, Edward, 8, 10, 13, 15, 19–22, 27–29, 31, 33, 34, 55, 156–157
Chalmers, George, 45
Chandler, Richard, 36–41, 43, 49, 97, 102
Chapman, R. W., and Allen T. Hazen, 45, 158
"Characters of the Lilliputian Senate," 138
Chesterfield, Philip Dormer Stanhope, 4th Earl of, 13, 43–44, 48, 51, 112–113, 114, 119–120, 126, 137, 159
Cholmondeley, George, 3d Earl of, 74–76, 118, 125, 134
Cobbett's Parliamentary History, 31, 50–52, 159
Commons. *See* House of Commons
Corn bill, debate on, 24, 49, 52
Cornbury, Henry Hyde, Viscount, 80, 82
Cornwall, Velters, 46–47
Courtney, W. P., and D. Nichol Smith, 35

Cowse, B., 42–43
Coxe, William, 49, 95, 96–97, 99–103, 127–128
Crosby, Brass, 31

Defoe, Daniel, 139–140
Diurnals, 4
Doddington, George Bubb, 80, 126
Dyer, John, 1–3

Egmont, John Percival, 1st Earl of, 123, 127

Fazakerly, Nicholas, 196–197
Foote, Samuel, 33, 34
Fox, Henry, 79, 81, 83–90, 93–95, 104, 108, 134
Francis, Philip, 33–34

Gage, Thomas, 1st Viscount, 22, 126–127
Gent, Thomas, 39
Gentleman's Magazine, 10–12; Johnson's connection with, 15; initiated *Debates,* 17–20; rivalry with *London Magazine,* 21–22; *Debates* translated, 23, 26; *Debates* discontinued, 30; *Debates* reprinted, 37–38, 40, 43; lack of bias in debate reports, 77–78, 129–130
Gordon, Thomas, 17
"Gulliver's Account, Appendix to," 17–19, 144, 145, 171–181
Guthrie, William, 19, 27, 49
Gybbon, Philip, 81, 120

Haddock, Admiral Nicholas, 88, 127
Halifax, George Montagu, 2d Earl of, 74
Hanoverian troops, debate on, (Commons) 26, 122–123, (Lords) 115–117
Hansard, T. C., 50
Hardwicke, Philip Yorke, 1st Earl of, 13, 59, 60, 73–74, 113, 115, 137, 157
Harley, Edward, 37, 52, 80, 82, 104–107, 120
Harrington, William Stanhope, 1st Earl of, 112
Hawkesworth, John, 26, 144, 145

[225]

Index

Hawkins, Sir John, 15, 22, 25, 26, 28, 29, 32, 35, 44–45, 131–132, 136–137, 139
Hay, William, 190–191
Heathcote, George, 82, 109, 134
Hervey, John, Lord, 52, 59, 60, 75, 113–114, 116, 118, 144, 145
Hill, George Birkbeck, x, 19–20, 26, 57, 131–133, 137–139
Historical Register, 9–10, 154, 158
Hooker, John, 3
House of Commons: *Votes and Proceedings*, 5, 7; *History and Proceedings*, 36–39, 41, 43, 49; ritual of choosing Speaker, 124; *Journals*, 154
House of Lords: *History and Proceedings*, 39–41, 43, 49; *Journals*, 154
Howe, John, 81, 82, 109

Indemnifying evidence on Walpole, bill for, debate on, 113–115

Johnson, Samuel, 15; "Appendix to Capt. Lemuel Gulliver's Account," 17–19, 144, 145, 171–181; "Anagrammata Rediviva," 20, 183–184; "author" of debates, 23–28, 33–34, 35, 129, 158; revision of Guthrie's debates, 24, 27; hurried composition of debates, 26, 156; materials used in writing debates, 28–29, 56–57, 76 ff., 129, 138; speeches compared to classical orations, 33–44, 140, 159, 164; *Literary Magazine*, 34; *Debates* reprinted by Chandler, 36–41, 43, 49, 97, 102, by Torbuck, 36, 41–43, by Timberland, 39–41, 43, 49, in Chesterfield's *Works*, 43–44, 159; Johnson's *Works*, 44, 50, 52–53; bias in *Debates*, 55–57, 77–78, 130; *Debates* as moral essays, 78, 130, 140–141; *London Magazine*, 129; emphasis on the general and universal, 130, 135, 141, 149–150; *The Rambler*, 131, 142, 147; debate-like qualities, 132 ff.; "tart replies" in *Debates*, 133–135, 139; speeches as isolated units, 135, 136, 140; lack of variety in speeches, 137–138; audience of *Debates*, 139; lack of realistic detail in *Debates*, 139, 150; relation of *Debates* to his conversation, 141; parallelism in style, 143–145, 149; *Taxation No Tyranny*, 144, 145; antithesis in style, 145–146, 149; philosophic and abstract diction, 146–149; inversion in style, 148; chiasmus in style, 148–149; "Debate between the Committee of the House of Commons in 1657, and O. Cromwell," 157; "Historical Design," 157–158

Licensing Act, 4
"Lilliputian Senate, Characters of the," 138
Limerick, James Hamilton, Viscount, 21, 79, 81, 121–122
London Magazine, 11, 12; "Proceedings of the Political Club," 16–17, 19, 23, 56, 129; rivalry with *Gentleman's Magazine*, 21–22; *Debates* discontinued, 30; *Debates* reprinted, 37, 40, 43; bias in debate reports, 77–78, 120, 129–130
Lords. *See* House of Lords
Lyttleton, George, 1st Baron, 80, 121, 133

MacDonagh, Michael, 57
Mantoux, Paul J., 53
Montagu, Wortley, 79–80, 81
Murphy, Arthur, 28, 33, 50, 55, 111, 138

Newcastle, Thomas Pelham Holles, 1st Duke of, 59, 60, 69–72
Nichols, John, 23, 28
Norris, Admiral Sir John, 127, 134

Oliver, Richard, 31
Onslow, Arthur, 13, 124
Oxford, Edward Harley, 3d Earl of. *See* Harley

Parliament, privilege of secrecy of, 1–5, 13–14. *See also* House of Commons; House of Lords
Paul, Herbert, 53
Pelham, Henry, 37, 82, 104–105, 121, 124, 203–204
Perry, Micajah, 193–194
Phillips, Sir John, 121, 123
Pitt, William (Earl of Chatham), 79–80, 82, 95–96, 108, 121–122, 127–128, 133, 136, 185–188, 200–202
"Political Club," 16–17, 19, 23, 56, 129
Political State of Great Britain, 6–9, 11, 12–15
Powell, L. F., 27
Pulteney, William (Earl of Bath), 17, 37, 81–82, 104, 106–107, 122, 126–128, 134, 146

Index

Quartering of soldiers, debate on, 120–121

Raikes, Robert, 8
Rambler, The, 131, 142, 147
Ransome, Mary, 10, 12, 15, 57
Reade, A. L., 27
Regiments, raising of new, debate on, 126
Ryder, Sir Dudley, 197–198

St. Aubyn, Sir John, 22, 121, 122, 123
Sandys, Samuel, 37, 79–95, 104, 108, 138
Scots Magazine, 23, 155
Seamen's bill, debate on, 127–128, 184–204
Secker, Archbishop Thomas: *Journal* of, 51–52, 58–78, 111–120, 125–126, 136–137; speech of, 118–119
Sherlock, Thomas (Bishop of Salisbury), 49, 75
Shippen, William, 52, 80, 81, 128
Smollett, Tobias, 158
Somerset, Noel, Lord, 17, 128
Southwell, Edward, 80, 81
Spirituous liquors bill, debate on, 24, 26, 43, 117–120, 137
Stockdale, John, 44–49
Stokes, Jeremiah, 3

Talbot, William, 1st Earl of, 75–76, 115, 136
Taxation No Tyranny, 144, 145
Thrale, Hester Lynch, 35

Timberland, Ebenezer, 39–41, 43, 49
Torbuck, John, 36, 41–43
Trade and navigation bill, debate on, 125
Tyers, Thomas, 44

Vernon, Admiral Edward, 88

Wager, Admiral Sir Charles, 52, 80, 81
Walesby, Francis Pearson, 52
Walpole, Horace (1st Baron Walpole of Wolverton), 126–128, 133, 136, 198–201
Walpole, Horace (4th Earl of Orford), 35, 122, 128, 201
Walpole, Sir Robert (1st Earl of Orford), 16, 37; motion to remove, (Commons) 47, 78–110, (Lords) 25, 58–78, 136; speeches, 79–82, 96–104, 126, 128, 191–192; anti-Walpole pamphlet, 103; bill for indemnifying evidence on, 113–115
Wedderburne, Alexander, 33
Wilkes, John, 31
Williams, Basil, 53
Wilson, Mona, 53
Wimsatt, W. K., 142–143, 145, 147
Winchelsea, Daniel Finch, 7th Earl of, 125
Winnington, Thomas, 121, 202
Wright, John, 51

Yonge, Sir William, 121, 133, 195–196
Yorke, Philip. *See* Hardwicke

www.ingramcontent.com/pod-product-compliance
Lightning Source LLC
Chambersburg PA
CBHW021944240426
43668CB00037B/721